# Ethical Approaches to Physical Interventions

## Responding to Challenging Behaviour in People with Intellectual Disabilities

*Edited by David*

Consultant Clinical
Bro Morgannwg N
University of Glam

British Library Cataloguing in Publication Data

A CIP record for this book is available from the Public Library

ISBN 1 904082 01 7

© Copyright 2002 BILD Publications

BILD Publications is the publishing office of the
British Institute of Learning Disabilities
Campion House
Green Street
Kidderminster
Worcs
DY10 1JL

Telephone: 01562 723010
Fax: 01562 723029
e-mail: enquiries@bild.org.uk
Website: www.bild.org.uk

Please contact BILD for a free publication catalogue listing BILD books, reports and training
materials.

BILD Publications are distributed worldwide by
Plymbridge Distributors Limited
Plymbridge House
Estover Road
Plymouth
United Kingdom
PL6 7PZ
Telephone: 01752 202301
Fax: 01752 202333

# CONTENTS

# CONTRIBUTORS

**David Allen,**
Consultant Clinical Psychologist and
Professor of Intellectual Disability
Bro Morgannwg NHS Trust and
University of Glamorgan
Special Projects Team
Unit 3, Cowbridge Court
58–62 Cowbridge Road West
Cardiff CF5 3BS

**Peter Baker,**
Consultant Clinical Psychologist,
Community Learning Disability
Service,
Hastings and Rother NHS Trust,
Gambier House,
West Hill Road,
St. Leonards-on-Sea,
East Sussex TN38 0NG

**Paul Cambridge,**
Senior Lecturer in Learning
Disability,
Tizard Centre,
University of Kent at Canterbury,
Beverly Farm,
Canterbury CT2 7LZ

**Tony Doyle,**
Clinical Manager,
Intensive Support Service,
Bro Morgannwg NHS Trust,
Welsh Centre for Learning
Disabilities,
Meridian Court, North Road,
Cardiff CF14 3BG

**Eric Emerson,**
Professor of Clinical Psychology,
Institute for Health Research,
Alexandra Square,
Lancaster University,
Lancaster LA1 4YT

**John Harris,**
Chief Executive,
British Institute of Learning
Disabilities,
Campion House
Green Street
Kidderminster,
Worcestershire DY10 1JL

**Alan Jefferson,**
Regional Director,
North West,
National Care Standards
Commission,
St. Nicholas Building,
St. Nicholas Street,
Newcastle upon Tyne NE1 1NB

**David Jones,**
Clinical Psychologist,
Community Opportunities
Consortium,
143 Station Road,
Llandaff North,
Cardiff CF14 2XF

**Neil Kaye,**
Training Co-ordinator,
Bro Morgannwg NHS Trust,
Hensol,
Nr. Pontyclun,
Mid Glamorgan CF72 8YS

**Amanda Kelly-Pike,**
Research Worker,
The Tizard Centre,
Beverly Farm,
University of Kent at Canterbury,
Canterbury CT2 7LZ

**Gary LaVigna,**
Clinical Director,
Institute for Applied Behaviour
Analysis,
5777 West Century Boulevard,
Suite 675,
Los Angeles,
California 90045,
USA

**David Leadbetter,**
Director,
CALM Training Services Ltd.,
Menstrie Business Centre,
Elmbank Mill,
Menstrie,
Clackmannanshire FK11 7BU

**Donal MacIntyre,**
BBC,
White City,
201 Wood Lane,
London W12 7TS

**Jim Mansell,**
Professor in the Applied
Psychology of Learning Disability,
The Tizard Centre,
Beverly Farm,
University of Kent at Canterbury,
Canterbury CT2 7LZ

**Andy McDonnell,**
Clinical Psychologist,
Studio III Training Systems,
32 Gay Street,
Bath BA1 2NT

**Peter McGill,**
Director,
The Tizard Centre,
Beverly Farm,
University of Kent at Canterbury,
Canterbury CT2 7LZ

**Ann Palen McGlynn,**
Chief Psychologist,
Lubbock State School,
Lubbock,
Texas 79408–5396,
USA

**Glyn Murphy,**
Professor of Clinical Psychology of
Learning Disabilities,
The Tizard Centre,
Beverly Farm,
University of Kent at Canterbury,
Canterbury CT2 7LZ

**Peter Sturmey,**
Associate Professor,
Queens College and Graduate
Centre,
City University of New York,
65–30 Kissena Boulevard,
Flushing, NY 11367,
USA

**Tony Waters,**
Behavioural Advisor,
Studio III Training Systems,
32 Gay Street,
Bath BA1 2NT

**Tom Willis,**
Associate Director,
Institute for Applied Behaviour
Analysis,
5777 West Century Boulevard,
Suite 675,
Los Angeles,
California 90045,
USA

# Foreword

Challenging behaviour is the product of individual and environmental factors, both of which are quite widespread. Many families, and most service settings (schools, residential homes, day services etc) will include people who present a challenge. Proactive strategies for challenging behaviour require well-organised and managed services, employing enough well-trained staff supported by enough well-trained professional specialists (psychology, speech and language therapy, psychiatry etc). In Britain, all of these are in short supply. Therefore, in many situations, it seems likely that carers (family members, friends, staff) are coping with incidents of challenging behaviour outside the kind of comprehensive framework which represents good practice. Very often, 'coping' will include the use of physical interventions to prevent the person with a learning disability from hurting themselves or other people or from damaging property. Even where comprehensive strategies are in place, limitations in our understanding, and therefore in our ability to prevent challenging behaviour, mean that physical interventions sometimes have to be used.

Given this, it is better that physical intervention is planned and regulated. Better for people with intellectual disabilities, in that what are likely to be relatively risky and unpleasant experiences are only used when appropriate and are carried out competently; better for carers and staff, in that they follow recognised good practice in a safe way. A large part of this book concerns the planning and regulation of physical interventions. In considering the task, the authors of this volume face some uncertainty. This is partly because of inadequate legal and policy frameworks: for example, several contributors point to the long awaited reform of English law on capacity and the multiple sources of general policy guidance from government departments and professional bodies. It also partly because of the current lack of evidence as to what constitutes best practice in this complex field. Nevertheless, this book presents a sophisticated picture of the relationship required between law, policy, procedures, training, management, monitoring and audit if this aspect of the care of people with intellectual disabilities is to be carried out well. It will be required reading for decision-makers planning services, those advocating for and representing the interests of people with intellectual disabilities, as well as for practitioners working directly with service users.

In setting out the way in which these different activities together contribute to the quality of practice at the interface between staff and service users, the message of this book is consistent with the picture emerging in other areas of service delivery. In the area of protection from abuse, for example, the same emphasis on integrating the legal and policy framework with detailed procedural guidance and monitoring has arisen. Similarly, the provision of staff support to enable people with intellectual disabilities to participate fully in life at home and in the community, through active support, total communication environments, positive behavioural support and so on, entails a relatively high degree of specification of the work of staff and of fidelity in its execution. One of the central beliefs originally held by some proponents of community services – that supporting people with complex needs to live a good life in the community required an unskilled, 'ordinary' workforce unencumbered by special knowledge or skill – is giving way to a more considered view. Services now face the challenge of how to integrate the relatively structured, prescriptive ways of working that people with intellectual disabilities need to live a good life, with the highly individualised, self-effacing style that is consistent with social inclusion and empowerment. So this book presents an important challenge as well as a guide.

In facing this challenge, evidence is going to be of central importance. The second major theme of this book is that evidence is needed to guide decision-making and that its absence is a serious hindrance to making progress. Every contributor notes the relative paucity of evaluative research that describes what is happening now, which approaches to physical intervention work best, what individual and service characteristics matter, what is the best kind of training etc. It seems inevitable, given the direction indicated by legislation such as the Care Standards Act and the Health and Safety at Work Act, that the collection of detailed, comprehensive information will become a more important part of social and health care activity in future. It will be important to use this information as the basis for the kind of applied research that will address the questions raised by the authors of this book.

Service evaluation research is important, but this book also identifies some much more fundamental questions about challenging behaviour and its management that research should address. These are questions about the relationship between carers and people with intellectual disabilities: about whose psychological needs are being met by particular ways of working (who should be 'in control'?), about whether the methods commonly justified by reference to behaviour analysis are really being properly understood, and about whether more careful analysis would yield alternatives to physical intervention. This is every bit as important a research agenda as service evaluation.

This is a timely, relevant and accessible book that combines solid practical guidance based on good experience with thought-provoking reflection and argument. It should be read by everyone interested in building a better life for people with intellectual disabilities and those who provide care and support to them.

Jim Mansell
*University of Kent at Canterbury*

# Preface

Producing a book on this topic would have been virtually impossible a decade ago. Although the planning of services for people with learning disabilities and challenging behaviour had been forced onto both national and local planning agendas, these agendas were quite appropriately preoccupied with basic issues of service design and the emerging technology of positive behavioural support.

The latter had equipped clinicians with a set of intervention tools that were compatible with and supportive of social role valorisation. The 'rediscovery' of antecedent interventions had reduced our historical dependency on contingency management strategies. At the same time new approaches, such as functional communication training, together with the application of therapeutic approaches pioneered with other populations, for example, self-control and cognitive behavioural techniques, offered new hope and promise.

All these interventions had good social validity, and hence were more acceptable to service users, carers and therapists than the aversive interventions that had dominated both the scientific literature and clinical practice up until the late 1980s. Allied with the changes taking place in care services, with the significant shift away from institutional care and towards community living, these therapeutic options helped fuel a new found optimism concerning our ability to meet the needs of this most vulnerable group of service users. One major area of difficulty remained however. Although psychologists, psychiatrists and others were increasingly able to produce constructional intervention plans that could help change behaviour over time, they remained unable in most cases to answer the simple question:

> 'What do we do in the meantime if the person hits out at us, or self injures or generally loses control?'

As no national guidelines were in existence to inform practitioners as to what advice they should give, their frequent inability to make recommendations was understandable. In the absence of formal advice, solutions were typically improvised by direct carers, sometimes with appropriate results, but more often than not with ad hoc responses to difficult behaviours that increased risks for both service users and carers. On those comparatively rare occasions that formal guidance and training was provided, it frequently came from individuals with no experience of intellectual disability and, consequently, it was often inappropriate to the needs of both service users and their carers. The net result was that in many service settings, severe challenging behaviours were managed in ways that were potentially dangerous, unethical and unlawful.

Very few practitioners openly expressed an interest in the area of reactive behaviour management in these early days. Those who did often assumed the role of 'closet' pioneers who recognised the importance of the issue, but who were sometimes reluctant to speak too openly about a taboo subject that was frequently (and understandably) portrayed as being in conflict with the values base and aspirations of the day. Gradually this situation has changed, and an increasing number of commissioners, providers and clinicians have come to acknowledge that this is an area that we ignore at our peril.

Since 1993, the British Institute of Learning Disabilities (BILD) has, with the support of the Department of Health and, more recently, the Department for Education and Skills, been at the forefront of national initiatives to improve practice in this hugely contentious area. This is the fourth publication from BILD to concern itself with physical interventions, following as it does on the heels of *Physical Interventions: A Policy Framework* (1996), *Training Carers in Physical Interventions* (2001) and *BILD Code of Practice for Trainers in the Use of Physical Interventions* (2001) and *BILD Directory of Physical Interventions Training Organisations* (2003).

In ten years, we have come a long way. It feels that the time is right to try and take stock of our current knowledge and to identify objectives for the immediate future. This book is an attempt to do just that.

I would like to express my deep personal thanks to all those who helped in the task of producing the book. All the contributors are incredibly busy people who gave freely of their time and ideas. They responded to my repetitive badgering with an unerring calm and good humour. It was a pleasure to work with a group of people who were singing from the same hymn book, even if, at this still early stage in the development of our knowledge, we are not all on exactly the same page.

Special thanks are also due to staff at BILD, particularly John Harris, Sharon Powell, Lucy Bennett and Catherine Allsopp, for their generous help and enthusiasm for this subject. Out of the seemingly myriad of people involved in shaping BILD's work on physical interventions, Marion Cornick deserves a special mention for her continued support and insight.

At a more personal level, my thanks due to my close colleagues over last 13 years, whose own interest in this topic has, at various times, stimulated, informed and inspired much of my own work in this area. Again, a large group of staff have contributed at this level, but my gratitude is due especially to Tony Doyle, Colin Dunn, John Hadley, Wendy James, Neil Kaye, Linda Newton and Wendy Dutton.

Final, and most importantly, I need to thank my home support team – Dyfi, Caitlin, Abigail & Madelaine – for their patience in allowing me to undertake one more 'little project'.

David Allen,
January 2003

# SECTION 1:
## Introduction

Chapter 1

# Behaviour Change and Behaviour Management

David Allen

## Introduction

This chapter will provide an introduction to and overview of the management of difficult or dangerous challenging behaviours in people with intellectual disabilities. The defining characteristics of challenging behaviour will be briefly described, and the effectiveness and limitations of current therapeutic approaches summarised. Factors that determine the need for the development of safe, ethical responses to such behaviours will be outlined, and a synopsis of the contents of the remainder of the book will then follow.

## Defining 'Challenging Behaviour'

The term 'challenging behaviour' came to prominence within the UK largely as a result of its use within a series of influential reports from the King's Fund Centre (Blunden & Allen, 1987; Allen, Banks & Staite, 1991) and via the work of the Special Development Team, University of Kent (1987). The term had been originally coined by the North American organisation, the Association for Persons with Severe Handicaps. It was designed to stress the fact that difficult behaviours shown by service users should be viewed most appropriately as the product of an interaction between characteristics of the individual and characteristics of their service settings. Hence, '. . . such behaviours represent challenges to services rather than problems which individuals with learning disabilities somehow carry around with them. If services could rise to the "challenge" of dealing with these behaviours they would cease to be "problems"' (Blunden & Allen, 1987, p14).

A number of attempts have been made to define the characteristics of challenging behaviour in people with intellectual difficulties more precisely. Emerson's definition, used within the King's Fund reports, and then revised by the author in 1995, is undoubtedly the most commonly cited within the UK. This describes challenging behaviour as:

*'culturally abnormal behaviour(s) of such an intensity, frequency or duration that the physical safety of the person or others is likely to be placed in serious jeopardy, or behaviour which is likely to seriously limit*

*use of, or result in the person being denied access to ordinary community facilities.'*

(Emerson, 1995, p4)

An alternative definition was provided by Zarkowska and Clements (1996) who suggested that behaviour could be viewed as problematic if it satisfied some of the following criteria:

- The behaviour itself or its severity is inappropriate given the person's age and level of development

- The behaviour is dangerous either to the person or others

- The behaviour constitutes a significant additional handicap for the person by interfering with the learning of new skills or by excluding the person from important learning opportunities

- The behaviour causes significant stress to the lives of those who live and work with the person and impairs the quality of their lives to an unreasonable degree

- The behaviour is contrary to social norms.

These definitions vary slightly in the criteria by which they identify behaviour as 'challenging'. Emerson stresses that behaviour rate, duration and severity, in addition to behavioural topography (that is, what the behaviour looks like), will be important determinants of whether a behaviour is viewed as problematic. A particular behaviour would also have to fall outside accepted cultural norms in order to be identified as 'deviant'; hence, while both smoking and consuming alcohol are potentially self-injurious activities, they are tolerated within society (albeit increasingly less so in the case of smoking), and would therefore not usually be regarded as challenging. Finally, Emerson suggests that challenging behaviour may lead to the individual concerned being excluded from services and communities.

The Zarkowska and Clements definition includes the additional concepts that behaviour may be viewed as challenging if it forms a barrier to further learning on the part of the individual, if it is out of step with a person's chronological age, or if it acts as a major source of stress to the person or their carers.

Central to both definitions is the notion of dangerousness. Challenging behaviours frequently pose significant risks either to the person displaying the behaviours or to those around them. Self-injury and physical aggression are the two forms of challenging behaviour which most obviously fulfil this criterion. They are also, along with destructive behaviour towards the environment, the most prevalent forms of challenging behaviour reported in epidemiological studies (Borthwick-Duffy, 1994; Emerson et al, 1997; Harris & Russell, 1989). Not surprisingly, they also tend to be the forms of challenging behaviour which are most commonly referred to specialist intervention services (Colond & Wieseler, 1995; Emerson et al, 1988; Toogood et al, 1994).

The consequences of severe self-injury are obviously largely internally directed. They may include auditory and visual sensory damage, permanent scarring and oedema, secondary neurological impairments and increased mortality (Hillery, 1999).[1] In contrast, as physical aggression is externally directed, its immediate consequences are experienced by those individuals supporting the service user in question. Injuries to family members (Adams & Allen, 2001; Qureshi, 1990) and paid carers (Emerson & Hatton, undated; Department of Health & Social Security, 1988; Royal College of Nursing & NHS Executive, 1998) are therefore common consequences of physical aggression, while both immediate and longer-term psychological trauma may also result from exposure to aggressive user behaviour (Bowie, 1999; Robb, 1997; Rowett & Breakwell, 1992).

The difficulties of supporting a person with severely challenging behaviour are illustrated well in the following quotes from Qureshi's study on parents caring for young adults with such behaviours:

> 'He had a spell when he was attacking everybody and everything, me included. You see this scarred eye I've got? That's where he had me. But I must admit, you can't say when he's going to have these moods. They just come on. Like he nearly choked me – it sounds awful – he nearly choked me on Blackburn Road a couple of months ago. If my husband hadn't have been there, then I'd have been dead, I'm sure'.

> 'She hit me in my ribs so hard. Oh, I was in such pain . . .'

> 'Like I say, it could be anything, anything could set her off. Sometimes if she's really bad, she'll come up to me, and she's big . . . I'm a bit frightened of her really sometimes, but I think I can't let her see that. And she'll come right up to my face and she'll say, 'I've told you, Mum, I've told you!'. And I think, God, you know, she's going to lash out'.
>
> (Qureshi, 1990, p 31)

On the basis of the above, it is apparent that effective support plans for people with intellectual disability and challenging behaviour need to contain two key elements. The primary aim of services must be to improve the quality of life of people with challenging behaviour and their carers by ameliorating the behaviours shown. Strategies for helping to change challenging behaviour and to develop more appropriate alternative behaviour over time are therefore a central component of effective care. In addition, strategies for responding to difficult behaviours when they occur will also be required if the safety of service users and carers is to be ensured, if abusive practice is to be reduced, and if employers are to discharge their statutory duties towards their employees. Furthermore, it is totally unrealistic to expect carers to persist with the implementation of longer-term behaviour change strategies in the absence of crisis management plans (Carr et al, 1994; McDonnell, 1997). Both elements are necessary, but not sufficient, components of effective intervention. This will become more apparent if the strengths and limitations of each element are considered further.

---

[1] Murphy & Wilson (1985) provide a number of chapters that deal with reactive approaches to self-injurious behaviour.

## Strategies for Changing Challenging Behaviour

The most effective strategies for challenging behaviour known at the present time are derived from Applied Behaviour Analysis. There are a number of thorough meta-analytical studies that have reviewed the strengths and weaknesses of these approaches (Scotti et al, 1991; Didden et al, 1997). The most recent, by Carr et al (1999), focussed on the use of positive behavioural strategies (ie those that avoided the use of aversive procedures). The review found that, using a criterion of a 90% reduction in challenging behaviour from baseline levels, these strategies were successful approximately 52% of the time. If a criterion of an 80% reduction was applied, this rate increased to around 68%.

Personal perspective determines whether this particular therapeutic 'glass' is viewed as being 'half full' or 'half empty'. Although the potential for improvement is readily apparent, these figures should be viewed as very encouraging when the full severity and complexity of challenging behaviour is taken into account.

Given the evidence for their effectiveness, it is alarming to note that these technologies appear to be considerably under-utilised in services for people with intellectual disabilities. Research suggests that only between 2–20% of people with severe challenging behaviours are in receipt of such interventions (Harris & Russell, 1989; Oliver et al, 1987; Qureshi, 1994; Emerson, 2001). This in itself may be one reason why challenging behaviours often appear to endure over long periods of time (Kiernan & Alborz, 1996; Lowe & Felce, 1995; Toogood et al, 1994). In contrast, approaches with little or no empirical support in terms of their specific effect on challenging behaviour, but which are easier to apply, appear to be used at much higher rates. Most notably, psychotropic medications, which have no evidence in favour of their use as a specific treatment for challenging behaviour (Brylewski & Duggan, 1999), are prescribed on average to around 50% of people showing such behaviour (Fleming et al, 1996; Kiernan et al, 1995). Likewise, the use of physical interventions in services generally exceeds the use of appropriate behavioural change strategies (as evidenced in Chapter 2). A major challenge for both commissioners and providers is therefore to ensure that these positive behaviour change strategies are more routinely implemented within mainstream services. Without this investment, rates of use of reactive procedures will inevitably rise. To use a simple analogy, the lower the investment in fire prevention, the greater the investment that will be required in fighting fires - and fighting fires is by far the more risky and demoralising option. As Carr et al (1994) state:

> '. . . if you focus on crisis management alone, what you typically find is that problem behaviours occur again at some future time, thereby making more crisis management necessary. You can become trapped in a scenario that has no end, except frustration and despair.'
>
> (Carr et al, 1994, p 12)

Behaviour change strategies are not the primary focus of the present volume, although some chapters inevitably and appropriately make reference to them.

There are already in existence a number of excellent texts on this subject. Readers seeking further practical information on constructing positive behavioural support plans are directed to the work of Donnellan et al (1988), Meyer & Evans (1989), Durand (1990), McBrien & Felce (1992), Carr et al (1994), Zarkowska & Clements (1996) and O'Neill et al (1997). All of these authors provide excellent advice on both behavioural assessment and intervention.

Although the general evidence in favour of behavioural interventions is encouraging, a number of qualifications arise from the outcome data available to date which draw attention to the need to construct strategies for managing as well as changing behaviour:

- Outwardly directed challenging behaviours, such as physical aggression, form the class of challenging behaviour that is least responsive to behavioural intervention (Scotti et al, 1991; Didden et al, 1997).

- Even with successful intervention, zero rates of challenging behaviour post-intervention are rare (Scotti et al, 1991; Didden et al, 1997: Whitaker, 1993). This means that behaviours of concern will still occur from time to time, and will therefore continue to pose challenges to carers.

- Aggression sometimes occurs at low frequency but high intensity (Harris & Russell, 1989; Sigafoos et al, 1994); evidence of successful behavioural intervention for low frequency aggression is lacking (Whitaker, 1993).

It is therefore very clear that, at certain times, and despite our best therapeutic efforts, carers supporting people who challenge will be faced with difficult behaviours that pose a significant risk of harm to themselves or others. Although positive behavioural change strategies provide considerable information about the actions needed to bring about medium to long-term behavioural improvements, they provide little or no information as to what should be done at the point that target behaviours occur.

## Strategies for Managing Challenging Behaviour

To summarise the above, behaviour management strategies would appear necessary because behaviours that pose direct risk either to the person performing the behaviour or to those caring for them tend to be the most common forms of challenging behaviour, and even successful interventions are unlikely to completely eliminate these behaviours. Despite this seemingly obvious need, reactive behaviour management has historically received scant attention from professionals working in the field of intellectual disability.

Managers and clinicians have to a large extent been able to adopt a 'head in the sand' attitude to this issue, insulated from the reality of caring for severely challenging people by the knowledge that, when behaviours of concern occurred, it would be front-line carers who would be called upon to cope with them. This avoidance of the issue has also been partly fuelled by a concern that training staff in physical interventions such as restraint may serve to encourage the use of such procedures and the somewhat naïve corollary that, in the absence of training, restraint will not take place.

A number of factors have combined to prompt a change of attitude towards behaviour management:

- The major changes in service provision within the last two decades, with the move away from institutional care and towards community care, has made people with challenging behaviour a far more visible group. While challenging behaviour had previously been contained within institutional settings, more creative and appropriate responses are now required if such individuals are to be successfully supported within community settings.

- The problem of violence in human care services has received increasing attention (Bowie, 1996) and this has been accompanied by important changes in legislation (described in chapter 5) that require employers to take steps to provide safer working environments for their employees.

- Growing concerns have been expressed about certain forms of training in reactive management, most notably with regard to procedures deliberately designed to inflict pain upon service users (Allen et al, 1997), resulting in calls for more ethical approaches to crisis management.

- Major anxieties about the deaths of service users in restraint have emanated in the United States (Weiss, 1998), and similar concerns have arisen about the abuse of physical interventions following a television documentary shown in the UK (MacIntyre, 1999).

Both individually and collectively, these factors have helped to force the issue of behaviour management on to the agenda of service commissioners and providers at a local, national and international level.

## The Nature of Behaviour Management Strategies

Emergencies occur in all walks of life and range from the minor (eg a factory worker sustains a cut to their hand while operating machinery) to the major (eg a train crashes on the outskirts of a large city). When people are faced with such crises, adrenaline levels will rise, thereby precipitating a whole range of significant physiological reactions (Rowett & Breakwell, 1992). Panic will often result. This panic is likely to be exacerbated if no clear premeditated plans of action are available for responding to the crisis. This panic will militate against clear thinking and bad decisions will often be made as a result. Hence, considerable time and effort is often invested in constructing action plans to cover such contingencies. Again, these might be quite small in scale (eg having a trained first aider on site to provide initial support to the worker with the cut hand prior to escorting them to the local casualty department), or much more dramatic (eg a disaster plan that specifies the co-ordinated response to be made by all emergency services in the light of a train crash). At both levels, crisis drills will be worked out and rehearsed under non-crisis conditions so that, if and when required, they can be put into place in a calm fashion that helps ensure the safety of all those involved, rather than in panic mode, which may increase, rather than reduce, risks.

Behaviour management strategies for responding to severe challenging behaviour are another example of proactive crisis planning. Having identified the challenges posed by a particular service user, bespoke plans for responding to the behaviours can be constructed and rehearsed. In addition to helping to ensure the safety of both carers and service users, clear behaviour management policies and plans help set a benchmark for ethical practice. This is vitally important given that persons with intellectual disabilities and challenging behaviour are at increased risk of physical abuse from carers and that these carers are likely to experience strong emotional reactions to this behaviour (Baker & Allen, 2001). Adopting a 'head in the sand' attitude to these issues will invariably help promote poor and potentially abusive practice.

Behaviour management strategies therefore have one simple objective. Their only goal is to achieve rapid and safe control over high-risk behaviours (Willis & LaVigna, 1999). They are not constructive, and they are not concerned with changing behaviour in the long term. They only provide temporary control over difficult behaviour. Accordingly, their use is never justified without the parallel use of behavioural change strategies. As Carr et al (1994) observe, they may be best viewed as helping to provide a window of opportunity through which more constructive intervention plans can be implemented. The relationship between the two components may therefore be described as symbiotic. They are interdependent.

As with other types of crisis management, behaviour management plans need to cover situations of varying severity. For some service users, reactive management plans will simply consist of mapping out verbal and non-verbal strategies for diverting the person away from escalating patterns of agitation. In other instances, the plans may focus on the use of proxemics (personal space) as a major reactive strategy. When carers are likely to be subject to brief physical attacks, physical interventions that enable carers to escape from such attacks may need to be identified. Finally, where more severe and longer duration risk behaviours are identified, safe restraint procedures may need to be implemented.

## About this book

The aim of this book is to complement the available literature on behavioural change strategies by focussing entirely on the topic of non-pharmacological approaches to behaviour management.[2] A secondary aim is to bring together various elements of the programme of work undertaken by the British Institute of Learning Disabilities (BILD) in the area of physical interventions since 1993. The book is not a 'how to do' text; there are plenty of these around in the shape

---

[2] General advice on the use of as required medication for behaviour management is provided by the Royal College of Psychiatrists (1998) and limited intellectual disability specific information in contained in Reiss & Aman (1998).

of training manuals offered by a plethora of training organisations. Rather, the book is an attempt to more towards a more 'evidence based' overview of the complex issues involved in behaviour management.

The chapters that follow are divided into five major sections. Eric Emerson completes this introductory overview by providing summary data on rates of physical intervention use within UK services. This chapter clearly demonstrates that the use of such interventions is fairly widespread in services, and reinforces the need to develop good practice standards as a consequence.

A significant problem for service commissioners and providers until comparatively recently has been the dearth of policy guidelines available governing the use of such interventions. In section two, John Harris gives an account of the British Institute of Learning Disabilities' initiative to improve policy making and Glyn Murphy and colleagues report on the initial evaluation of the impact of this work.

As stated above, physical interventions are only one element of developing effective, ethical responses to challenging behaviour. The section on intervention practice that follows therefore has an appropriately broad perspective. An initial chapter on risk assessment and risk management is followed by an account of non-physical reactive strategies by Gary LaVigna and Tom Willis, and on low arousal approaches to challenging behaviour by Andy McDonnell and colleagues. David Leadbetter then describes current thinking on best practice regarding the provision of safe and ethical physical interventions, and draws attention to particular procedures that appear to carry high risks for service users. Despite an increasingly significant investment in training by services supporting challenging individuals, until very recently there have been no clear guidelines governing the provision of training, nor has there been any universally accepted procedure for accrediting training. The delivery of training is therefore lead entirely by market forces and commissioners currently have no means of differentiating between the products on offer. John Harris concludes this section by describing the work that has been undertaken to construct a code of conduct for trainers in physical interventions, and describes how this relates to an accreditation procedure.

The fourth section of the book addresses some of the potential problems that may arise from this area of work. In particular, it examines the thin line that exists between the use of physical interventions and abusive practice. While the thoughts of staff working with challenging individuals are becoming increasingly well documented (Bromley & Emerson, 1995; Hastings et al, 1995: Whittington & Wykes, 1994), the views of service users about being subject to physical interventions are very under-researched. Peter Baker looks at the available literature on this topic, and also examines implications for good practice. Some of the themes identified by Baker are explored further by Paul Cambridge, who describes a number of organisational lessons arising from a case study involving the physical abuse of persons with intellectual disabilities in a community home. Alan Jefferson then brings this section to a close by reviewing the implications of the MacIntyre investigation for monitoring and inspection in social care settings.

In the final section, two accounts are provided on service initiatives to improve practice in behaviour management. Peter Sturmey and Ann Palen McGlynn look at restraint reduction in long-stay care, and David Allen and colleagues describe a research programme concerning the delivery of training in behaviour management within adult community services. While neither of these accounts claims to describe a definitive approach to behaviour management, together they illustrate how some of the good practice principles illustrated both throughout this book and in previous BILD publications can be realised. These chapters also provide evidence of important differences in approaches to behaviour management between the UK and the USA.

## References

Adams, D & Allen, D (2001) Assessing the need for reactive behaviour management strategies in children with learning disabilities and severe challenging behaviour. *Journal of Intellectual Disability Research*, 45, 4, 335–343.

Allen, D, Banks, R & Staite, S (Eds) (1991) *Meeting the Challenge. Some UK perspectives on community services for people with learning difficulties and challenging behaviour*. London: King's Fund Centre.

Allen, D, McDonald, L, Dunn, C & Doyle, T (1997) Changing care staff approaches to the prevention and management of aggressive behaviour in a residential treatment unit for persons with mental retardation and challenging behaviour. *Research in Developmental Disabilities*, 18, 2, 101–112.

Baker, P & Allen, D (2001) Physical abuse and physical interventions in learning disabilities: an element of risk? *The Journal of Adult Protection*, 3, 2, 25–31.

Blunden, R & Allen, D (1987) *Facing the Challenge: An Ordinary Life for People with Learning Difficulties and Challenging Behaviours*. London: King's Fund Centre.

Borthwick-Duffy, SA (1994) Prevalence of Destructive Behaviours: A Study of Aggression, Self-Injury, and Property Destruction. In Thompson, T, & Gray, DB (Eds) *Destructive Behaviour in Developmental Disabilities*. Sage: Thousand Oaks, CA, pp. 2–23.

Bowie, V (1996) *Coping with Violence. A guide for the human services*. London: Whiting & Birch.

Bowie, V (1999) Providing Staff with Adequate Support: Health workers as Survivors of Assault and Aggression. In Turnbull, J & Paterson, B (Eds) *Aggression and Violence. Approaches to Effective Management*. Basingstoke: Macmillan, pp. 148–178.

Bromley, J & Emerson, E (1995) Beliefs and emotional reactions of care staff working with people who challenge. *Journal of Intellectual Disability Research*, 39, 341–352.

Brylewski, J & Duggan, L (1999) Antipsychotic medication for challenging behaviour in people with intellectual disability: a systematic review of randomized controlled trials. *Journal of Intellectual Disability Research*, 43, 504–12.

Carr, EG, Levin, L, McConnachie, G, Carlson, JI, Kemp, D C, & Smith, CE (1994) *Communication-Based Intervention for Problem Behaviour. A User's Guide for Producing Positive Change*. Baltimore: Paul H. Brookes.

Carr, EG, Horner, RH, Turnbull, AP, Marquis, JG, McLaughlin, DM, McActee, ML, Smith, CE, Ryan, KA, Ruef, MB, & Doolabh, A (1999) *Positive Behavior Support for People with*

*Developmental Disabilities: A Research Synthesis*. Washington: American Association on Mental Retardation.

Colond, JS, & Wieseler, NA (1995) Preventing restrictive placements through community support services. *American Journal on Mental Retardation*, 99, 201–206.

Department of Health & Social Security (1988) *Violence to Staff. Report of the DHSS Advisory Committee on Violence to Staff*. London: HMSO.

Didden, R, Duker, PC, & Korzilius, H (1997) Meta-analytic study on treatment effectiveness for problem behaviours in individuals who have mental retardation. *American Journal on Mental Deficiency*, 101, 387–399.

Donnellan, A, LaVigna, GW, Negri-Scoultz, N, & Fassbender, LL (1988) *Progress without Punishment. Effective approaches for learners with behaviour problems*. New York: Teachers College Press.

Durand, VM (1990) *Severe Behaviour Problems. A Functional Communication Training Approach*. New York: Guilford Press.

Emerson, E (1995) *Challenging Behaviour: Analysis and Intervention in People with Learning Disabilities*. Cambridge: Cambridge University Press.

Emerson, E (2001) Utilization of psychological services and psychological interventions by people with learning disabilities and challenging behaviours. Clinical Psychology, 8, 25–29.

Emerson, E, Alborz, A, Reeves, D, Mason, H, Swarbrick, R, Kiernan, C, & Mason, L (1997) *The HARC challenging behaviour project. Report 2. The prevalence of challenging behaviour*. Manchester; Hester Adrian Research Centre, University of Manchester.

Emerson, E, Cummings, R, Barrett, S, Hughes, H, McCool, C, & Toogood, A (1988) Who are the people who challenge services? *Mental Handicap*, 16, 16–19.

Emerson, E & Hatton, C (undated) *Violence against social care workers supporting persons with learning difficulties: A review*. London: National Task Force. Violence against Social Care Staff.

Fleming, I, Caine, A, Ahmed, S, & Smith, S (1996) Aspects of the use of psychoactive medication among people with intellectual disabilities who have been resettled from long-stay hospitals into dispersed housing. *Journal of Applied Research in Intellectual Disabilities*, 9, 194–205.

Harris, P & Russell, O (1989) *The prevalence of aggressive behaviour among people with learning difficulties (mental handicap) in a single health district*. Interim report. Bristol; Norah Fry Research Centre, University of Bristol.

Hastings, RP, Remington, B, & Hopper, GM (1995) Experienced and inexperienced health care workers' beliefs about challenging behaviours. *Journal of Intellectual Disability Research*, 39, 474–483.

Hillery, J (1999) Self-injurious behaviour and people with developmental disabilities. In Bouras, N (Ed) *Psychiatric and Behavioural Disorders in Developmental Disabilities and Mental Retardation*. Cambridge: Cambridge University Press, pp.109–120.

Kiernan, C, Reeves, D, & Alborz, A (1995) The use of anti-psychotic drugs with adults with learning disabilities and challenging behaviour. *Journal of Intellectual Disability Research*, 39, 263–274.

Kiernan, C & Alborz, A (1996) Persistence in challenging and problems behaviours of young adults with intellectual disability living in the family home. *Journal of Applied Research in Intellectual Disabilities*, 9, 181–193.

Lowe, K & Felce, D (1995) How do carers assess the severity of challenging behaviour? A total population study. *Journal of Intellectual Disability Research, 30*, 117–127.

MacIntyre, D (1999) *MacIntyre Undercover. One Man, Four Lives.* London: BBC.

McBrien, J & Felce, D (1992) *Working with People who Have Severe Learning Difficulty and Challenging Behaviour. A Practical Handbook on the Behavioural Approach.* Kidderminster: British Institute of Mental Handicap.

McDonnell, A (1997) Training care staff to manage challenging behaviour: An evaluation of a three day course. *British Journal of Developmental Disabilities, 43*, 156–161.

Meyer, L & Evans, IM (1989) *Nonaversive intervention for behaviour problems. A manual for home and community.* Baltimore: Brookes.

Murphy, G & Wilson, B (1985) *Self Injurious Behaviour. A collection of published papers on prevalence, causes and treatment in people who are mentally handicapped or autistic.* Kidderminster: BIMH Publications.

Oliver, C, Murphy, G, & Corbett, JA (1987) Self-injurious behaviour in people with mental handicap: A total population study. *Journal of Mental Deficiency Research, 31*, 147–162.

O'Neill, R, Horner, RH, Albin, RW, Storey, K, Sprague, JR (1997) *Functional Analysis and Program Development for Problem Behavior.* Pacific Grove, CA: Brooks/Cole.

Qureshi, H (1994) The size of the problem. In Emerson, E, McGill, P & Mansell, J (Eds.) *Severe learning disabilities and challenging behaviours. Designing high quality services.* London: Chapman & Hall, pp. 17–36.

Qureshi, H (1990) *Parents caring for young adults with mental handicap and behaviour problems.* Manchester: Hester Adrian Research Centre.

Reiss, S & Aman, MG (1998) *Psychotropic Medications and Developmental Disabilities. The International Consensus Handbook.* Ohio: Nisonger Center, Ohio State University.

Robb, E (1997) Post-incident care and support for assaulted staff. In Kidd, B, & Stark, C (Eds) *Management of Violence and Aggression in Health Care.* London: Gaskell, pp. 140 –162.

Rowett, C & Breakwell, G (1992) *Managing Violence at Work. A course leader's guide.* Windsor: NFER Nelson.

Royal College of Nursing & National Health Service Executive (1998) *Safer Working in the Community: A guide for NHS managers and staff on reducing the risks from violence and aggression.* Wetherby: Department of Health.

Royal College of Psychiatrists (1998) *Management of Imminent Violence. Clinical practice guidelines to support mental health services. Occasional Paper OP41.* Glasgow: Bell & Bain.

Scotti, JR, Evans, IM, Meyer, LM, & Walker, P (1991) A meta-analysis of intervention research with problem behaviour: Treatment validity and standards of practice. *American Journal on Mental Retardation, 96*, 233–256.

Sigafoos, J, Elkins, J, Kerr, M, & Atwood, T (1994) A survey of aggressive behaviour among a population of persons with intellectual disability in Queensland. *Jourrnal of Intellectual Disability Research, 38*, 369–381.

Special Development Team (1987) *Developing Services for People with Severe Learning Difficulties and Challenging Behaviours.* University of Kent at Canterbury: Institute of Social and Applied Psychology.

Toogood, S, Bell, A, Jacques, H, Lewis, S, Sinclair, C & Wright, L (1994) Meeting the challenge in Clwyd: the Intensive Support Team, part 2. *British Journal of Learning Disabilities, 22,* 46–52.

Weiss, EM (1998) Deadly Restraints. *Hartford Courant,* October 11–15, 1998.

Whitaker, S (1993) The reduction of aggression in people with learning difficulties: A review of psychological methods. *British Journal of Clinical Psychology, 32,* 1–37.

Whittington, R & Wykes, T (1994) 'Going in Strong': Confrontive coping by staff. *Journal of Forensic Psychiatry, 5,* 3, 609–614

Willis, TJ & LaVigna, GW (1999) *Emergency Management and Reactive Strategies within a Nonaversive Framework.* Facilitator's Manual. Los Angeles: Institute for Applied Behaviour Analysis.

Zarkowska, E & Clements, J (1996) *Problem Behaviour and People with Severe Disabilities. The STAR Approach.* London: Chapman & Hall.

Chapter 2

# The Prevalence of Use of Reactive Management Strategies in Community-based Services in the UK

Eric Emerson

## Introduction

Approximately 10–15% of people with intellectual disabilities show behaviours which present a significant challenge to carers and support agencies (Emerson et al, 2001a; Kiernan & Qureshi, 1993; Qureshi & Alborz, 1992). Expression of these behaviours is associated with an increased risk of exposure to a range of negative outcomes. These include:

- physical injury to the person, to other people with intellectual disabilities and to care staff

- social exclusion, isolation and neglect

- abuse from caregivers

- exposure to restrictive treatment and management practices

- increased stress and strain among caregivers

- increased cost of service provision (cf, Ball & Bush, 2000; Emerson, 2001; Meyer & Janney, 1989; Meyer & Evans, 1993).

A key component in responding appropriately to these challenges is that the strategies used to manage episodes of challenging behaviour (eg, physical restraint) are effective, well planned and appropriately implemented. Failure to provide such strategies exposes both people with intellectual disabilities and caregivers to significant additional risks (Allen & Tynan, 2000; General Accounting Office, 1999; Harris, 1996; Harris, Allen, Cornick, Jefferson & Mills, 1996; McDonnell & Sturmey, 1993).

In this chapter I will use the results from a series of studies undertaken by colleagues at the Hester Adrian Research Centre and, more recently, at the Institute for Health Research, to try to answer two questions:

- How commonly are different reactive management strategies used in community-based services?

- What do we know about who is at greatest risk of being exposed to various forms of reactive management strategies?

I will try to answer these questions separately for children and adults with learning disabilities. Unless specified otherwise, the term 'children and adolescents' will be used to refer to young people under the age of 18 years.

## Reactive Management Strategies Applied to Children and Adolescents With Intellectual Disabilities

### Study 1: The HARC Challenging Behaviour Project

In 1994 the Department of Health commissioned colleagues at the Hester Adrian Research Centre to undertake two inter-linked projects to investigate the prevalence and persistence of challenging behaviours shown by people with intellectual disabilities. These projects built upon a large-scale epidemiological study on the prevalence of challenging behaviour undertaken in North West of England in 1988 (Kiernan & Qureshi, 1993; Qureshi, 1994; Qureshi & Alborz, 1992).

In the first part of this project we replicated the procedures used in 1988 and undertook a total population survey to determine the prevalence of challenging behaviour in two localities in the North West of England (Emerson et al, 2001a). In the second part of the study we attempted to follow up all people who had been identified as showing severe challenging behaviour in the original 1988 study (Emerson et al, 2001b; Kiernan et al, 1997).

The replication of the original prevalence survey identified a total of 107 children and adolescents with intellectual disabilities as showing challenging behaviour. Information was collected for each participant on whether physical restraint, mechanical restraint, seclusion and sedation were 'usually', 'sometimes', 'rarely' or 'never' used for the immediate control of episodes of challenging behaviour. The resulting data showed that 67% of children & adolescents' behaviour was 'sometimes' or 'usually' managed by physical restraint, 68% by seclusion, and 6% by sedation. Five per cent of individuals showing self-injury had this behaviour 'sometimes' or 'usually' managed by mechanical restraint.

Logistic regression was used in this study and those which follow to identify whether particular characteristics of the person (eg gender, age, severity of intellectual disability, type of challenging behaviour) or their service settings (eg size, staffing levels, availability of day care) were associated with increased risk of exposure to particular reactive strategies. In the present study, this analysis only involved physical restraint and seclusion, as insufficient numbers were available to undertake these analyses on exposure to sedation or use of mechanical restraint. The results of these analyses are summarised in Table 2.1.

**Table 2.1:** Personal characteristics associated with the use of physical restraint and seclusion in the management of challenging behaviours shown by children and adolescents with intellectual disabilities (HARC Challenging Behaviour Project)

| Intervention | Personal Characteristic | Significance (P) |
|---|---|---|
| Physical Restraint (79% correct classification; model $\chi^2 = 23.9$, df=3, p<0.001) | (greater) overall severity of challenging behaviour | 0.0002 |
| | (less) severe intellectual disability | 0.005 |
| | (more restricted) expressive communication | 0.045 |
| Seclusion (84% correct classification; model $\chi^2 = 26.2$, df=2, p<0.001) | (greater) self-care ability | 0.009 |
| | (more likely to show) stereotyped behaviour | 0.066 |

The use of restraint was associated with more severe overall challenging behaviour, higher levels of overall ability, and greater impairments in expressive communication. Seclusion use was linked with greater self-care skills and with the presence of stereotypic behaviour.

## Study 2

In 2000 we were commissioned by a local NHS Trust to undertake a similar total population survey in a third locality in the North West (Emerson et al, 2001c). This project identified 68 children and adolescents with intellectual disabilities as showing challenging behaviour. Information was collected for each participant on whether physical restraint, mechanical restraint, seclusion and sedation had been used 'once or twice in the last 6 months', 'once or twice in the last month', 'at least once a week' or 'every day' for the immediate control of episodes of challenging behaviour. Using these criteria, 46% had experienced physical restraint, 67% seclusion, 2% sedation and 4% medication.

Seclusion rates were comparable with study 1, although rates of restraint were slightly lower; sedation and mechanical restraint were again infrequently applied. Logistic regression showed that the only personal characteristic associated with restraint use was the presence of behaviour likely to result in injury to other children (69% correct classification; ($\chi^2 = 7.5$, df=1, p= 0.0006; significance 0.052). No associations were discovered for seclusion use.

## Study 3

In 2000 we were commissioned by a large city to help assess the health and social care needs of children with intellectual disabilities from minority ethnic groups. This involved collecting information on a total of 909 children. Of these, 69%

belonged to 'South Asian' ethnic groups, 20% to 'Black' ethnic groups and 11% to 'Other' minority ethnic groups (Emerson & Robertson, in press). Information was collected for 656 children on the severity of challenging behaviour and the strategies used to manage episodes of challenging behaviour.

Of the 656 children, 42% were reported to have shown at least one form of 'severe' challenging behaviour in the previous month. Information was collected on the use of reactive strategies for each participant using the same criteria utilised in study 2. The resulting data are summarised in Table 2.2.

**Table 2.2:** Aspects of the management and treatment of challenging behaviours shown by children and adolescents with intellectual disabilities from minority ethnic groups (Study 3)

| Children & Adolescents with Challenging Behaviour who in the last 6 months had been subject to: | % children with Challenging Behaviour | % of all Children |
|---|---|---|
| Physical Restraint | 28% | 12% |
| Seclusion | 32% | 13% |
| Sedation | 1% | <1% |
| Mechanical Restraint | 3% | 1% |

The use of both restraint and seclusion were lower than in the previous studies, although almost a third of children had experienced each form of intervention during the preceding six months. The results of the logistic regression analysis are shown in table 2.3.

Restraint use was associated with the presence of more severe irritable behaviours and conduct disorders, less severe anxiety problems, and attending special classes. Similar relationships were found between irritable behaviours, attendance at special classes and seclusion. The latter was also associated with the presence of less severe ritualistic behaviours, more severe self-injury, older chronological age and membership of a 'black' minority ethnic group.

**Table 2.3:** Personal & service characteristics associated with the use of reactive procedures in children and adolescents from minority ethnic groups (Study 3)

| Intervention | Personal Characteristic | Significance (P) |
|---|---|---|
| Physical Restraint (79% correct classification; model $\chi^2 = 74.5$, df=4, p<0.001) | Greater severity of challenging behaviour (irritability) | <0.001 |
| | Lesser severity of challenging behaviour (anxiety) | <0.001 |
| | Greater severity of challenging behaviour (conduct disorder) | 0.005 |
| | Attending special classes | 0.039 |
| Seclusion (87% correct classification; model $\chi^2 = 104.4$, df=9, p<0.001) | Lesser severity of challenging behaviour (isolated/ritualistic) | <0.001 |
| | Attending special school | 0.001 |
| | Greater severity of challenging behaviour (conduct disorder) | 0.001 |
| | Greater severity of challenging behaviour (self-injury) | 0.001 |
| | Greater severity of challenging behaviour (irritability) | 0.014 |
| | Older age | 0.015 |
| | Belonging to 'black' minority ethnic group | 0.036 |

## Reactive Management Strategies Applied to Adults With Intellectual Disabilities

### Study 1: The HARC Challenging Behaviour Project

The replication of the HARC total population prevalence survey identified a total of 156 adults with intellectual disabilities as showing challenging behaviour

(Emerson et al, 2001a). As noted above, information was collected for each participant on whether physical restraint, mechanical restraint, seclusion and sedation were 'usually', 'sometimes', 'rarely' or 'never' used for the immediate control of episodes of challenging behaviour. Physical restraint was used 'usually' or 'sometimes' to manage the behaviour of 49% of the sample, seclusion for 38% and sedation for 27%. Seven per cent of adults with self-injury were 'sometimes' or 'usually' subject to mechanical restraint.

Logistic regression (table 2.4) showed that physical restraint use was linked to the presence of dangerous behaviours that were more likely to harm the service user and others and to the presence of mobility problems. Seclusion use was associated with increased severity of aggressive behaviour and incontinence. Sedation was also associated with increased severity of aggression, diagnoses of psychosis and autism, and increased problems in expressive communication.

**Table 2.4:** Personal characteristics associated with the use of physical restraint, seclusion and sedation in adults with intellectual disabilities and challenging behaviour (HARC Challenging Behaviour Project)

| Intervention | Personal Characteristic | Significance (P) |
|---|---|---|
| Physical Restraint (79% correct classification; model $\chi^2$ = 43.2, df=3, p<0.001) | Challenging behaviour more likely to result in injury to the person or others | <0.001 |
| | Challenging behaviour more likely to put person in danger | 0.020 |
| | (less restricted) mobility | 0.042 |
| Seclusion (70% correct classification; model $\chi^2$ = 15.5, df=2, p<0.001) | (greater) severity of aggression | 0.001 |
| | (more likely to show) incontinence | 0.040 |
| Sedation (75% correct classification; model $\chi^2$ = 27.9, df=4, p<0.001) | (greater) severity of aggression | <0.001 |
| | (more restricted) expressive communication | 0.023 |
| | Reported diagnosis of psychosis | 0.028 |
| | Reported diagnosis of autism | 0.053 |

The second part of the HARC Challenging Behaviour Project sought to follow up all people who had in 1988 been identified as showing severe challenging behaviour. In the event we followed up 265 adults with intellectual disabilities (Kiernan et al, 1997). As in the first part of this study, information was collected for each participant on whether physical restraint, mechanical restraint, seclusion and sedation were 'usually', 'sometimes', 'rarely' or 'never' used for the immediate control of episodes of challenging behaviour. The combined rates for the 'sometimes' and 'usually' categories in this study were 57% for physical restraint, 37% for seclusion and 35% for sedation. Seventeen per cent of those with self-injurious behaviour experienced mechanical restraint 'sometimes' or 'usually'.

Again, logistic regression was used to identify whether particular personal characteristics or support arrangements were associated with increased risk of exposure to physical restraint, seclusion and sedation. The results of these analyses are summarised in Table 2.5.

**Table 2.5:** Personal and service characteristics associated with the use of physical restraint, seclusion and sedation in adults with intellectual disabilities and challenging behaviour (HARC Challenging Behaviour Project Follow-up)

| Intervention | Characteristic | Significance (P) |
|---|---|---|
| Physical Restraint (72% correct classification; model $\chi^2$ = 39.8, df=3, p<0.001) | Challenging behaviour more likely to result in injury to the person or others | 0.003 |
| | Greater overall severity of challenging behaviour | 0.003 |
| | Male | 0.052 |
| Seclusion (69% correct classification; model $\chi^2$ = 18.1, df=2, p<0.001) | Challenging behaviour more likely to put person in danger | 0.002 |
| | Diagnosis of autism | 0.004 |
| Sedation (68% correct classification; model $\chi^2$ = 30.9, df=4, p<0.001) | Challenging behaviour more likely to result in injury to person or others | 0.014 |
| | Person living in residential care | 0.020 |
| | (less restricted) mobility | 0.042 |
| | Challenging behaviour more likely to put person in danger | 0.056 |

Physical restraint use was associated with the presence of behaviours likely to cause injury, more severe challenging behaviour and male gender. Seclusion was again associated with dangerous behaviours and, interestingly, autism. For persons for whom social contact is potentially aversive, seclusion would be likely to act as a reinforcer, thereby strengthening the frequency, intensity or duration of any behaviour that it was contingent upon. Sedation was also associated with dangerous behaviours likely to cause injury to the service user or others, increased mobility problems and placement in residential care.

## Study 2

As noted above, we undertook a similar total population survey in a third locality in the North West of England in 2000 (Emerson et al, 2001c). This project identified 68 adults with intellectual disabilities as showing challenging behaviour. Forty one per cent of these people had been subject to restraint, 27% to seclusion, 26% to sedation and 2% mechanical restraint over the preceding six months. Logistic regression (table 2.6) showed that physical restraint was associated with behaviours more likely to injure staff and to seriously injure the person themselves, lower levels of functional ability, being placed in residential and not being in receipt of a day service. Seclusion was linked to the number of challenging behaviours shown, and sedation to the presence of self-injury, higher levels of receptive communication, the use of weapons, residential care placement and membership of minority ethnic groups.

## Study 4: Quality and Costs of Community-Based Supported Accommodation

In 1997 the English Department of Health commissioned us to undertake a study of the quality and costs of different forms of supported accommodation (Emerson et al, 2000; 2001d). This included an analysis of approaches to the treatment and management of challenging behaviour among 281 adults with intellectual disabilities supported by nominated 'better' providers of community-based supported accommodation, 46% of whom were reported to have shown one moderate or serious form of challenging behaviour in the previous month (Emerson et al, 2000a). As in the HARC Challenging Behaviour Project, information was collected for each participant on whether physical restraint, mechanical restraint, seclusion and sedation were 'usually', 'sometimes', 'rarely' or 'never' used for the immediate control of episodes of challenging behaviour. In this study, 8% of the study group's behaviour was 'sometimes' or 'usually' managed by physical restraint, 15% by seclusion, 15% by sedation, and 2% by mechanical restraint. Physical restraint use was associated with greater overall severity of challenging behaviour, modified home environments, the absence of a diagnosis of autistic spectrum disorder, and the implementation of active support strategies. Sedation was linked with the presence of a dual diagnosis, more severe challenging behaviour and, once more, the absence of autistic spectrum disorder (see table 2.7).

## Study 5: NW Audit

In 1996 the North West Regional Office of the NHSE commissioned colleagues in the Hester Adrian Research Centre and the National Development Team to develop procedures and materials for auditing the quality of supported accommodation for people with intellectual disabilities (Bliss, Emerson, Quinn

**Table 2.6:** Personal and service characteristics associated with physical restraint, seclusion and sedation (Study 2)

| Intervention | Characteristic | Significance (P) |
|---|---|---|
| Physical Restraint (85% correct classification; model $\chi^2 = 64.5$, df=5, p<0.001) | Challenging behaviour likely to result in more serious injury to staff | <0.001 |
| | Less able (general adaptive behaviour) | 0.001 |
| | Person not attending day centre for persons with intellectual disabilities | 0.002 |
| | Person living in residential care | 0.003 |
| | Challenging behaviour likely to result in more serious injury to person themselves | 0.028 |
| Seclusion (65% correct classification; model $\chi^2 = 7.8$, df=5, p<0.001) | (greater) number of challenging behaviours | 0.008 |
| Sedation (75% correct classification; model $\chi^2 = 33.6$, df=5, p<0.001) | Person shows self-injury | <0.001 |
| | Person living in residential care | 0.005 |
| | (more able) receptive communication | 0.014 |
| | Person may use weapons during episodes of aggressive behaviour | 0.025 |
| | Person belongs to minority ethnic group | 0.044 |

& Thomas, 1999). Since 2000, we have worked with eight Local Authorities and three Health Authorities in northern England to use components of these materials to monitor the quality of supports provided to 1,466 people with intellectual disabilities. Of these, 416 (28%) were identified as showing moderate or severe challenging behaviour.

**Table 2.7:** Personal and service characteristics associated with physical restraint, seclusion and sedation (Study 4)

| Intervention | Characteristic | Significance (P) |
|---|---|---|
| Physical Restraint (95% correct classification; model $\chi^2 = 33.3$, df=4, p<0.001) | (More severe) challenging behaviour overall | 0.001 |
| | Person's home has less normative architectural features | 0.004 |
| | Person does not have autism | 0.006 |
| | Implementation of active support | 0.022 |
| Seclusion (no variables identified) | | |
| Sedation (87% correct classification; model $\chi^2 = 29.9$, df=3, p<0.001) | Person screens positively for mental health problems | 0.001 |
| | (More severe) challenging behaviour overall | 0.004 |
| | Person does not have autism | 0.051 |

As in Studies 2 and 3, information was collected for each participant on whether physical restraint, mechanical restraint, seclusion and sedation had been used 'once or twice in the last 6 months', 'once or twice in the last month', 'at least once a week' or 'every day' for the immediate control of episodes of challenging behaviour. Twenty six percent were subject to physical restraint, 39% to seclusion, 28% to sedation and 2% to mechanical restraint within the six-month period prior to data collection.

In this study, physical restraint use was associated with greater numbers of staff, younger chronological age and lower levels of adaptive behaviour; seclusion with greater levels of challenging behaviour and admission from a non-institutional setting, and sedation with greater levels of challenging behaviour, larger scale services and an absence of day services (table 2.8).

**Table 2.8:** Personal characteristics associated with the use of physical restraint and seclusion (Study 5: NW Audit)

| Intervention | Personal Characteristic | Significance (P) |
|---|---|---|
| Physical Restraint (65% correct classification; model $\chi^2$ = 32.6, df=3, p<0.001) | (higher) overall staffing ratio | <0.001 |
| | (younger) age | 0.020 |
| | (lower) overall ability | 0.034 |
| Seclusion (64% correct classification; model $\chi^2$ = 22.4, df=2, p<0.001) | (greater) overall severity of challenging behaviour | <0.001 |
| | (did not) move into home from hospital ward | 0.005 |
| Sedation (71% correct classification; model $\chi^2$ = 29.2, df=3, p<0.001) | (greater) overall severity of challenging behaviour | <0.001 |
| | (greater) number of people with intellectual disabilities living together | 0.007 |
| | (does not) attend day centre for people with intellectual disabilities | 0.007 |

## Summary

Making comparisons across these studies is made problematic by the use of different sampling strategies (eg total populations, people in receipt of supported accommodation services etc), different approaches to identifying people as showing 'challenging behaviour' and the use of different measures of exposure to particular reactive management strategies ('usually' or 'sometimes' used vs. frequency of use in previous six months). Nevertheless, a number of conclusions may be tentatively drawn from these data.

First, it is clear that significant numbers of children and adults with intellectual disabilities are exposed to reactive management strategies. Between half and two thirds of children with challenging behaviour (as defined in the HARC Challenging Behaviour Project) were 'sometimes' or 'usually' subject to physical restraint (see also Adams & Allen, 2001), two thirds were 'sometimes' or 'usually' subject to seclusion. Just over one in ten of all children with intellectual disabilities from minority ethnic groups had been subject to physical restraint or seclusion in the previous six months.

Similarly high reports of use of physical restraint were apparent among adults (approximately half of adults with challenging behaviour as defined in the HARC Challenging Behaviour Project, one in four of adults with some degree of challenging behaviour in supported accommodation). Among adults, however, there was less reported use of seclusion (one in four to one in three adults with challenging behaviour), but significantly higher reported use of sedation (also one in four to one in three adults with challenging behaviour).

Second, analyses of the risk of exposure to different reactive management strategies identified a number of personal and environmental factors that were associated with increased risk of exposure. Personal factors (other than severity or form of challenging behaviour) included:

- **Severity of intellectual disability or severity of impairments in adaptive behaviour.** Less severe intellectual disability was associated with increased risk of physical restraint and seclusion in children (Study 1). More severe intellectual disability was associated with increased risk of physical restraint in adults (Study 2, Study 5).

- **Communication abilities.** Having more restricted expressive communication was associated with increased risk of physical restraint in children (Study 1) and increased risk of sedation in adults (Study 1).

- **Age.** Older age was associated with increased risk of seclusion in children (Study 3). Younger age was associated with increased risk of physical restraint in adults (Study 5).

- **Gender.** Men were at greater risk of exposure to physical restraint (Study 1).

- **Ethnicity.** Black children were at greater risk of seclusion (Study 3). Adults from minority ethnic groups were at increased risk of sedation (Study 2).

- **Autism.** A diagnosis of autism was associated with increased risk of seclusion (Study 1) and sedation (Study 1), but decreased risk of physical restraint and sedation (Study 4) in adults.

- **Psychiatric diagnosis.** Having a diagnosis of psychosis (Study 1) or any mental health problem (Study 4) was associated with increased risk of sedation in adults.

Environmental factors (other than severity of challenging behaviour) included:

- **Attending a special school.** Was associated with increased risk of physical restraint and seclusion in children (Study 3).

- **Living in residential care.** Was associated with increased risk of physical restraint (Study 2) and sedation (Study 1, Study 2) in adults.

- **Not attending a day centre** was associated with increased risk of physical restraint (Study 2) and sedation (Study 5) in adults.

- **Living in a home with less normal architectural features** was associated with increased risk of physical restraint in adults (Study 4).

- **Higher overall staffing ratio** was associated with increased risk of physical restraint in adults (Study 5).

- **Living in a home with more people with intellectual disabilities** was associated with increased risk of sedation in adults (Study 5).

It is important that the social significance of these relationships is interpreted with caution. These relationships are only correlational. As such, no direction of causality can be assumed and any such relationships may reflect the operation of other (unmeasured) variables. Nevertheless, the association between certain personal characteristics (eg gender, ethnicity) and environmental characteristics (eg use of non-inclusive services) clearly warrants further investigation.

## References

Adams, D & Allen, D (2001) Assessing the need for reactive behaviour management strategies in children with intellectual disability and severe challenging behaviour. *Journal of Intellectual Disability Research* 45, 335–343,

Allen, D & Tynan, H (2000) Responding to aggressive behaviour: The impact of training on staff knowledge and confidence. *Mental Retardation*, 38, 97–104

Ball, T & Bush, A (2000) *Clinical Practice Guidelines: Psychological Interventions For Severely Challenging Behaviours In People With Learning Disabilities.* Leicester: British Psychological Society.

Bliss, V, Emerson, E, Quinn, H, & Thomas, D (1999) *Monitoring Quality in Supported Accommodation for People With Learning Disabilities.* Manchester: Hester Adrian Research Centre, University of Manchester. (Now available through the Institute for Health Research, Lancaster University).

Emerson, E (2001) *Challenging Behaviour. Analysis and Intervention in People with Intellectual Disabilities. (2nd Edition)* Cambridge: Cambridge University Press.

Emerson, E & Robertson, J (In press) *An Analysis of the Current and Future Needs of South Asian and Black Children With Learning Disabilities.* Lancaster: Institute for Health Research, Lancaster University.

Emerson, E, Alborz, A, Kiernan, C, Mason, H, Reeves, D, Swarbrick, R, & Mason, L (1997) *The HARC Challenging Behaviour Project. Report 5: The Treatment and Management of Challenging Behaviour.* Manchester: Hester Adrian Research Centre, University of Manchester. (Now available through the Institute for Health Research, Lancaster University)

Emerson, E, Robertson, J, Gregory, N, Kessissoglou, S, Hatton, C, Hallam, A, Knapp, M, Järbrink, K, Walsh, P, & Netten, A. (2000) The quality and costs of village communities, residential campuses and community-based residential supports in the UK. *American Journal of Mental Retardation,* 105, 81–102.

Emerson, E, Robertson, J, Gregory, N, Hatton, C, Kessissoglou, S, Hallam, A, & Hillery, J (2000a) The treatment and management of challenging behaviours in residential settings. *Journal of Applied Research in Intellectual Disabilities,* 13, 197–215.

Emerson, E, Kiernan, C, Alborz, A, Reeves, D, Mason, H, Swarbrick, R, Mason, L & Hatton, C (2001a) The prevalence of challenging behaviours: a total population study. *Research in Developmental Disabilities, 22,* 77–93.

Emerson, E, Alborz, A, Kiernan, C., Reeves, D, Mason, H, Swarbrick, R, Mason, L & Hatton, C (2001b) Predicting the persistence of severe self-injurious behavior. *Research in Developmental Disabilities, 22,* 67–75.

Emerson, E, Green, K, Crossley, R, & Rand, R (2001c) *A Survey of the Needs of and Supports Received by People With Learning Disabilities and Challenging Behaviour in Blackburn, Hyndburn and Ribble Valley.* Lancaster: Institute for Health Research, Lancaster University.

Emerson, E, Robertson, J, Gregory, N, Hatton, C, Kessissoglou, S, Hallam, A, Järbrink, K, Knapp, M, Netten, A, & Walsh, P (2001d) The quality and costs of supported living schemes and group homes in the UK. *American Journal of Mental Retardation,* 106,5,401–415.

General Accounting Office (1999) *Mental Health: Improper Restraint or Seclusion Use Places People At Risk.* Washington, DC: United States General Accounting Office.

Harris, J (1996) Physical restraint procedures for managing challenging behaviors presented by mentally retarded adults and children. *Research in Developmental Disabilities, 17,* 99–134.

Harris, J, Allen, D, Cornick, M, Jefferson, A & Mills, R (1996) *Physical Interventions: A Policy Framework.* Kidderminster: BILD/NAS.

Kiernan, C, Reeves, D, Hatton, C, Alborz, A, Emerson, E, Mason, H, Swarbrick, R, & Mason, L (1997) *The HARC Challenging Behaviour Project. Report 1: Persistence and Change in the Challenging Behaviour of People with Learning Disability.* Manchester: Hester Adrian Research Centre, University of Manchester. (Now available through the Institute for Health Research, Lancaster University.)

McDonnell, AA, & Sturmey, P (1993) Management of aggression and violence. In RSP Jones & CB Eayrs (Eds) *Challenging Behaviours and People With Learning Disability: A Psychological Perspective.* Clevedon: BILD, pp. 148–171.

Meyer, LH & Evans, IM (1993) Meaningful outcomes in behavioural intervention: evaluating positive approaches to the remediation of challenging behaviours. In J. Reichle & D.P. Wacker (Eds), *Communicative Approaches to the Management of Challenging Behaviour.* Baltimore: Paul H. Brookes, pp. 407–428.

Meyer, LH & Janney, R (1989) User-friendly measures of meaningful outcomes: evaluating behavioural interventions. *Journal of the Association for Persons with Severe Handicaps,* 14, 4, 263–270.

Qureshi, H (1994) The size of the problem. In E Emerson, P McGill & J Mansell (Eds). *Severe Learning Disabilities and Challenging Behaviours: Designing High Quality Services.* Chapman & Hall: London, pp. 17–36.

Qureshi, H, & Alborz, A (1992) Epidemiology of challenging behaviour. *Mental Handicap Research, 5,* 130–145.

# SECTION II:
## Shaping Policy

# Chapter 3

## From good intentions to improved practice – developing effective policies

John Harris

## Introduction

Consider the following domestic scenes involving Mrs Walters and her daughter Chloe:

**7:00 pm. Friday**
Mrs. Walters: *'Your father and I are going out tonight – be good'*

**10:00am Saturday**
Mrs. Walters: *'I'm really disappointed in you Chloe. Bob and Sally next door have just been round to complain about the noise that you and your friends made last night. On top of that, you left a load of dishes in the sink, and there's popcorn all over the carpet.'*

Chloe: *'Sorry mum.'*

**7:00pm Saturday**
Mrs. Walters: *'We've been invited out to dinner tonight. Be good while we're away – that means: keeping the noise down, washing your dishes and clearing up any crumbs on the carpet.'*

Chloe: *'OK, Mum – but is it OK if I have a few friends round while you're out?'*

To anyone who has close contact with teenagers, this is a fairly familiar scenario. While there are many possible interpretations about the relationship between Chloe and her parents, two points stand out. First, Mrs Walters needs to find a way of communicating her expectations to Chloe and second, the success of Mrs Walter's attempts to persuade Chloe to comply with expectations will depend on a number of additional considerations including:

- Whether Chloe wants to comply with her mother's expectations. For example, does she think her mother is being unreasonable?

- How Chloe's friends behave. This is turn will be affected by the extent to which Chloe can explain her parent's expectations to her friends, and how far she can persuade them to comply if they are used to different parental expectations in their own homes.

- Mr Walters' views – whether he agrees with his wife and supports her in giving a clear and unambiguous message to Chloe.

The problem with Mrs Walters' first statement is not what she said, but rather what was implied but not stated explicitly. We might infer that, for Mrs Walters, behind the phrase 'be good' was a whole set of assumptions about what 'being good' means for a teenager like Chloe when her parents are out of the house. Some of these assumptions are made more explicit on Saturday morning, but even then, the list of expectations is probably incomplete. And until the general request to 'be good' is 'unpacked' and re-stated in terms of the things that Chloe should and shouldn't do, there is always room for misunderstanding.

As Mrs Walters and Chloe grapple with the problems of adolescence, it is likely that they will, over time, establish a shared understanding of just what 'being good' means. They will probably never write anything down, but it is fair to say that they will have developed a 'policy'.

While this chapter provides an overview of policy development in the context of services for people with an intellectual disability, the conversations between Chloe and her mother will provide a useful link between the everyday world of family experience and the more formal, sometimes bureaucratic, and often complex, settings for service provision. The term 'policy' can be applied to an unwritten understanding or set of mutual expectations as illustrated in the case of Mrs Walters and Chloe, or the term can be used specifically to refer to a formal written document. Throughout the remainder of this chapter the term will be used to refer to the latter.

The chapter is based upon the author's experience of working on the BILD *Physical Interventions: A Policy Framework* (Harris et al, 1996), the recent guidance from the Department of Health and Department of Education and Skills[1] on Physical Interventions (Department for Education and Skills and Department of Health, 2002) and the *BILD Code of Practice for Trainers* (2001). I am greatly indebted to the many colleagues who contributed to the preparation of these documents and, in doing so, provided me with an opportunity to extend my own knowledge of the role policies play in shaping practice. Needless to say, while this chapter reflects the insights of many different people, its limitations are entirely of my own devising. The chapter begins by addressing the following topics:

- Why are policies needed?

- What is the context in which policies operate?

- Policies with a purpose

- Developing policies

- What makes a good policy?

[1] Formerly the Department of Education and Employment.

It then goes on to outline BILD's contribution to the development of organisational policies on physical interventions before closing with a brief commentary on the relationship between policy and research on this topic.

## Why are policies needed?

Typically, services seek to marry a number of overarching and sometimes competing objectives. While it is important that services are tailored to meet the needs of individual service users, other priorities include:

**Equality** – everyone using the service has access to the same care and support and no one is arbitrarily denied opportunities that are available to other service users

**Consistency** – the level and quality of service does not fluctuate when services operate in different settings and are provided by different members of staff

**Reliability** – the quality of the service should be maintained in the light of changing needs or specific challenges presented by service users.

A service which simply exhorts its staff to 'be nice to the people you work with' or to 'encourage independence' is unlikely to be any more successful than Mrs Walters giving instructions to Chloe. This is partly because terms like 'independence' are open to a number of different interpretations. Even when they are clearly defined, the way in which they may be applied to different service users, living in different settings, is likely to require further elaboration. A policy is a way of describing how broad aims can be achieved for a variety of different service users, being supported by different members of staff, working in different settings, in a way that reflects the overarching priorities of equality, consistency and reliability.

In addition, services must be able to monitor the way in which staff carry out their duties and, if necessary, justify the actions taken. This is particularly important in the event that service users are harmed or concerns are raised about service quality. For example, if a service user is injured while on a fairground ride, staff might be asked to explain how the person concerned came to be on the ride and whether their actions had been guided by the service policy on managing risk. The policy is an important point of reference for all parties who might subsequently wish to explore the sequence of events leading up the incident, whether the injury was avoidable and if so, whether anyone should be held responsible. The policy helps to ensure that the service user is provided with support for independence and choice, while at the same time minimising the foreseeable risks that might arise.

Similarly, for staff, a policy offers protection against unfair accusations of negligence. For the service, the policy provides a reference point against which to evaluate the appropriateness of actions taken by individual members of staff. Finally, to the extent to which the policy reflects current thinking (as evidenced by a recognised professional body), and practice in other services, it will be an important part of any explanation offered to the person concerned and his or her representatives or family members. In the event of legal proceedings in the civil or criminal courts, it is likely to be a key document for both parties. For all these reasons, the importance of service policies is readily apparent.

## What is the context in which policies operate?

Given that it is possible to create a policy on almost anything and that the development and implementation of an effective policy requires considerable time and resources, it is inevitable that judgements will be made regarding the relative importance of a policy on topic X compared to a policy on topic Y. The emphasis placed on organisational policies and the importance attributed to a policy in any particular area will reflect both the practical considerations which operate within the service and the wider political and legal context. Each of these will be addressed in turn.

Factors within an organisation which influence the importance attributed to policies in general include:

- The size of the service, with larger services developing a greater number of policies

- The range and complexity of needs presented by service users

- The extent to which the service perceives its practice as being vulnerable to criticism or to legal challenge.

Factors within an organisation that affect the particular topics selected for policy development include:

- The characteristics of the people who use the service, for example, adults are likely to need different policies compared to children

- The values and broad aims of the service

- The settings in which service users live and spend their time.

External factors which influence the importance attributed to policies in particular areas include:

- Specific legal requirements, for example, arising from Health and Safety legislation

- Guidance from government departments

- Influence from commissioning authorities.

## Policies with a Purpose

Policies help the service provider to ensure that the experiences of individual service users reflect the broad aims of the service and that the service is provided in a way which is fair, consistent and reliable. For these outcomes to be achieved, not only must the policy address issues that have potential significance for service quality, but they must also be used in ways that have an impact on practice. An effective policy will influence a service in a number of different ways.

### Raising awareness

The process of developing a policy should, in itself, carry a strong message about the importance of the topic to all involved in the service. A consultation exercise is one way of informing everyone concerned about the new policy, gather information about specific issues which might need to be addressed in the policy and, also, highlight limited knowledge and poor practice which might subsequently be addressed as part of the implementation procedure.

### Shaping good practice

To the extent that a policy makes explicit expectations, which might previously have been implicit or only expressed verbally, it is, in itself, a vehicle for improving practice. To be effective it will need to dovetail with organisational structures, management lines of responsibility and accountability, job descriptions, care plans and other existing policies. In order to achieve consistency, a policy usually comprises general statements, which are applicable across a service or agency. In shaping good practice, the policy will often be used to establish more specific procedures, which apply to certain parts of the service or to particular service users (see Harris, 2001, for a description of the relationship between policies and procedures on physical interventions). Staff should be able to interpret their job descriptions in the context of the policy, and service users should have care plans that make reference to relevant policies.

### Highlighting staff training needs

The process of developing a policy may well reveal concerns about staff knowledge, attitudes or skills. Successful implementation may require additional staff training at different levels within the organisation.

### Focussing service evaluation and audit

Any attempt to determine how successfully a service meets the needs and aspirations of its users will involve a review of service policies, with respect to their relevance, accessibility, and effectiveness. In some services, policies are used as a starting point to evaluate organisational performance and each part of the policy is translated into specific measurable objectives.

### Improving the service

Finally, one of the main justifications for policies is that they can be used as part of a process of continuous service improvement. At each stage – raising awareness; shaping good practice; highlighting staff training needs and service evaluation – there are two opportunities for improving the service. One, there is an opportunity for staff and managers to evaluate and revise *the policy* in the light of experience. Two, what actually happens in *practice* can be measured against the policy and changes made where there are inconsistencies.

This process of continual feedback, evaluation and revision is summarised in Figure 3.1.

## Developing policies

In the preceding sections, it is suggested that a policy can be viewed in two ways: firstly as a document which sets out explicit expectations regarding how the service is provided and, secondly, as a tool that can be used both to evaluate the extent to which the service meets its aims and as a way of identifying weaknesses and limitations in the policy itself.

If policies are to succeed in addressing these dual objectives, particular care must be taken when developing and introducing them. Policies are rarely if ever developed in a vacuum. Instead they are usually introduced to clarify ongoing practice against a background of service values, legal requirements, and research evidence. These background factors may be more or less well defined and may or may not indicate a consensus regarding the main issues to be addressed and what constitutes good practice.

It is a considerable advantage if, at the outset, an up to date summary of the law, and associated government guidance affecting the area of practice under consideration is available, together with a commentary regarding the implications for those responsible as owners or managers of services. In the

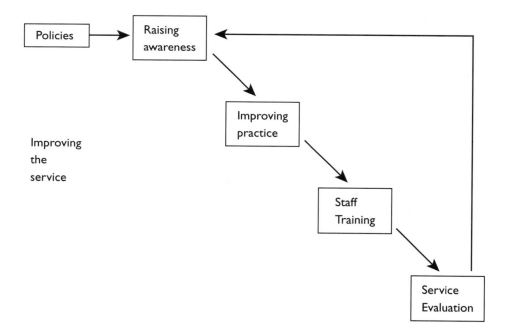

**Figure 3.1:** The Policy Feedback Loop

absence of this material, service managers will need to decide whether legal expertise is available within the service or, if it is appropriate to appoint an external consultant. It is however, worth stressing the inadvisability of proceeding without legal advice.

Not only will a policy need to be consistent with the underlying values of the service, but as the policy takes shape, clarification about what constitutes good practice and what might be regarded as unacceptable conduct, will need be guided by these underlying values. Service users have a key role to play in shaping service policies and a joint exploration of service values in relation to the policy under consideration by staff, service users and their families can provide a useful platform for further consultation.

Thirdly, theoretical and empirical research can often make a significant contribution to the creation of clear conceptual frameworks and to our understanding of good practice. Relevant literature on the topic under consideration should be subjected to a critical review and the implications for practice summarised.

Beyond the matter of placing the policy in the context of an agreed values base, relevant legal requirements and current research knowledge, there remains the question of the process by which the policy will be developed and evaluated. Policies are more likely to achieve the purposes set out above if they are prepared in close consultation with all those who might be affected, and particularly service users, their families or supporters and members of staff. Others who may wish to be involved in the consultation process include: advocacy groups; commissioners; professional bodies; trade unions; other services which contribute to the well-being of service users.

There is little doubt that consultation requires considerable time, a range of interpersonal and organisational skills and the ability to negotiate solutions that satisfy different points of view without compromising values, legal requirements or the evidence from research. Among the many different ways of developing a policy in consultation with different stakeholders, the summary in Table 3.1 represents the most widely used.

## What makes a good policy?

If the aim of a policy is to promote good, consistent, reliable practice for all service users, anything that contributes to this objective will be helpful. Hence, the importance of extensive consultation when developing a policy. In terms of a policy document, there are at least four critical features. These are summarised below.

### Consensus support

Irrespective of the formal status of a service policy and the sanctions that may apply if the policy is not followed, the policy will be more effective if those responsible for implementation are committed to making it work. Commitment from staff and service users is more likely when:

**Table 3.1:** Stages in developing an organisational policy

- Set up a working group with representatives from the main stakeholders and allocate tasks, including the key task of preparing and revising drafts. The working group should include people with direct experience of the issues under consideration, both as staff and as service users.

- Circulate information describing the area of practice under consideration and the reasons for reviewing the existing policy or creating a new policy. Indicate:
  - the process of consultation
  - how anyone interested can contribute
  - those involved in the working group
  - the time scale for each stage of the work.

- Prepare the first draft in the light of the value base of the service, relevant legal requirements, research and the shared experiences of those involved in the working group.

- Circulate the draft. The early stages of consultation might include everyone who could be affected by the policy or it might be restricted to those who responded to the initial announcement.

- Revise the policy in the light of feedback.

- Depending on the complexity of the policy and the level of interest aroused by the previous steps, it is often extremely helpful to organise meetings at which current thinking on the policy can be presented and discussed.

- After one or more rounds of consultation and revision, a final draft document should be circulated to everyone who might be affected by the policy and anyone else who has expressed an interest. When any final comments have been considered, the final version is issued.

- The policy is consistent with personal values as well as those espoused by the service. For example, policies on sexual relationships that support safe sex may conflict with the personal values of staff with particular religious beliefs.

- Staff and service users were actively involved in developing the policy

- The policy is seen to improve the quality of life for service users, for example, a policy on service user's money might create greater scope for individualised community activities.

- The policy has potential benefits for staff, for example, a policy on risk management might be seen as offering protection to staff in the event of an accident.

- The policy is seen as sensible and practical by staff and service users.

## Relevance

The policy should be clearly related to the issues which staff and service users are routinely required to address. The values, principles and research on which the policy is based should be described and the relationship between this knowledge and the service policy should be explained. It is helpful if the policy includes examples illustrating how it can be used to influence practice.

## Clarity

The policy should be written in plain English and available in other formats including large print or symbols so that it is accessible to all those who need to use it. Technical terminology and complex grammatical constructions should be avoided.

## Comprehensiveness

The policy should address all aspects of practice which arise within the identified area and should indicate other policies which impinge upon the issues being addressed.

## The development of service policies on physical interventions

In an ideal world, policies on physical interventions would be created against a background of agreed values, unambiguous legal advice, consistent government guidance and a strong evidence base from research. Gaps in the background would be filled in systematically so that those responsible for organisational policies could work in a logical and informed way.

In reality, when the BILD work on physical interventions began the only acknowledged frame of reference was the values base which had emerged following the work of O'Brien in the USA (O'Brien, 1987; Blunden, 1987). In contrast to the consensus around a set of core values, there were embarrassing gaps in other areas. The legal context for staff working in services was unclear. There was no government guidance which specifically addressed schools or adult services for people with an intellectual disability. Research evidence as a basis for developing good practice in the use of physical interventions was patchy and unreliable.

In these circumstances, it may have been wise to plug some of the gaps in the evidence base before trying to help services develop policies. In the event, logical analysis was overtaken by the availability of funding. However, developments over the last eight or nine years bear testament to the merits of pragmatism as a basis for achieving progress. In retrospect, it is clear that efforts to establish a policy framework provided an impetus for research rather than being a logical outcome of an emerging evidence base.

## Promoting local policies

In 1993 BILD, in collaboration with the National Autistic Society, began a modest project to develop advice for organisations seeking to develop organisational policies on the use of physical interventions. This involved an extended process of consultation with practitioners in the field and the establishment of an advisory group to review current practice and develop draft guidelines for consideration and comment. Initially, seventeen existing organisational policies on the use of 'physical restraint' in both schools and adult services were analysed and the work programme was announced in the BILD newsletter which, at that time, had a circulation of approximately 7,000. Subsequently, 170 copies of a final draft document were circulated with a feedback questionnaire to practitioners who had indicated an interest in the work and 48 were returned with comments. After minor amendments this was published by BILD in 1996 under the title *Physical Interventions: A Policy Framework* (Harris et al, 1996).

The Policy Framework highlights key areas for consideration by any organisation developing a local policy on the use of physical interventions. It is based upon 32 principles organised under nine headings. These are summarised in the table below. The Policy Framework includes a brief explanation of the relevance of each principle to practice, examples of good and poor practice and a checklist of questions to help organisations test the adequacy of the policies.

## Clarifying the law on the use of physical interventions

An earlier BILD project in schools for pupils with severe intellectual difficulties (Harris, Cook & Upton, 1996) had revealed the need for greater clarity regarding the legal protection for staff in schools who needed to physically intervene with their pupils. This resulted in the Mental Health Foundation (MHF) inviting Christina Lyon to undertake a review of the law relating to the care and control of children with severe learning difficulties and challenging behaviour (Lyon, 1994a).

**Table 3.2:** BILD Policy Principles

---

**The Law and Physical Interventions**

Any physical intervention should be consistent with the legal obligations and responsibilities of care agencies and their staff and the rights and protection afforded to people with intellectual disabilities under the law.

Working within the 'legal framework', services are responsible for the provision of care, including physical interventions, which are in a person's best interest.

**A Common Values Base**

Physical interventions should only be used in the best interest of the service user.

Service users should be treated fairly and with courtesy and respect.

Service users should be helped to make choices and be involved in making decisions which affect their lives.

There should be experiences and opportunities for learning which are appropriate to the person's interests and abilities.

---

**Prevention of Violence and Aggression**
Challenging behaviours can often be prevented by the careful management of the setting conditions.

The interaction between environmental setting conditions and personal setting conditions should be explored for each service user who presents a challenge. Setting conditions should be modified to reduce the likelihood of challenging behaviours occurring.

Establish secondary prevention procedures to ensure the problematic episodes are properly managed with non-physical interventions before service users become violent or aggressive.

For each service user who presents a challenge there should be individualised strategies for responding to incidents of violence and aggression. Where appropriate the strategy should include directions for using physical interventions.

**Promoting the Best Interest of Service Users**
Individualised procedures should be established for responding to service users who are likely to present violent or reckless behaviour. The procedures should enable care staff to respond effectively to violent or reckless behaviours while ensuring the safety of all concerned.

Physical interventions should only be used in conjunction with other strategies designed to help service users learn alternative non-challenging behaviours.

Planned physical interventions should be justified in respect of: what is known of the client from a formal multidisciplinary assessment; alternative approaches which have been tried; an evaluation of the potential risks involved; references to a body of expert knowledge and established good practice.

The use of physical interventions should be subject to regular review.

**Physical Interventions and Risk Assessment**
The potential hazards associated with the use of physical interventions should be systematically explored using a risk assessment procedure. Physical interventions should not involve unreasonable risk.

**Minimising Risk and Promoting the Well-Being of Service Users**
Physical interventions should be employed using the minimum reasonable force.

Any single application of physical intervention should be employed for the minimum period of time consistent with the best interests of the service user.

For individual service users, the use of physical interventions should be sanctioned for the shortest period of time consistent with his or her best interests.

Physical interventions should not cause pain.

Service users should have individual assessments to identify contra-indications to physical interventions before they are approved.

Service users who receive a physical intervention should be routinely assessed for signs of injury or psychological distress.

**Management Responsibilities**
Policy implementation: service managers are responsible for developing and implementing policies on the use of physical interventions.

The use of any physical intervention should be clearly set out in the form of written guidance for staff.

Monitoring and recording: service managers are responsible for ensuring that all incidents which involve the use of a physical intervention are clearly, promptly and comprehensively recorded.

All service users and their families and representatives should have ready access to an effective complaints system.

Careful consideration should be given to the impact of resource management on the use of physical interventions.

**Employers' Responsibility**
Employers and managers are responsible for the safety and well-being of staff.

Staff should be encouraged to monitor all physical interventions and to report any incidents which give cause for concern.

**Staff Training**
Staff who may be required to use physical interventions should receive regular training on knowledge, skills and values.

Training should be provided by an instructor with appropriate experience and qualifications.

Staff should only employ physical interventions which they have been trained to use.

Staff deployment should be organised to ensure that appropriately trained staff are available to respond to any incident which requires physical intervention.

Prior to the publication of Lyon's work, there was considerable confusion regarding both the circumstances in which physical interventions could be justified and the possible consequences of not intervening. This confusion can be attributed to the following:

- The absence of government guidance from either the Department of Health or the Department for Education and Employment in respect of adults and children with an intellectual disability and/or autism.

- A widespread misunderstanding of the implications of the Children Act and, in particular, the assumption that the emphasis placed upon, 'the paramount interests of the child', excluded the use of any kind of physical force whatsoever.

- The numerous Acts of Parliament which affect people receiving different kinds of care and the extensive body of case law which has evolved as this legislation has been tested in the courts.

While Lyon's work introduced a much needed legal manual, together with an invaluable guide for parents and carers (Lyon, 1994b), its relevance to the field was somewhat limited by its focus upon children under the jurisdiction of English Law. Furthermore, with the passage of time, the law has also changed dramatically so that much of the 1994 volume has been superseded by new legislation and associated guidance. A revised and updated version of Lyon's review, extended to address the law affecting adults with an intellectual disability and children with special educational needs throughout the UK, has recently been commissioned.

## The role of government

The simultaneous publication of the BILD Policy Framework (Harris et al, 1996) and the Mental Health Foundation's practical guide for carers and staff (Lyon, 1994b) not only assisted many services in shaping their own policies, but they also served to increase awareness about the use of physical interventions generally. Part of this interest was focussed on how best to train staff in the use of physical interventions and provided a stimulus for the development of the *BILD Code of Practice for Trainers* (BILD, 2001) and the creation of a formal scheme for the accreditation of trainers (see chapter 9).

Increased awareness among service staff also highlighted the absence of guidance from central government. However, it required legislation primarily concerned with the management of pupil behaviour in mainstream secondary schools (Education Act, 1996) to initiate guidance from the Department for Education and Employment (1998). Similarly, the Department of Health was only persuaded to prepare guidance by the public outcry following a BBC television programme 'MacIntyre under Cover' (BBC, 1999), which showed people with intellectual disabilities in a private care home being physically abused by staff under the guise of 'restraint'.

By this time, as a result of ongoing work and continued involvement with a growing network of experts on the use of physical intervention, BILD was in a good position to contribute to the development of draft guidance issued separately by both the Department of Health and the Department for Education and Employment. Representations were made from many sources, including BILD, on the potential for confusion arising from two different sets of guidance and the benefits of joint guidance to ensure a consistent approach within services working together to support children and young people with intellectual disabilities and/or special educational needs. The ministers concerned responded by agreeing to issue one set of guidance endorsed by both the Department of Health and the Department of Education and Skills. A consultation exercise was also conducted with service users with an intellectual disability prior to the guidance being submitted for ministerial approval.

Notwithstanding good progress in respect of the law affecting the use of physical interventions and the development of joint guidance from two government departments, the research evidence remains disturbingly sparse. The final section of this chapter considers why this gap remains in research on physical interventions and outlines some of the research questions which still need to be addressed in the future.

## Research & Evaluation

If one accepts the standard view that empirical research provides the 'gold standard' for evidence in social care practice as well as in medicine, at the time of writing (July 2001), good practice in the use of physical interventions is rather precariously balanced upon an extremely narrow evidence base (Allen, 2001). A reluctance by government and charitable bodies to fund research which may prove controversial, together with problems which arise when any attempt is made to examine clandestine care practices have been the main reasons for this unfortunate state of affairs. However, there is a well-defined research agenda which needs to be addressed if the work on policy development and implementation, and the growing consensus around good practice in the use of physical interventions, is to be based on anything more substantial than a distillation of personal experiences.

### Service audit

The role of a service audit is to collect information that will permit an objective evaluation of the service performance against agreed criteria. In the light of research which shows that as many as 50% of people who present challenging behaviour will be exposed to physical interventions (Emerson, 2000), it is reasonable to suppose that both the performance criteria and the audit information will address this topic. Table 3.3 shows how an organisational policy on physical interventions can be used to generate specific measurable outcomes. The example is concerned with one service standard on the provision of staff training.

Audit data should provide services with information on:

- the number of incidents which result in the use of physical interventions within a given period of time

- the names of staff involved in using physical interventions

- the level of training undertaken by all staff who may be required to use a physical intervention

- any injuries incurred by service users and staff as a consequence of physical interventions

- the physical and psychological consequences of restrictive physical interventions for service users and for members of staff.

This data should be routinely analysed to indicate:

**Table 3.3:** Relating service policy to service outcomes

| Service standard | Structure | Process | Outcome | Criteria | Audit Method |
|---|---|---|---|---|---|
| Adequate training is given to all staff in dealing with, and the prevention of, challenging behaviour, violence and aggression. | • Staff who are required to use physical interventions should receive regular training on knowledge, skills and values<br>• Staff should only employ physical interventions which they have been trained to use<br>• Training should be provided by an instructor with appropriate experience and qualifications<br>• Staff deployment should be organised to ensure that appropriately trained staff are available to respond to any incident which requires physical intervention | • A programme of training on dealing with violence and aggression, breakaway techniques and restraint is organised and implemented for all appropriate staff<br>• An ongoing programme for training and updating instructors is formulated<br>• A procedure on deployment of staff is drawn up for use during incidents of challenging behaviour, violence and aggression<br>• Staffing levels in areas at most risk are reviewed in line with changes in clients and client behaviour. | • The service provides a programme of training for staff who work with service users who present challenging behaviours and all those likely to come into contact with those service users<br>• The instructors who provide training have appropriate experience and qualifications<br>• Staff are informed about who can and cannot use physical interventions with service users and this is documented<br>• Adequate staff, with appropriate experience and training, are available to respond to incidents of challenging behaviour. | • An ongoing programme of training for staff who work with service users who present challenging behaviours is formulated and provided<br>• An ongoing programme of training and updating for instructors is agreed upon and provided<br>• Clear guidelines are drawn up informing staff who can and cannot use physical interventions with service users<br>• A clear policy is drawn up regarding immediate response to incidents of challenging behaviour<br>• Complaints regarding the use of physical interventions are investigated following the organisation's complaints procedure. | • Survey patient records<br>• Recording of reviews<br>• Quality visits<br>• Spot checks on management minutes<br>• Untoward incident audit<br>• Complaints reviews |

- Trends over time in the use of physical interventions

- Variations across the service in the use of restrictive physical interventions (for example, comparing different units or different staff shifts)

- The impact of training on the frequency with which physical interventions are used (effective training should result in a decrease in the use of physical interventions).

Over and above the benefits arising from each service reviewing its own audit information, much could be learned from national statistics. Notwithstanding the advice from government and other national bodies encouraging services to collect information on the use of physical interventions, there are no data available to permit the charting of national trends. Currently, it is simply not possible to provide any objective evidence regarding even the most basic questions, for example:

- Nationally, how often are physical interventions used to manage the behaviour of adults and children with an intellectual disability or pupils with special educational needs?

- How many injuries are sustained by service users and by staff as a result of using physical interventions?

- Do staff who have been trained to use physical interventions actually resort to physical interventions less often than staff who have not been trained?

- Do physical interventions applied by trained staff result in fewer injuries compared to physical interventions applied by untrained staff?

There are two main reasons why national statistics on the use of physical interventions are not available. First, there is considerable anecdotal evidence to suggest that recording is subject to wide variations of interpretation, both within and between services. The introduction of a nationally agreed approach, using reliable methods of data collection, similar to that being developed by the Royal College of Psychiatry (2001), is therefore essential for generating meaningful evidence both locally, within organisations, and nationally. Secondly, no organisation has a responsibility, or indeed the resources, to collect and analyse information collected locally to establish a broader picture. Until these two deficiencies are addressed, there is little prospect of any systematic monitoring of trends in the use of physical interventions.

## Techniques for physical intervention

By definition, a physical intervention involves direct contact between a member of staff and a service user. Situations in which the member of staff decides to use some degree of force to restrict the movements of the service user are inherently risky. That decision should be based on an assessment of likely outcomes in a least two scenarios: firstly, if the physical intervention is employed and secondly if the physical intervention is not employed, but some other non-physical way of managing the situation is adopted.

The risks associated with *using* a physical intervention will be influenced by a whole host of factors. Among these should be a clear understanding of the specific techniques which might be employed and the relative risks and benefits associated with each technique. Unfortunately, once again, this is a topic on which the published research literature has almost nothing to contribute. Many of the techniques taught as physical interventions for staff working in schools and services for people with an intellectual disability originated in the martial arts and have been gradually modified as a result of trial and error within a variety of different service settings (Lindsay & Hosie, 2000). Apart from internal evaluations conducted by some of the training companies, there is little research evidence available to indicate whether some positions, holds or techniques are more or less risky for those involved. The data produced from national surveys (for example, the Hartford Courant Study 1998) clearly highlight the potential risks associated with certain positions, for example prone restraint, but they do not provide sufficient data to draw definitive conclusions.

Professional trainers are best placed to make judgements about the level of risk associated with different ways of holding or positioning someone during a physical intervention. Unfortunately, many of those with extensive experience as trainers are also those with a commercial interest in perpetuating particular techniques. Without evidence regarding the adverse outcomes associated with different types of physical intervention (see above), or detailed studies to document bio-mechanical risk factors, there is little scope for separating commercial self interests from the best interests of service users and staff.

## Efficacy of training

Agency policies and draft government guidance (Department of Health, 2000; Department of Education and Employment, 2000) place great emphasis on staff training as a vehicle for improving practice in the use of physical interventions. While there is some empirical support for the view that well organised staff training is a necessary condition for raising standards of practice in services, there is very little evidence to indicate the circumstances that are associated with consistent positive outcomes from training staff in the use of physical interventions.

After carrying out a systematic review of 45 papers from peer-reviewed journals and the 'grey literature' Allen (2001) drew two rather pessimistic conclusions. First, much of the published research on this topic is of poor quality owing to methodological limitations and a lack of detail about the training methods employed. Second, while some research reports positive changes in staff knowledge, confidence and skills, none of these can be guaranteed. Moreover, some research studies found that training produced a negative impact on these outcome measures.

While there is general agreement that training is needed, in the absence of sound research based knowledge, it really is anybody's guess as to how much training to provide, on what topics and techniques, over what period of time, with what combination of training methods and with what levels of refresher training to follow. In comparison, the choice between different leading 'brands' of training is probably of only minor significance.

In view of the scale of training which is currently delivered and the promise of increasing resources being committed to training in the future (Department of Health, 2001) this reliance on poorly informed subjective judgements is potentially wasteful of both staff time and scarce financial resources. More importantly, it places at risk the whole strategy of raising standards by investing in staff training. If nothing much changes after three or four years of funding for poorly targeted staff training initiatives, there will be little justification for continued support. This will be the case even if it is possible to demonstrate that some trainers working in some services, by luck or good judgement, actually achieved positive long-term outcomes.

## Impact of policies

Finally, it is worth asking whether anything is achieved by policy initiatives and, in particular, attempts to influence the design, development and implementation of organisational policies. The BILD publication *Physical Interventions: A Policy Framework* was produced against a background of very limited research, and much of that which was available was undertaken in controlled clinical conditions in the United States (Harris, 1996). It therefore summarises best current knowledge and has helped to set the agenda for subsequent work on the evidence base, the need for government guidance, staff training and the development of organisational policies. The question as to the impact of the BILD Policy Framework on service planning, service policies and staff practices has been addressed by an independent research evaluation which is described in chapter 4.

## Summary

This chapter has provided a short overview of the issues that services need to address when developing organisational policies. While it is desirable that policy development is firmly based on shared values, a clear appreciation of the legal framework, a knowledge of relevant government policies and a good understanding of the available research evidence, this is seldom possible in practice. Above all policies should be practical tools that help organisations and their staff to achieve positive outcomes for service users. To this end they need to be based upon current knowledge, bearing in mind that, very often, such knowledge will itself be based on what works in everyday practice. When used effectively, policies become part of an iterative process that enables the service to both monitor its performance against the policy and review the policy in the light of evolving practice.

## Acknowledgements
My thanks to Alison Wall and David Allen for their helpful comments on a draft version of this chapter. I also like to thank the Department of Health and the Department for Education and Skills who have funded much of the work described.

# References

Allen, D (2001) *Training Carers in Physical Interventions: Research Towards Evidence Based Practice*. Kidderminster: BILD Publications

BILD (2001) *Code of Practice for Trainers in the Use of Physical Interventions*, Kidderminster: BILD Publications.

Blunden, R (1987) Quality of life in persons with disabilities: issues in the development of services. In Brown, RI (Ed) *Quality of Life for Handicapped People*. Beckenham: Croom Helm, pp.37–55.

Department of Education and Employment (1998) *Circular 10/98 Guidance on Section 550A of the 1996 Education Act*. London: Department for Education and Employment.

Department of Education and Employment (2000) *Promoting Positive Handling Strategies for Pupils with Severe Behavioural Difficulties (Draft for consultation)*. London: Department for Education and Employment.

Department for Education and Skills and Department of Health (2002) *Guidance for Restrictive Physical Interventions. How to provide safe services for people with learning disabilities and autistic spectrum disorder*. London: Department of Health.

Department of Health (2001) *Valuing People: A New Strategy for Learning Disability for the 21st Century*. London: Department of Health.

Emerson, E (2000) Treatment and management of challenging behaviour in residential settings. *Journal of Applied Research in Intellectual Disabilities*, 13, 4, 197–215.

Harris, J C, Cook, M & Upton, G (1996). *Pupils with Severe Learning Disabilities and Challenging Behaviour: A Whole School Approach to Assessment and Intervention*. Kidderminster: BILD Publications.

Harris, J (1996) Physical restraint procedures for managing challenging behaviours presented by mentally retarded adults and children. *Research in Developmental Disabilities*, 17, 2, 99–134.

Harris, J (2001) Physical abuse and physical interventions – from policy to practice. *Journal of Adult Protection*, 3,2, 18–24.

Harris, J, Allen, D, Cornick, M, Jefferson, A & Mills, R (1996) *Physical Interventions: A Policy Framework*. Kidderminster: BILD Publications

Hartford Courant (1998) *Deadly Restraint: National Restraint Death Database*, http://courant.ctnow.com/projects/restraint/death_data.stm

Lindsay, M & Hosie, A (2000) *The Edinburgh Inquiry – Recommendation 55, The Independent Evaluation Report*. Glasgow: The University of Strathclyde and the former Centre for Residential Child Care.

Lyon, CM (1994a) *Legal Issues Arising from the Care, Control and Safety of Children with Learning Disabilities who also present Challenging Behaviour*. London: Mental Health Foundation.

Lyon, CM (1994b) *Legal Issues Arising from the Care and Control of Children with Learning Disabilities who also present Severe Challenging Behaviour: A Guide for Parents and Carers*. London: Mental Health Foundation.

O'Brien, J (1987) A Guide to Lifestyle Planning. In Wilcox, BW, & Bellamy, GT (Eds) *The Activities Catalogue: An Alternative Curriculum for Youth and Adults with Severe Disabilities*. Baltimore: Paul H Brookes.

Royal College of Psychiatry (2001) *National Multi-centre Audit of the Management of Violence in Services for People with Learning Disabilities. Newsletter No.1*. London: RCP, Multi-Centre Audit Team.

# Chapter 4

# Assessing the impact of the BILD/NAS Policy Framework

Glynis Murphy, Amanda Kelly-Pike and Peter McGill

## Introduction

Staff often feel at a loss when faced with severe challenging behaviour which may result in harm to themselves or others. At such times, physical interventions such as restraint may be necessary, although ideally such techniques should only be used within a framework of planned programmes of positive behavioural support, as both Allen et al, (1997) and Stirling (2001) have commented.

Physical interventions are known to present risks to both staff and service users (Hill and Spreat, 1987), particularly when the interventions are 'unplanned' (Spreat et al, 1986), and the long term effects of such procedures are poorly understood (Harris, 1996). Indeed, some service users have died as a result of physical interventions being inappropriately applied (DHSS, 1985; Community Care, 1997). In addition, cases have come to light where physical interventions or restraint appear to have been used in an abusive manner (MacIntyre, 1999).

It could be argued that such poor practice would be less likely were there a clear policy framework for the use of physical interventions. Such a framework has, however, been slow to develop in the UK, with many services relying on 'in-house' policies at best.

As a result of the recommendations of the Ritchie report (DHSS, 1985) into the death of Michael Martin, NHS staff in mental health and intellectual disability services were increasingly offered training in 'Control and Restraint' (C&R), a method of physical intervention originally developed in the prison service (Wright, 1999). A number of other approaches have developed over the last decade, but there has been very little guidance available for staff about the relative merits of the different methods, either in terms of their content (Beech, 2001) or their effectiveness (Allen et al, 1997; Baker & Bissimire, 2001; McDonnell, 1997).

In 1996, funding from the Department of Health enabled the British Institute of Learning Disabilities and the National Autistic Society to draw up a policy framework for the use of physical interventions with people with intellectual disabilities (Harris et al, 1996). The framework defined physical interventions and provided guidance on the law, values, prevention of violence, best interests, risk assessment, minimising risks, managers' and employers' responsibilities and staff training. Subsequently, BILD and the NAS were interested in establishing the extent to which their policy document was affecting practice in services and an independent evaluation of the impact of the policy document was commissioned from the Tizard Centre at the University of Kent. This chapter reports on some of the outcomes of this evaluation.

## Staff and services involved in the evaluation

Two of the most important issues for the evaluation were the extent to which staff in intellectual disability services knew about the policy document (Harris et al, 1996) and the degree to which staff used the document in their services. BILD and the NAS hoped that by running a series of three conferences on physical interventions, at which the policy framework was presented and copies of the document distributed to delegates, knowledge about and use of the framework would become widespread. The conferences were held in London, Manchester and Birmingham in 1996 and 1997.

In the evaluation, it was decided to survey the staff attending these conferences; in the analyses that follow, these staff made up *Group 1*. In addition, it was reasoned that other samples of staff needed to be included in the study, since those attending the BILD/NAS conferences may have already had a special interest in physical interventions and thus constitute a rather biased sample. Two further groups of staff were therefore included:

- A geographical sample (*Group 2*), consisting of staff managing educational, day, residential and peripatetic services for children and adults with intellectual disabilities in two boroughs in south east London served by one NHS Trust (the total population of the two boroughs together amounted to approximately 435,000) and a rural county in south east England (total population 499,000).

- A special assessment and treatment service sample (*Group 3*), consisting of staff managing services that offered short-term specialist assessment and treatment for people with intellectual disabilities in England. It was reasoned that these services would be the ones most likely to be in need of comprehensive information about physical interventions and training in physical interventions.

All three groups of staff were sent a questionnaire that sought the following information:

- Name, age, gender, job title, workplace and ethnic background of the respondent

- Professional qualifications and years working in services for people with autism and/or intellectual disabilities

- Details of the type of service that respondents were working in

- Training in methods of physical intervention received by the respondent

- Methods of physical intervention used in the respondent's service

- Whether the respondent had attended one of the BILD/NAS conferences and, if so, their view of its usefulness to their work (on a five point rating scale)

- Their views of the document *Physical Interventions: A Policy Framework,* both overall and section by section (on five point rating scales)

- Their opinions on the strengths and weaknesses of the policy document (free response section)

- Their views on what additional guidance was required, in terms of further principles, more depth and/or new issues (free response sections)

- Their thoughts on what their own organisation needed to do to promote the safety and wellbeing of service users (and staff) exposed to physical interventions

- Their ideas as to what BILD and other such organisations needed to do to promote the safety and wellbeing of service users (and staff) exposed to physical interventions

- Whether their service had a written policy on the use of physical interventions

- An indication of whether they would be prepared to complete a second questionnaire regarding physical interventions (results from this second questionnaire will not be presented here).

## Results of the evaluation

Postal questionnaires run the risk of producing very low response rates but the rates in this evaluation were relatively good: 34% (Group 1), 39% (Group 2) and 46% (Group 3). Staff responding to the questionnaires were generally very experienced in intellectual disability services and were relatively well qualified, though somewhat less so in Group 2 (see table 4.1).

In all three groups, staff were employed in a variety of different types of services, including schools, residential homes, day services and peripatetic teams, and in many different roles (see table 4.2). Not surprisingly, the precise balance of types of services varied a little from group to group (so that, for example, there were more hospital services in Group 3).

It appeared that respondents had been exposed to a large number of different methods or 'brands' of physical intervention training (see table 4.3). Many of

**Table 4.1:** Participant characteristics

| Variable | | Group 1 (conf) (n=115) | Group 2 (geog) (n=165) | Group 3 (SPAT) (n=61) |
|---|---|---|---|---|
| Age | Mean | 43.3 years | 44.3 years | 40.6 years |
| | Range | 30–65 years | 22–72 years | 29–54 years |
| | Std deviation | 6.7 years | 10.2 years | 6.1 years |
| Years worked in intellectual disabilities | Mean | 17.5 years | 13.9 years | 16.9 years |
| | Range | 3–31 years | 1–39 years | 2–32 years |
| | Std deviation | 6.0 years | 7.3 years | 7.0 years |
| Gender | Male | 53 (46%) | 59 (36%) | 25 (41%) |
| | Female | 63 (54%) | 106 (64%) | 36 (59%) |
| Ethnic origin (only categories for which there were entries are listed here) | White | 91% | 92% | 85% |
| | Irish | 5% | 1% | 3% |
| | Black Caribbean | 1% | 0% | 0% |
| | Black British | 2% | 0% | 2% |
| | Black other | 1% | 1% | 5% |
| | Other | 0% | 6% | 5% |
| Professional qualifications | Nursing (RMN/RNMH) | 32% | 16% | 71% |
| | Social work | 11% | 8% | 2% |
| | Clin Psychology | 7% | 1% | 5% |
| | Teaching | 38% | 25% | 10% |
| | Other | 10% | 22% | 12% |
| | None | 1% | 29% | 0% |

these methods included at least some training in breakaway skills and de-escalation skills and most participants in Groups 1 and 3 had been trained in these aspects, though fewer of Group 2 had either kind of training (see figure 4.1).

Similarly, the services of most respondents in Groups 1 and 3 used breakaway and de-escalation methods, while fewer services in Group 2 did so (see Figure 4.2). Many of these differences between Group 2 and the other two groups were significant (Murphy et al, submitted).

Respondents were themselves trained in a variety of different approaches to physical intervention training (see table 4.3 and figures 4.3 & 4.4). In all, 81% of Group 1, 61% of Group 2 and 87% of Group 3 had training in at least one specific method (excluding training in breakaway and de-escalation skills). It appeared that the 'market leaders' in terms of the methods of physical intervention in which respondents were trained were either a variation of Control and Restraint (including Care and Responsibility, Dignified Control and

**Table 4.2:** Service characteristics

| | Group 1 (conf) participants (n=115) | Group 2 (geog) participants (n=165) | Group 3 (SPAT) participants (n=61) |
|---|---|---|---|
| **Sector worked in** | | | |
| NHS Trust | 30% | 5% | 57% |
| Local Education Authority | 26% | 11% | 0% |
| Social Services Department | 15% | 18% | 2% |
| Voluntary or 'not for profit' org | 14% | 26% | 10% |
| Private hospital | 0% | 0% | 13% |
| Other private organisation | 10% | 36% | 18% |
| Other (eg HE; indep. consultancy) | 6% | 4% | 0% |
| **Care role on an everyday basis** | | | |
| Residential home (care worker, manager, etc) | 15% | 69% | 43% |
| Day service (eg instructor, manager) | 4% | 9% | 3% |
| Educational (school, FE college) | 28% | 13% | 13% |
| Peripatetic (eg CTLD) | 25% | 2% | 5% |
| Care manager | 2% | 0% | 0% |
| Management (no contact w. SUs) | 16% | 6% | 8% |
| Other (eg service managers w. contact with SUs, training, inspection) | 11% | 1% | 28% |

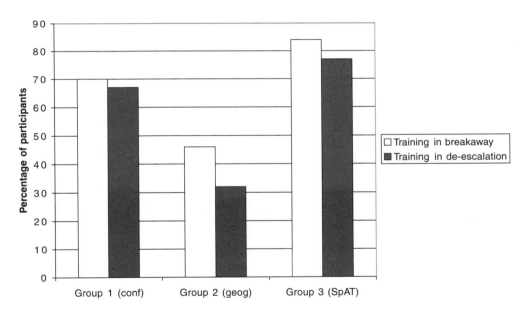

**Figure 4.1:** Percentage of respondents with training in breakaway and de-escalation skills across the three groups

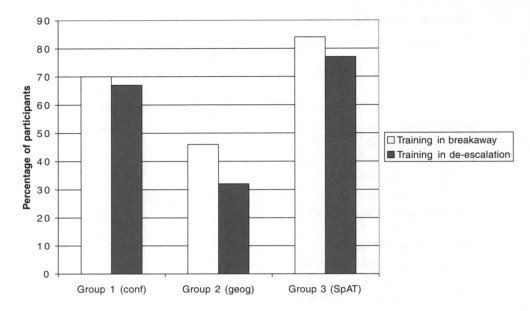

**Figure 4.2:** Percentage of respondents using breakaway and de-escalation skills in their services across the three groups

Restraint, General Services Control and Restraint) or SCIP (Strategies for Crisis Intervention and Prevention). This was true for all three samples (see table 4.3). These methods were also the most commonly used methods in services, for all three samples, although C&R and its variants were relatively more common in Group 3 services than the other services (Murphy et al, submitted).

It was noticeable that, across groups, staff in certain settings appeared more likely to have been trained in or to use particular techniques. For instance:

- More NHS* staff (76%) than LEA staff (51%) or other staff (57%) were trained in breakaway techniques

- More NHS staff (76%) than LEA staff (55%) or other staff (42%) were trained in de-escalation skills

- More NHS staff were trained in C&R (58%) than LEA (32%) or other staff (40%)

- LEA staff seemed to be more often trained in SCIP (43%) than NHS (22%) or other staff (33%).

Not surprisingly, these differences in training were reflected in the extent to which the various types of services actually used the different methods (Murphy et al, submitted).

When it came to service policies on the use of physical interventions, most participants said they either had a written policy or were actively developing a written policy on the use of physical interventions (71% of Group 1, 58% of Group 2 and 80% of Group 3 said this). The remainder of each group had no written policy.

---

\* For simplicity here private hospital services & staff are included under 'NHS'

**Table 4.3:** Comparison of respondents' own training in physical interventions

| Method | Group 1 (conf): % of participants trained in this method (n=115) | Group 1 (geog): % of participants trained in this method (n=165) | Group 3 (SPAT): % of participants trained in this method (n=61) |
|---|---|---|---|
| Control & restraint | 45% | 33% | 66% |
| Care & responsibility | 16% | 16% | 20% |
| Strategies for Crisis Intervention and Prevention (SCIP) | 37% | 32% | 20% |
| STUDIO–III | 6% | 1% | 7% |
| Non-aversive Psychological & Physical Interventions (NAPPI) | 11% | 10% | 7% |
| Protection of Rights in Care Environments (PRICE) | 5% | 6% | 3% |
| Preventing and responding to aggressive behaviour (Welsh Centre method) | 5% | 7% | 3% |
| Natural Therapeutic Holding/Options method | 5% | 2% | 0% |
| Timian training | 3% | 1% | 0% |
| Crisis Aggression Limitation and Management (CALM) | 1% | 4% | 0% |
| Other methods (eg Team Teach; in house methods) | 17% | 10% | 13% |
| None | 19% | 39% | 13% |

As stated above, Group 1 were specifically selected as people who had attended the BILD/NAS conferences on physical interventions (76%) or who had purchased the policy document (24%). Far fewer of the other groups had been to the training conferences (2% of Group 2 and 7% of Group 3), suggesting that the dissemination of the framework may not have been as widespread as had

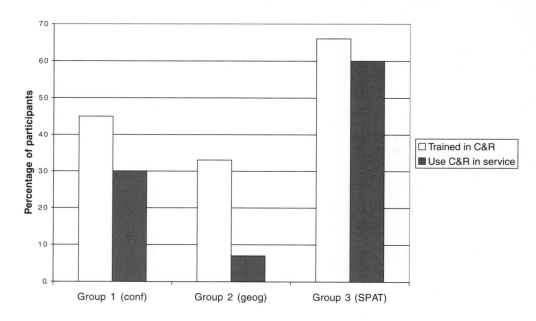

**Figure 4.3:** Percentage of respondents with training in C&R and using C&R in their services across the three groups

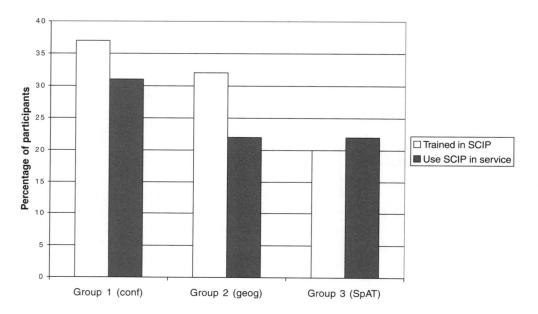

**Figure 4.4:** Percentage of respondents with training in SCIP and using SCIP in their services, in the three groups

been hoped. Of those who had attended the conferences (from any group), the vast majority rated the conference as 'extremely useful' (18%), 'very useful' (50%) or 'quite useful' (25%) to their work, only 4% rating the conferences as 'a little useful' or 'not at all useful' to their work (see figure 4.5).

Almost all of the respondents in Group 1 (97%) said that they had read or partly read the BILD/NAS policy framework document, whereas fewer of Group 3 had

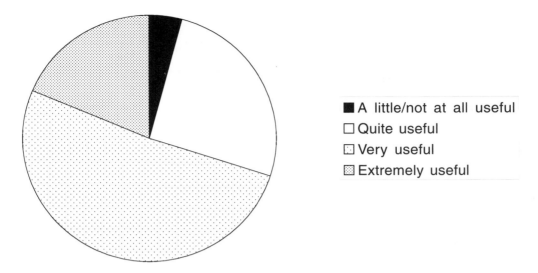

**Figure 4.5:** Respondents' views of the usefulness of the BILD/NAS conferences on physical interventions to their work

done so (39%) and only 13% of Group 2 had done so. Respondents mostly found the document 'extremely easy' (28%) or 'very easy' (51%) to understand (19% rated it as 'quite easy' to understand and only 1% rated it as harder than this). Group 2 seemed to find the document somewhat more difficult to understand than the other two groups (see table 4.4) but this was not statistically significant.

The majority of participants were overwhelmingly positive about the usefulness of the Policy Framework document to their work (see figure 4.6), with 22% rating it as extremely useful, 40% rating it as very useful, 35% rating it as quite useful (and only 7% rating it less than this). The various sections were also highly rated (see table 4.5). The groups did not differ significantly on any of these aspects of the policy framework.

Participants in all of the groups noted various strengths of the Policy Framework, including the broad overall perspective, the fact that it was useful for staff training and policy development, the fact that summaries were provided for each section, the 'good' and 'bad' practice examples and the action points. Respondents were generally extremely positive in their comments and some examples from Group 1's comments are given below (see also Murphy et al, 2001):

*'The document is a landmark and should be required reading for all ... The DfEE should be distributing it free of charge to all schools where physical interventions are an unfortunate fact of life. Similarly (for) Health and Social Services'.*

*'Excellent for reference and reminding (us) of all the key issues relating to such a complex area. We've used it for the basis of our current policy development.... Always on my desk'*

**Table 4.4:** Ratings of the readability and usefulness of the Policy Framework document

| Group | Not at all | A little | Quite | Very | Extremely |
|---|---|---|---|---|---|
| Group 1: readability (n=103) | 0% | 0% | 18% | 52% | 31% |
| Group 2: readability (n=15) | 7% | 0% | 40% | 40% | 13% |
| Group 3: readability (n=22) | 0% | 0% | 14% | 59% | 27% |
| Group 1: usefulness (n=102) | 1% | 6% | 30% | 41% | 22% |
| Group 2: usefulness (n=15) | 7% | 7% | 40% | 33% | 13% |
| Group 3: usefulness (n=22) | 0% | 9% | 32% | 27% | 32% |

'(It) raises issues that matter. For too long there has been a culture that has not 'challenged' the status quo'.

'As you can see from our policies, copies enclosed, the document was fantastic! I couldn't have done my work without it'

Participants were also asked to comment on the weaknesses of the Policy Framework. Most people noted no weaknesses. Of those who did note weaknesses, it was very rare for these to be direct criticisms. Some respondents did consider that the framework was somewhat idealistic (n=4), but only one person was thoroughly negative, saying that 'It seemed to me that BILD has very tunnel vision. It advocates SCIP which I know doesn't work with adults that are violent'. In fact, of course, BILD does not 'advocate' any particular technique,

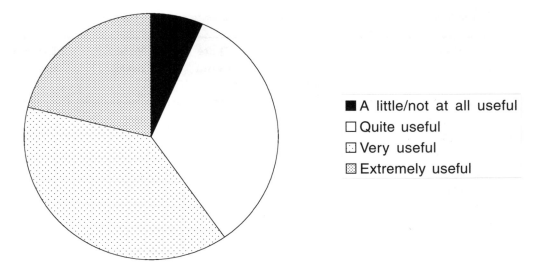

**Figure 4.6:** Respondents' views of the usefulness of the BILD/NAS policy framework on physical interventions to their work

and this in itself was an aspect of the policy framework that drew some criticisms (see below).

Most often, under 'weaknesses', the plea was for more guidance on:

- The law

- Risk assessment

- How to consult with service users and/or parents on physical interventions

- Health and Safety requirements and/or employer responsibility

- Setting events or triggers

- Debriefing and/or staff counselling

- The role of medication as a form of physical intervention

- How to deal with physical interventions in public.

Some respondents also asked for abbreviated versions of the framework for all staff to read. By far the most common comment, however, related to the need for guidance on training methods. These were variously phrased, for example:

*'It is not prescriptive of what you can actually do... More guidance could be given regarding the confusion between the various types of training available and the legal status they hold if something goes wrong, ie if trained people then become trainers and disseminate information to others, what level of expertise is recognised as ... sufficient?'*

**Table 4.5:** Ratings of the usefulness of the different sections of the Policy Framework document

| Section | 'Not at all' or 'A little useful' | Quite useful | Very useful | Extremely useful |
|---|---|---|---|---|
| Guidance on law (n=136) | 7% | 35% | 40% | 18% |
| Guidance on values (n=134) | 6% | 30% | 53% | 11% |
| Guidance on prevention of challenging behaviour (n=135) | 12% | 40% | 38% | 10% |
| Guidance on promoting best interests (n=135) | 7% | 31% | 44% | 18% |
| Guidance on risk assessment (n=137) | 8% | 32% | 46% | 14% |
| Guidance on risk minimisation (n=134) | 10% | 31% | 43% | 16% |
| Guidance on management responsibility (n=134) | 8% | 30% | 45% | 17% |
| Guidance on employer responsibility (n=134) | 10% | 40% | 35% | 15% |
| Guidance on staff training (n=134) | 16% | 33% | 36% | 15% |

*'The real problem is which training to use – there seems to be no independent evaluation available of the different types, which to my knowledge are very different. Also what is the legal position in relation to different techniques/types of training?'*

*'(The) policy framework document does not look at the various alternatives available for restraining individuals – an evaluation of the various models to look at their efficacy from a research evidence point of view would be useful.'*

*'There is no reference to specific acceptable or unacceptable interventions. There is a need to give more specific guidelines which could enhance the national standards already established for RCN and ENB.'*

One respondent also identified a possible reason for the proliferation of methods, in the absence of any national co-ordination or control: the commercial motive, since most training is provided by independent agencies. She said:

*'How do you deal with the 'hard sell' of people running physical interventions? They all seem to want to put the others down, rather than look at service and client needs.'*

When asked what they thought their organisation needed to do to improve the safety and wellbeing of service users and staff in relation to physical interventions, by far the most common tasks named were the provision of more staff training on physical interventions and the development or improvement of the organisation's own policy documents on physical interventions. Some respondents took a broad and constructive view and commented that they felt they needed to improve the service quality generally because of the impact this would in turn have upon the use of physical interventions. For example, one deputy head teacher said:

*'To further extend and develop the facilities available to pupils in the hope of reducing anxiety and providing enough variety of enjoyable activities to lower the rate of incidents. To establish a variety of safe places where students can go to calm or relax at stressful times. To further improve our approaches to communication, social understanding, curriculum delivery, physical exertion, so pupils have less need to become anxious.'*

When asked what they thought BILD and other similar organisations should do to improve the safety and wellbeing of service users and staff in relation to physical interventions, a number of respondents asked that BILD act as an information centre and network promoter. There were also some pleas for up-dated versions of the policy document, since a number of other related publications had appeared, including the Royal College of Nursing (1999 and 2000) and the Royal College of Psychiatrists (1998) guides on physical interventions; the Mental Health Act revised codes of practice (Department of Health and the Welsh Office, 1999) and the 1997 Education Act (care and control), section 550A, circular 10/98, which gave guidance for LEAs on the use of physical interventions. However, the most frequent pleas were for BILD/NAS to provide low cost training, to mandate training and/or to provide advice on approved training courses. There were also suggestions that BILD could identify how training could be monitored for quality and efficiency. Two people seemed to sum up many respondents' concerns, asking BILD for:

*'Clarification regarding the various approaches to physical intervention – some core shared content and uniformity relating to interventions used, their legal acceptability and all the preventative approaches. Why do we have so many different systems? It is confusing to parents and staff...'*

*'If practice is to be challenged there must be agreed standards for trainers, including a directory of physical skills. Currently the whole area of physical skills training is a mess, with all sorts of weird and/or potentially dangerous practices being taught by a variety of trainers.'*

## Conclusions

The results of the evaluation need to be viewed with some caution since not all those who were sent questionnaires returned them. However, the results do provide some initial information on staff training in physical interventions in intellectual disability services and they do show what staff thought of the BILD/NAS policy framework document on physical interventions.

It appeared that by no means all staff in intellectual disability services were trained in the simple physical interventions of breakaway and de-escalation skills. Nor did all staff have any specific training in a particular method or 'brand' of physical interventions, even when they worked in a specialist assessment and treatment service, where it is known that physical interventions are likely to be commonly employed (Emerson et al, 2000; Adams & Allen, 2001). This was worrying as it seemed likely that, if anything, the evaluation overstated the degree of training in physical interventions that was typical in the organisations surveyed, since the respondents were relatively senior and well qualified.

There appeared to be a large number of different types of physical interventions training available, including at least three based on C&R. Variants of C&R and SCIP appeared to be 'market leaders' in intellectual disability services and it seemed that C&R was utilised particularly in NHS and specialist assessment and treatment services. However, whether this was because C&R is actually more effective than the other methods or whether it merely reflects the historical events surrounding cases such as that of Michael Martin is not known.

A remarkably large number of services surveyed (about one third of participants in all) did not have written policies for the use of physical interventions. This was particularly worrying in the case of specialist assessment and treatment services, as they were very likely to be using physical interventions regularly.

Overall, staff who had read the BILD/NAS policy framework document very much welcomed it. They mostly rated it as highly readable and very useful. In general, they seemed to want more guidance on a number of key areas and they often voiced concerns about the plethora of methods of physical interventions available and the lack of information and research into their relative efficacy. It was of concern, though, that very large numbers of respondents in Groups 2 and 3 seemed to be unaware of the existence of the policy framework document (less than a sixth of Group 2 and a little over a third of Group 3 had read or even partly read the document). Of course, this would be immaterial if there were numerous other guides around but, at the time of the survey, there were very few (apart from that by Lyon, 1994, which was concerned exclusively with legal issues).

Since the BILD & NAS framework was published, a number of other related documents have been produced (see above) and BILD has developed a database of trainers (BILD, 2000) and a code of practice for trainers in physical interventions (BILD, 2001), partly in response to comments made by staff in this evaluation study. In addition, the Department for Education and Skills and the Department of Health have produced codes of practice for physical interventions (see chapter 3). However, none of these government guides tackles the issue of whether particular methods or 'brands' of intervention are preferable to others, even though there are often strong views amongst practitioners on such matters (for example, on the use of prone restraint and the likelihood of pain, particularly in C&R – Stirling, 2001). There is remarkably little hard evidence to hand on whether the different methods differ in effectiveness (Allen et al, 1997; Baker & Bissimire, 2001; McDonnell, 1997), nor much evidence on what service user's views are of physical interventions (Murphy et al, 1996) or on what the effects of training are in relation to staff skills, morale and behaviour (Allen & Tynan, 2000). In short, there remains a long way to go.

## Acknowledgements

We are very grateful for the help and advice of Professor John Harris of BILD and we wish to extend our thanks to all those participants who completed questionnaires for us, to Samantha Jones and James Byatt, who helped at various stages of the study, and to the Department of Health, who funded the study.

## References

Adams, D & Allen, D (2001) Assessing the need for reactive behaviour management strategies in children with intellectual disability and severe challenging behaviour. *Journal of Intellectual Disability Research*, 45, 335–343.

Allen, D, McDonald, L Dunn, C & Doyle, T (1997) Changing care staff approaches to the prevention of aggressive behaviour in a residential treatment unit for persons with mental retardation and challenging behaviour. *Research in Developmental Disabilities*, 18, 101–112.

Allen, D & Tynan, H (2000) Responding to aggressive behaviour: the impact of training on staff knowledge and confidence. *Mental Retardation*, 38, 97–104.

Baker, P & Bissmire, D (2000) A pilot study of the use of physical intervention in the crisis management of people with intellectual disabilities who present challenging behaviour. *Journal of Applied Research in Intellectual Disabilities*, 13, 38–45.

Beech, B (2001) Managing aggression and violence in care settings: a review of the legal and ethical content of staff training courses. *Journal of Adult Protection*, 3, 8–17.

British Institute of Learning Disabilities (2003) *BILD Directory of Physical Interventions Training Organisations*. Kidderminster: BILD.

British Institute of Learning Disabilities (2001) *BILD Code of Practice for Trainers in the Use of Physical Interventions*. Kidderminster: BILD

Community Care (1997) Inquest told of death 'under restraint'. *Community Care, 2nd–8th October*, 3.

Department of Health and Social Services (1985) *Report to the Secretary of State for Social Services Concerning the Death of Mr Michael Martin at Broadmoor Hospital (The Ritchie Report)*. London: HMSO.

Department of Health and the Welsh Office (1999*) Code of Professional Practice: Mental Health Act 1983* (3rd edition). London: HMSO.

Emerson, E, Robertson, J, Gregory, N, Hatton, C, Kessissoglou, S, Hallam, A, & Hillery, J (2000) Treatment and management of challenging behaviours in residential settings. *Journal of Applied Research in Intellectual Disabilities*, 13, 197–215.

Harris, J (1996) Physical restraint procedures for managing challenging behaviours presented by mentally retarded adults and children. *Research in Developmental Disabilities*, 17, 99–134.

Harris, J, Allen, D, Cornick, M, Jefferson, A & Mills, R (1996) *Physical Interventions: A Policy Framework*. Kidderminster: British Institute of Learning Disabilities Publications

Hill, J & Spreat, S (1987) Staff injury rates associated with the implementation of contingent restraint. *Mental Retardation*, 25, 141–145.

Lyon, C (1994) *Legal Issues Arising from the Care, Control and Safety of Children with learning Disabilities Who Also Present Severe Challenging Behaviour*. London: Mental Health Foundation

MacIntyre, D (1999) *MacIntyre Undercover. One Man, Four Lives*. London: BBC.

McDonnell, A (1997) Training care staff to manage challenging behaviour: an evaluation of a three day training course. *British Journal of Developmental Disabilities*, 43, 156–162.

Murphy, G, Estien, D & Clare, ICH (1996) Services for people with mild intellectual disabilities and challenging behaviour. *Journal of Applied Research in Intellectual Disabilities*, 9, 256–283.

Murphy, G, Kelly-Pike, A & McGill, P (2001) Physical interventions for people with intellectual disabilities: initial survey of training and evaluation of a policy framework. *Journal of Applied Research in Intellectual Disabilities*, 14, 401–411.

Murphy, G, Kelly-Pike, A & McGill, P, Jones, S & Byatt, J (submitted) Physical interventions for people with intellectual disabilities: staff training and policy frameworks. *British Journal of Psychiatry*.

Royal College of Nursing (1999) *Restraining, Holding Still and Containing Children: Guidance for Good Practice*. London: RCN.

Royal College of Nursing (2000) *Restraint revisited - Rights, Risks and Responsibility* London: RCN

Royal College of Psychiatrists (1998) *Management of Imminent Violence: Clinical Practice Guidelines*. London: Royal College of Psychiatrists.

Spreat, S, Lipinski, DP, Hill, J & Halpin, M (1986) Safety indices associated with the use of contingent restraint procedures. *Applied Research in Mental Retardation, 7*, 475 – 481.

Stirling, C (2001) Physical interventions in the management of aggression and violence: legal, ethical, professional and ethical considerations. *Journal of Adult Protection, 3*, 30–40.

Wright, S (1999) Physical restraint in the management of violence and aggression in in-patient settings: A review of issues. *Journal of Mental Health, 8*, 459–472.

# SECTION III:
## Shaping Practice

# Chapter 5

## Devising individualised risk management plans

David Allen

### Introduction

Although this book is primarily concerned with reactive responses to challenging behaviour, the main focus of high quality services must be on preventing challenging behaviours occurring in the first instance. It is clearly both more appropriate and less risky for services to strive to reduce or avoid episodes of aggressive behaviour than it is to respond to episodes as they occur. By adopting a preventative culture, services can reduce the immediate impact of challenging behaviour in terms of distress and injuries, and can also impact on the frequency of use of and dependence on reactive procedures. Indeed, the implementation of reactive strategies in the absence of equivalent preventative strategies constitutes unethical and unacceptable practice.

Central to this notion of preventative working is the concept of risk assessment. As Quinsey & Walker (1992) have observed, intervention for violent behaviour is inexorably bound to prediction, and the ability to predict when violent behaviour will occur is central to risk assessment. As described below, risk assessment for challenging behaviour can sometimes be corrupted, and used purely as a means of justifying very restrictive care regimes or excluding people from services. If used appropriately however, the process of risk assessment and management can be a very constructive and positive one.

This chapter reviews good practice principles in relation to the assessment and management of challenging behaviours. The legislative frameworks governing risk management will be outlined, and the basic elements of clinical risk analysis will be described. A framework for positive risk assessment and management will then be provided. Finally, the importance of assessing risk in relation to the use of specific physical interventions will be briefly discussed.

### Statutory Responsibilities

As stated in Chapter 1, there has been a historical tendency to deny the problems posed by the management of challenging behaviours such as physical aggression in human care services. This situation has changed quite dramatically over the last decade or so, partly as a result of high-profile campaigns such as that recently involving violence towards staff in social care services (National Taskforce, 2000), and partly as the implications of changes in legislation have become increasingly realised and enforced by the Health & Safety Executive (HSE).

In the late 1980s, the European Commission set in train a series of initiatives to improve health and safety with the issue of a number of Directives to which the UK was obliged to respond. In particular, the UK implemented a series of regulations (known as the 'six pack' regulations) in 1992 which transformed health and safety law. Key to these changes was the duty to assess risk. Since then, further regulations have been issued and existing ones amended or revised. The major pieces of legislation that currently impact on the management of violence are:

### The Health & Safety at Work Act (1974)

Employers' duties with regard to the management of risky behaviours such as physical aggression are determined by the Health & Safety at Work Act, by regulations issued in response to European Health & Safety Directives and by the common law duty of care that they have towards their employees. The Health and Safety at Work Act only lays down general guidelines for the management of health and safety. It does not make any specific recommendations for the management of, for example, violence and aggression. The Act requires employers to ensure that its employees and other relevant people (such as visitors, contractors and, importantly, service users) are not exposed to risks to their health and safety so far as is reasonably practicable. Thus, while an employer is likely to be held liable for failing to train staff to manage incidents of violence effectively, they could in theory also be held liable under the Act for the provision of inappropriate training via which a service user becomes injured.

The Act specifies some aspects of the employer's duty that have a particular relevance to the management of high-risk user behaviours. These include:

- the preparation of written policies covering the arrangements for dealing with foreseeable risks

- the provision of a safe working environment

- the provision of safe systems of work

- the provision of information, instruction, training and supervision.

The Act also places important obligations upon employees. Section 7 states that an employee must take 'reasonable care for the health and safety of himself and of others who may be affected by his acts or omissions at work' and that 'as regards any duty or requirement imposed by his employer ... to co-operate with him in so far as is necessary to enable that duty or requirement to be performed or complied with'. Thus, while an employer's obligations include providing training that helps reduce risks in the workplace, it is incumbent upon an employee to work to the principles of that training in practice.

## The Management of Health & Safety at Work Regulations (1999)

The 1999 regulations replaced the original 1992 regulations which made the duties of employers more explicit. The current regulations specify that, in addition to assessing all risks to the health and safety of their employees, employers must:

- make arrangements for the management, planning, organisation, control, monitoring and review of the measures arising from such assessments

- appoint competent people to advise them on health and safety

- provide adequate health and safety training

- provide information for employees on risks and preventative or protective measures

- set up procedures for managing emergencies.

When the regulations were first introduced, the HSE enforcement policy took on board the fact that employers needed time to take action and formal enforcement notices were not utilised. However, the 'honeymoon' period is now over and the HSE is increasingly vigilant in scrutinising issues such as the adequacy of risk assessment and training leading to an increased use of improvement/prohibition notices and prosecution.

## The Reporting of Injuries, Diseases and Dangerous Occurrences Regulations (1995)

The RIDDOR regulations require employers to report to the enforcing authority (usually the HSE in the healthcare sector) all cases in which employees have suffered major injury or have been off work for three days or more following an assault which has resulted in physical injury. This is the case even if the absence is not due to the physical injury sustained per se. Interestingly, there is no requirement to report violent incidents to service users, visitors or members of the public (Health Services Advisory Committee, 1997). This is of great concern given the risks that users may be exposed to as a result, for example, of the use of inappropriate physical interventions (see chapter 8). The absence of a mandatory reporting mechanism for physical intervention related fatalities in the UK is a particular anxiety, although the biennial reports of the Mental Health Act Commission (1999) do make some provision for reviewing deaths by unnatural causes of persons formally detained under the mental health legislation.

## Clinical Risk Assessment & Management

Running in parallel to these legislative initiatives, a separate clinical approach has developed to the assessment and management of risk. Clinical risk assessment involves an analysis of the nature and conditions pertaining to previous risk behaviours and a prediction of future risk in the light of current circumstances. Risk management concerns the production of specific plans to help reduce or eliminate identified risks.

The present interest in clinical risk assessment emerged initially from forensic services, but this has increasingly extended into general mental health care. Much of the work in existence has focussed on the use of risk assessment as a tool to predict violent behaviour, although parallel work has been also undertaken in relation to suicidal behaviour and self-neglect. Morgan (1998) locates risk assessment firmly within the wider context of ongoing care assessment and planning:

> 'Placing risk assessment within the broader range of assessments should help us to maintain its focus on care rather than control'
>
> (Morgan, 1998, p 22)

General approaches to the prediction of violent behaviour have had two aspects, an actuarial (or statistically determined) element and a clinical element (Webster et al, 1994). The former involves the computation of a risk score based on a detailed analysis of case notes and background data, and a number of tools have been designed to help formulate such a score (Webster et al, 1994; Morgan, 1998). The latter involves the interpretation of these scores in conjunction with more contemporary data on mental health status and personal circumstances. Kemshall (1999) suggests that the broad components of an assessment for violent behaviour should include an analysis of predisposing hazards, individual motivation to engage in risky behaviours, access and proximity to potential targets, and the conditions and opportunities under which the behaviours are known to take place.

According to Morgan (1998), the present status of clinical risk assessment is as follows:

- Research can provide data on some of the more general indicators that are likely to increase the risk of certain behaviours occurring.

- While such group data provide helpful indicators, risk assessment must be individualised to the specific behaviours and context of the person concerned.

- It is misleading to think that assessment will lead to the accurate prediction and total elimination of risk given the general unpredictability of human behaviour.

Despite its limitations, group research data has identified a number of factors that appear to act as markers for aggression. These are of two main types, the first being concerned with the characteristics of individuals and the second with the characteristics of their environments. These factors have variously been viewed as predictive risk factors or as setting events, the presence of which increases the probability of aggressive behaviour occurring.

Personal risk factors for aggression commonly identified in the literature include:

- Age between 15–30

- Male gender (although evidence also exists which suggests that this may be an increasingly less reliable marker)

- Previous history of aggression

- Presence of mental health problems (most notably psychosis)

- Co-occurrence of self-destructive behaviour

- Concurrent substance abuse

- Recent stressful life events.

(Bowie, 1996; Kemshall, 1999; Linke, 1997; Morgan, 1998; Turns & Blumenreich, 1993)

It should be noted that these are risk factors for violence derived from research on the general population, and not risk factors specific to persons with intellectual disabilities. Equivalent associations have however been identified in research with intellectually disabled populations. For example, challenging behaviour in general appears to peak in this population between 15–34 years, and aggression is the single most common form of this behaviour (Emerson et al, 1997). Aggression occurs more commonly in males with intellectual disability (Borthwick-Duffy, 1994; Emerson et al, 1997). Aggressive behaviour is also very persistent over time (Kiernan & Alborz, 1996; Lowe & Felce, 1995), thus suggesting that a past history is predictive of future occurrence. It is associated with the presence of mental health concerns (Borthwick-Duffy, 1994; Reese et al, 1999; Szymanski et al, 1998) and correlated with the co-occurrence of self-injurious and other forms of challenging behaviour (Borthwick-Duffy, 1994; Emerson et al, 1997). Finally, it has been suggested that a broad range of life events (losses and changes, physical abuse, sexual abuse, bereavement, service transitions etc) may play a role in precipitating aggressive behaviour in persons with intellectual disabilities (Royal College of Psychiatrists, 1995). Increasing severity of intellectual disability is in itself a predictor of increasing rates of challenging behaviour (Kiernan & Qureshi, 1993; Rojahn, 1994), although aggression to others is more likely to be shown by those with less severe disabilities (Emerson et al, 1997). Other more specific markers that may be important in relation to this group of users include impaired receptive and expressive communication skills, poor impulse or anger control, and failure to recognise emotional cues (Allen, 2000).

Environmental factors that appear to act as setting events for aggression may be sub-divided into immediate situational and systems level variables. Situational risk factors include:

- The environment being crowded and hot

- There being few structured activities in place

- Carers employing inconsistent approaches with service users

- There being cues for violence present (both in terms of objects that may be used as weapons and aggressive behaviours being modelled by carers)

- Aggressive behaviour being purposeful (in that it achieves outcomes that non-aggressive behaviour fails to achieve)

- There is pressure from peers to engage in violent behaviour

- Carers displaying rejecting, authoritarian approaches

- Carers presenting aversive demands to service users.

Systems level risk factors include:

- Inexperienced staff

- High rates of usage of temporary staff

- An expectation of violence occurring.

(Bowie, 1996; Kemshall, 1999; Linke, 1997; Morgan, 1998; Turns & Blumenreich, 1993)

Again, it must be noted that many of the above findings have been derived from work within institutional settings and on non-intellectually disabled populations. It cannot therefore be assumed that exactly the same precipitants are relevant within smaller scale, community services supporting a different user group, even if intuitively this would seem likely to be the case. This qualification having been made, it would seem that many of the factors listed are fairly common features of care services in general and of services for people with intellectual disabilities in particular. For example, retaining staff in intellectual disability services is problematic and turnover is consequently high (LaVigna et al, 1994). Many staff are unqualified and receive little training once in post (Clements & Zarkowska, 1994). Low rates of structured activity and user engagement are almost defining characteristics of services for persons with intellectual disabilities (Allen & Felce, 1999). Demands from carers have been shown to be frequent precipitants of service user challenging behaviour (Emerson et al, 1988; Iwata et al, 1990), and a belief that encountering violence is all part of the job and to be expected is commonly reported (National Task Force Violence Against Social Care Staff, 2000).

## Individualised Risk Assessment & Management

Risk assessment for the challenging behaviour of people with intellectual disabilities has not as yet attracted the same kind of attention as has been the case with violent behaviour of offenders. Extensive work has been undertaken on the functional analysis of challenging behaviours in intellectual disabilities however (Miltenberger, 1998; O'Neill et al, 1997; Sturmey, 1996; Wacker et al, 1998), and much of the data derived from such analyses can be extremely helpful in constructing risk assessment and management plans. In particular, comprehensive functional analyses will yield information on: the specific forms of risk behaviour that need to be considered; how these behaviours may or may not link together to form a behavioural chain; their frequency, intensity and duration; their historical and current precipitants; the likely targets; the course of risk incidents; and immediate indicators that the behaviours are about to occur. These data can be employed to construct an individualised risk assessment and management plan.

The following example provides one model for such a plan. It is based on the Health & Safety Executive's (1994) five step plan for risk assessment, and therefore helps to address many of the requirements of good health and safety practice highlighted at the start of the chapter. It extends the model by taking into account particular aspects of risk planning that are relevant to consider when supporting people with intellectual disability and challenging behaviour:

## Step 1. Specify the behaviours of concern

The plan should start with a brief summary of the historical and recent appearance, rate, severity and duration of the risk behaviours.

## Step 2. Specify who might be at risk and how

This list might include the service users themselves, other users, carers, members of the public etc. To a large extent, the make up of this list will define the population of people who need to be informed of the risk management plan.

## Step 3. Identify the conditions under which the probability of the behaviour occurring is increased

This step will involve identifying both general setting events (eg illness, tiredness, transition points between activities, noise etc) that are associated with risk behaviours as well as their specific antecedents (eg being asked to complete a difficult task, being ignored, carer using complex language etc). Being aware of these possible precipitants for aggression is the first step in preventing aggression occurring as the vast majority of the environmental predictor variables identified above are modifiable to a greater or lesser extent. Even when this is not the case, a knowledge of the factors that trigger risk behaviours will help alert staff to the possibility of the behaviours occurring whenever they are present.

## Step 4. Specify what primary preventative strategies should be employed.

Primary prevention involves changing aspects of a service user's living, working, and recreational environments so that the probability of challenging behaviour occurring is reduced in the first instance. It also involves the use of interventions designed specifically to modify user behaviour (Doyle et al, 1996; Harris et al, 1996).

Consistent with the concept of challenging behaviour (see chapter 1), the premise that aggressive behaviour is typically the product of an interaction between the characteristics of individual service users and the characteristics of the service settings is central to the idea of primary prevention. Thus, the aggressive behaviour of a service user which is reliably precipitated by boredom is more likely to occur at times of the day when no activities are planned. Likewise, a user with autistic spectrum disorder who needs a predictable and reliable routine is more likely to be challenging when supported by relief staff who have no knowledge of his daily plan.

To a large extent, effective primary prevention can therefore be said to involve improving the 'goodness of fit' that exists between a person and their environment by reducing obvious discrepancies that may exist between them (Schalock & Kiernan, 1990). This may be achieved by changing the characteristics of one or both elements (ie the person and the setting).

Some examples of primary preventative strategies are given in table 5.1 below:

**Table 5.1:** Examples of primary prevention

| Identified antecendent condition | Possible Primary Preventive Strategies |
|---|---|
| James is more likely to engage in aggression in school if difficult academic tasks are presented after lunch. | i.  Schedule more difficult academic tasks for morning sessions.<br>ii.  Reduce levels of demand for afternoon activities.<br>iii. Schedule preferred activities for afternoon sessions.<br>iv. Increase the number of breaks in afternoon sessions.<br>v.  Use a functional communication training approach (Carr et al., 1994) to allow James to request help when he finds tasks difficult.<br>vi. Increase the help available on more difficult tasks.<br>vii. Teach James some simple relaxation procedures to use when he starts getting angry. |
| Penny appears more likely to hit out at her residential care staff when she's bored. | i.  Active Support Training (Jones et al, 1999) to be introduced into the house.<br>ii.  Full programme of leisure activities to be introduced.<br>iii. Teach Penny a range of recreational skills that she can undertake independently. |
| Sue's challenging behaviour is most common when she is in an unfamiliar situation and when activities are cancelled. | i.  Fade changes in Sue's activity plan in very slowly and in small steps.<br>ii.  Only plan activities that you can deliver with high reliability.<br>iii. If activities are cancelled, have a familiar fall-back activity available. Explain to Sue slowly and carefully what you are doing.<br>iv. Teach Sue to say 'I want to leave now' using her symbolic communication system. |
| Jenny is more likely to bite her mother when she has had a bad night's sleep. | Introduce sleep hygiene intervention (Durand, 1998) |

Prevention at this level can also involve environmental modifications that reduce the impact of incidents when it is not possible to prevent these occurring. Some examples here would include:

- If a user's aggressive behaviour involves throwing objects, limit the number of objects that can be thrown in the setting and ensure that available objects are less likely to cause injury.

- If the person pulls hair, staff members with long hair should tie their hair back, etc.

- If the person is likely to break windows, ensure that all glass is toughened.

- Avoid wearing jewellery and body piercings when supporting service users who may engage in aggressive behaviours (as they may increase the severity of any resulting injuries)

## Step 5. Clearly describe the early behavioural indicators that the person may be losing self-control

Descriptions of behavioural incidents are often initially described as coming 'out of the blue', yet further analysis will frequently reveal that the user shows a number of reliable indicators that all is not well prior to engaging in challenging behaviour. Using the simple analogy of a traffic signal, their behaviour moves from its normal baseline level (green), to a level that indicates that problems are about to occur (amber) prior to the occurrence of the challenging behaviour itself (red). These behaviours will be idiosyncratic, but will often include observable signs such as increased pacing, changes in vocalisations, or increased withdrawal. By producing clear operational definitions of behaviours seen at the amber stage, carers can be cued in to the need to take immediate action and thereby avoid passing on to 'red'. Many episodes of aggressive behaviour occur because carers fail to recognise these signs or, more commonly, fail to alter their own behaviour once the signs become evident.

## Step 6. Specify what secondary preventative strategies should be employed

Secondary prevention involves the identification of initial signs of agitation followed by early intervention to defuse agitation and alter the course of behaviour, thus avoiding a full-blown incident (Doyle et al, 1996; Harris et al, 1996). These strategies may include plans for terminating aversive events, distracting the person, defusion, and diversion to a reinforcing activity. The procedures described by LaVigna & Willis in chapter 6 fall into this category.

Classically, secondary preventative strategies are likely to involve verbal (eg limit setting, empathy, and constructive feedback) and non-verbal (personal space and touch) elements (Bowie, 1996; Clements & Zarkowska, 2000). However, the utility of verbal strategies is more limited when supporting persons with intellectual disabilities who are likely to have major difficulties in communication even at non-crisis points.

## Step 7. Specify what physical interventions may need to be employed

*Reactive Behaviour Management Strategies* consist of more physical responses that carers may be required to implement should it not prove possible to divert a user's behaviour via primary or secondary preventative strategies. This may be the case if, for example, diverting events are insufficiently powerful, if the user's challenging behaviour typically follows on very quickly from the occurrence of trigger events, or if the signals that a user's behaviour is escalating are not picked up by carers until a late stage in a behavioural chain.

The principal strategies employed here will include:

- Increasing personal space

- Self-protective breakaway procedures

- Minimal restraint.

Under the last two categories of intervention, the procedures prescribed should be directly tailored to the specific physical challenges posed by the service user.

## Step 8. Record any residual unmanaged risks

Having constructed an outline plan, it is important to consider whether it is adequate to cover the risks identified or whether more work needs to be done. Remember though that, while risk can be effectively minimised, it cannot be completely eliminated (Morgan, 1998). Ensuring that risk assessment and management plans are firmly anchored by a knowledge of what the person has done in the past (rather than on more speculative accounts of what they may do in future) represents one means of trying to ensure that plans are both comprehensive and realistic. If however there are significant unmanaged risks, there may be major implications for the model of care currently provided to the user.

## Step 9. Specify the procedures to be followed after an incident for both the service user and carers

For the service user, this section should specify any immediate behavioural actions that need to be implemented following incidents (eg giving the person more space, engaging in an activity etc), as well as procedures for ensuring their physical and emotional safety (via medical checks and debriefing counselling). These procedures need to be mirrored for carers in terms of any immediate medical checks and post-incident support (Bowie, 1999; Robb, 1995). The latter should be presented in the form of a menu from which carers can select an option most appropriate to their needs.

## Step 10. Specify how the risk management plan will be used to support access to community living

One of the main objectives of positive behavioural change strategies (Horner et al, 1990) is to improve the quality of life of service users with intellectual disabilities. Although it may appear incongruous in the context of discussing behaviour management strategies that may involve intrusive physical interventions, the same principle applies. Very easily, risk assessment and management plans can be used to justify very oppressive care regimes that manage risk by ensuring that no risks are ever taken. Morgan (1998) attributes this to a current societal climate in which blame needs to be apportioned when things go wrong:

> 'The fear of criticism and blame leads to an all too frequent, but understandable, retreat into defensive practice'
>
> Morgan (1998, p18)

Thus, in constructing behaviour management plans, steps must be taken to demonstrate that they are in the best interest of service users (Harris et al, 1996) and that they form part of a package of interventions that will lead to an enhanced lifestyle for the person concerned.

## Step 11. Specify how plans should be recorded and reviewed

Risk management plans that are not subject to effective recording and analysis procedures are worthless. Having identified risks and agreed strategies for minimising those risks, it is vital that feedback is sought on the effectiveness of the procedures advocated and their impact upon both the service user and their carers. Allen (2001) provides one example of a simple data form that can be used for this purpose and an illustration of the type of summary statistics that can be derived from its use.

## Step 12. Record Agreement with the Plan

Risk assessment and management plans should be the product of multi-disciplinary assessment. The plan should record who has been involved in its discussion and agreement, thus indicating that a broad range of views have been taken into account in its completion. Wherever possible, the service user should also be involved in this process.

## Step 13. Specify a review date

Risk management plans should be living documents. Data from step 11 should be used to regularly revise and update plans in the light of experience. In addition to setting dates for formal reviews, plans may need to specify the conditions under which plans are reviewed more urgently should the need arise.

These ideas can be condensed into a very simple behaviour intervention summary as shown in table 5.2 overleaf.

## Risk Assessment of Physical Interventions

As stated earlier in the chapter, the Health and Safety legislation requires employers to provide adequate training to help manage risks in the workplace and to establish procedures for managing emergencies. In services for persons with intellectual disabilities and challenging behaviour, the latter may involve training in physical interventions. As Paterson & Leadbetter (1999) state, risk assessment can also be used as a means of identifying reasonable responses in situations where such interventions may be required. Thus, the level of response required by carers can be matched to the level of challenging behaviour shown by a service user on the basis of a prediction of their future behaviour pattern.

As the use of physical intervention constitutes a risk event in itself (Harris et al, 1996; Spreat et al, 1986), and given that certain types of physical intervention appear to pose increased risks (Allen, 2001; Patterson, 1998; Leadbetter, chapter

**Table 5.2:** Summary Risk Plan

| Summary Risk Assessment & Management Plan | |
|---|---|
| Service User: Mr Peter Jenkins | |
| 1. Behaviours of Concern | Physical aggression – Peter will punch with his right hand and kick with either foot. Blows mostly occur singularly, but from time to time episodes of repeated aggression (up to 5 punches or kicks) will occur. This pattern has been consistent over the last two years; information concerning these behaviours prior to Peter's resettlement is very patchy. |
| 2. Who might be affected by these behaviours? | Mostly Peter's care staff (average rate of 4 incidents per month); very occasionally his co-tenants (one episode in the last 12 months). No members of the public have ever been involved. |
| 3. When are the behaviours most likely to happen? | Functional analysis has shown that Peter is more likely to be aggressive under the following conditions: when he is rushed getting up in the morning, when activities go on for more than 20 minutes, when he wants a drink of tea, and if there are too many people in the main lounge area. |
| 4. What primary preventative steps can be taken to avoid these behaviours occurring? | Actions:<br>1. Follow the agreed procedure for helping Peter get up (early call, one cup of tea in bed, 10 minutes 'coming to' time, bath before breakfast)<br>2. Activities should be 'chunked' into 15 minute periods, after which Peter has a 10 minute break.<br>3. Offer Peter up to 10 tea breaks a day (8 is the maximum he usually requires)<br>4. Encourage both staff and other tenants to use both lounges; additional TV to be bought for second lounge.<br>5. Continue with Anger Management sessions for Peter. |

**Table 5.2:** (continued)

| | |
|---|---|
| 5. Are there reliable signs that behaviour is moving off baseline? | Peter will always stare directly at staff prior to an incident; he will also rub the side of his head in an increasingly agitated fashion. Less reliably (staff estimate about 50% of the time) he will repeatedly utter 'bloody bloody' under his breath (but note that he will also do this when he's calm, although the pace of the comments is much slower). The build up to an incident can generally take between 5–30 minutes. |
| 6. What secondary preventative strategies should be introduced if the behaviours specified in 4 become apparent? | As appropriate : 1. Leave bedroom, telling Peter that you will come back and get him up in 5 minutes. 2. Terminate activity 3. Divert to tea break 4. Support other users to move out of main lounge 5. Encourage Peter to use his deep breathing and calm statement ('Gone now') in all of the above scenarios. |
| 7. What reactive strategies should be employed if required? | 1. Increase personal space 2. Blocks or deflection for punches & kicks 3. Inter-positioning if other users at risk. 4. Seated restraint if behaviour persists<br><br>All staff must receive induction training in these procedures prior to working at the house. |
| 8. Specify any major unmanaged risks | No significant unmanaged risks identified at this stage. Some potential risks to other users if Peter becomes agitated if staff are not in the immediate vicinity – to continue to monitor over next 6 months and modify staffing support to Peter if required. |
| 9. What should be the response following a behavioural incident?<br>a. Service User<br>b. Carers<br>c. Other users | a. Give Peter time & space to calm – don't try to tell him how he should have behaved differently at this point. Check hands for damage. Monitor vital signs during & following seated restraint. Debrief with Peter in Anger Management.<br>b. First aid as required. Staff to be offered support from the post-incident support menu as required.<br>c. Staff member to be allocated to spend time with affected user – follow individual support guidelines for person in question |

**Table 5.2:** (continued)

| | |
|---|---|
| 10. Specify how the plan supports access to community living | The plan will support Peter's continued residence at the house. The time limit on activities/ breaks/drinks will be incorporated into a new supported employment 'taster' session for Peter. |
| 11. What data need to be provided after the incident? | Standard incident form to be completed. Key worker to analyse forms and provide monthly feedback at team meeting. |
| 12. Agreed by: | S Smith (Team Manager)<br>A Jones (Locality Manager)<br>D Duncan (Psychologist)<br>V Jessop (Consultant) |
| 13. Review date | 1.2.02 or within two weeks if the use of restraint occurs more than once in a four week period. |

8, this volume), it also follows that interventions themselves need to be assessed with regard to the risks that they may pose. The key consideration is that techniques must be designed with the safety of both users and carers in mind. Questionable practice has sometimes been evident when the needs of one group have become predominant over the needs of the other. Hughes et al (in press) have summarised the possible combinations of risk factor for physical intervention techniques that may arise from this dual duty of care (see table 5.3).

A number of key questions therefore need to be addressed as part of the assessment of physical interventions. These include:

- How effective is the physical intervention procedure? What degree of control does it offer over very disturbed user behaviour?

- How technically complex is the procedure to execute? How many separate steps does it involve? How many steps require carers to make a sophisticated judgement (eg, how much pressure to exert when applying a hold)?

- What is the potential for harm to service users (in terms of physical pain, musculo-skeletal damage, respiratory distress, emotional distress etc)

- What is the potential for harm to carers in conducting the intervention (eg, back injury)?

- What is the margin for error? To what extent are these risks exacerbated if the intervention is performed incorrectly?

Unfortunately, this type of bio-mechanical assessment of physical interventions is very much in its infancy at the present time.

**Table 5.3:** Risk factors concerning physical interventions

| Conditions | Outcomes |
|---|---|
| Safe for staff – safe for users | Techniques offer a high degree of control over challenging behaviour and pose few or no risks to the physical and/or emotional health of users. |
| Safe for staff – unsafe for users | Techniques offer a high degree of control over challenging behaviour but pose significant risks to the physical and/or emotional health of users. |
| Unsafe for staff – safe for users | Techniques offer little control over challenging behaviour but pose few or no risks to the physical and/or emotional health of users. |
| Unsafe for staff – unsafe for users | Techniques offer little control over challenging behaviour and pose significant risks to the physical and/or emotional health of users. |

## Conclusions

The present chapter has presented a brief summary of a very complex and rapidly evolving topic. To date, risk assessment and management in services for people with challenging behaviour has often carried very negative connotations. The chapter has attempted to illustrate how good quality risk assessment and management plans can be a very positive element of providing effective support to people who challenge. It has also endeavoured to show how the requirements of Health and Safety legislation can be met within a clinical framework.

## Acknowledgement

My thanks are due to Tessa Shellens, Consultant in Healthcare and Public Sector Law, Morgan Cole Solicitors for her constructive comments on an earlier draft of this chapter.

# References

Allen, D (2000) Recent research on physical aggression in persons with intellectual disability: An overview. *Journal of Intellectual & Developmental Disability*, 25, 1, 41–57.

Allen, D (2001) *Training carers in physical interventions. Research towards evidence based practice*. Kidderminster: British Institute of Learning Disabilities.

Allen, D & Felce, D (1999) Service responses to challenging behaviour. In Bouras, N. (Ed.) *Psychiatric and Behavioural Disorders in Developmental Disabilities and Mental Retardation*. Cambridge: Cambridge University Press, pp. 279–94.

Borthwick-Duffy, SA (1994) Prevalence of destructive behaviours: A study of aggression, self-injury and property destruction. In Thompson, T & Gray, DB (Eds.) *Destructive Behaviour in Developmental Disabilities*. Thousand Oaks, CA: Sage, pp. 3–23.

Bowie, V (1996) *Coping with Violence. A Guide for the Human Services*. London: Whiting & Birch.

Bowie, V (1999) Providing staff with adequate support: Health workers as survivors of assault and aggression. In Turnbull, J & Paterson, B (Eds.) Aggression and Violence. Approaches to Effective Management. London: MacMillan, pp. 148–178.

Carr, EG, Levin, L, McConnachie, G, Carlson, JI, Kemp, DC, & Smith, CE (1994) *Communication-Based Intervention for Problem Behaviour: A User's Guide for Producing Positive Change*. Baltimore: P.H. Brookes

Clements, J & Zarkowska, E. (1994) *Care Staff Management. A Practitioner's Guide*. Chichester: Wiley.

Clements, J & Zarkowska, E (2000) *Behavioural Concerns & Autistic Spectrum Disorders. Explanations & Strategies for Change*. London: Jessica Kingsley.

Durand, MV (1998) *Sleep Better! A guide to improving sleep for children with special needs*. Baltimore: Paul H. Brookes.

Doyle, A, Dunn, C, Allen, D & Hadley, J (1996) *Preventing and Responding to Aggressive Behaviour. A Training Manual*. Cardiff: Welsh Centre for Learning Disabilities & Cardiff Community Healthcare NHS Trust.

Emerson, E, Alborz, A, Reeves, D, Mason, H, Swarbrick, R, Kiernan, C, & Mason, L (1997) *The HARC Challenging Behaviour Project. Report 2. The Prevalence of Challenging Behaviour*. Hester Adrian Research Centre: University of Manchester.

Harris, J, Allen, D, Cornick, M, Jefferson, A, & Mills, R (1996). *Physical Interventions. A Policy Framework*. Kidderminster: BILD & NAS.

Health & Safety Executive (1994) *Essentials of Health and Safety at Work*. Sudbury: HSE Books.

Health Services Advisory Committee (1997) *Violence and Aggression to staff in health services. Guidance on assessment and management*. Health and Safety Executive: Norwich.

Horner, RH, Dunlap, G, Koegel, RL, Carr, EG, Sailor, W, Anderson, J, Albin, RW, & O'Neill, RE (1990) Toward a technology of 'Nonaversive' Behavioural Support. *Journal of the Association for Persons with Severe Handicaps*, 15, 3, 125–132.

Hughes, JC, Berry, H, Allen, D, Hutchings, J, Ingram, E, & Tilley, EF (In press) *A review of the literature relating to safe forms of restraint for children with behaviour that is difficult to manage*. Cardiff: National Assembly for Wales.

Iwata, BA, Vollmer, TR, & Zarcone, JF (1990) The experimental (functional) analysis of behaviour disorders: Methodology, applications and limitations. In, Repp, AC & Singh, NN (Eds.) *Perspectives on the use of Nonaversive and Aversive Interventions for Persons with Developmental Disabilities.* Sycamore, Il. : Sage, pp. 301–330.

Jones, E, Perry, J, Lowe, K, Felce, D, Toogood, S, Dunstan, F, Allen, D, & Pagler, J (1999) Opportunity and the promotion of activity among adults with severe intellectual disability living in community residences: the impact of training in active support. *Journal of Intellectual Disability Research,* 43, 164–78.

Kempshall, H (1999) The Assessment and Management of Violent Offenders. In Kemshall, H & Pritchard, J (Eds) *Good Practice in Working with Violence.* London: Jessica Kingsley, pp. 50–73.

Kiernan, C & Alborz, A (1996) Persistence in challenging and problem behaviours of young adults with intellectual disabilities living in the family home. *Journal of Applied Research in Intellectual Disabilities,* 9, 181–193.

Kiernan, C, & Qureshi, H (1993). Challenging behaviour. In C. Kiernan (Ed). *Research to Practice? Implications of Research on the Challenging Behaviour of People with Learning Disabilities.* Kidderminster: British Institute of Learning Disabilities, pp. 53–87.

LaVigna, GW, Willis, TJ, Shaull, JF, Abedi, M & Sweitzer, M (1994) *The Periodic Service Review. A total quality assurance system for human services and education.* Baltimore: Paul H. Brookes.

Linke, S (1998) *Assessment and management of patients presenting risk to other. CORE Miniguides Series No.2.* London: Centre for Outcomes, Research and Effectiveness, British Psychological Society.

Lowe, K & Felce, D (1995) How do carers assess the severity of challenging behaviour? A total population study. *Journal of Intellectual Disability Research,* 30, 117–127.

Mental Health Act Commission (1999) *Eighth Biennial Report.* HMSO: Norwich.

Miltenberger, RG (1998) Methods for assessing antecedent influences on challenging behaviours. In J.K. Luiselli & M.J. Cameron (Eds.). *Antecedent Control: Innovative Approaches to Behavioural Support.* Baltimore: Paul H Brookes, pp. 47–66.

Morgan, S (1998) *Assessing and Managing Risk. Practitioner's Handbook.* Pavilion: Brighton.

National Taskforce Violence against Social Care Staff (2000) *Qualitative Research.* London: Department of Health.

O'Neill, RE, Horner, RH, Albin, RW, Storey, K, Sprague, JR (1997) *Functional Analysis and Program Development for Problem Behavior.* Pacific Grove, CA: Brooks/Cole.

Paterson, B (1998) Restraint and sudden death from asphyxia. *Nursing Times,* 94, 44, 62–64.

Paterson, B & Leadbetter, D (1999) De-escalation in the management of aggression and violence: Towards evidence-based practice. In Turnbull, J & Patterson, B (Eds) *Aggression and Violence. Approaches to Effective Management.* London: Macmillan, pp. 95–123.

Quinsey, VL & Walker, WD (1992) Dealing with Dangerousness: Community Risk Management Strategies with Violent Offenders. In Peters, RD, McMahon, RJ & Quinsey, VL (Eds) *Aggression and Violence Throughout the Lifespan.* Newbury Park, CA: Sage, pp. 244–262.

Reese, RM, Hellings, JA & Schroeder, SR (1999) Treatment methods for destructive and aggressive behaviour in people with severe mental retardation/ developmental disabilities. In Bouras, N. (Ed) *Psychiatric and Behavioural Disorders in Developmental Disabilities and Mental Retardation.* Cambridge: Cambridge University Press, pp. 249–261.

Robb, E (1995) Post-incident care and support for assaulted staff. In Kidd, B, & Stark, C (Eds.) *Management of Violence and Aggression in Health Care*. London: Gaskell, pp.140–162.

Rojahn, J (1994) Epidemiology and topographic taxonomy of self-injurious behaviour. In Thompson, T, & Gray, DB, (Eds.) *Destructive Behaviour and Developmental Disabilities. Diagnosis and Treatment*. Thousand Oaks, CA: Sage, pp. 49–67.

Royal College of Psychiatrists (1995) *Strategies for the management of disturbed and violent patients in psychiatric units* (Council Rep. CR 41, p. 6). London: Royal College of Psychiatrists.

Schalock, RL, & Kiernan, WE (1990) *Habilitation Planning for Adults with Disabilities*. New York: Springer-Verlag.

Spreat, S, Lipinski, DP, Hill, J, & Halpin, M (1986) Safety indices associated with the use of contingent restraint procedures. *Applied Research in Mental Retardation*, 7, 475–481.

Sturmey, P (1996) *Functional Analysis in Clinical Psychology*. Chichester:Wiley.

Szymanski, LS, King, B, Goldberg, B, Reird, A, Tonge, B & Cain, N (1998). Diagnosis of mental disorders in people with mental retardation. In S. Reiss & M G Aman (Eds), *Psychotropic medications and developmental disabilities. The international consensus handbook*. Columbus, Ohio: Ohio State University, Nisonger Centre, pp. 3–17.

Turns, DM & Blumenreich, PE (1993) Epidemiology. In Blumenreich, PE & Lewis, S (Eds) *Managing the Violent Patient. A Clinician's Guide*. New York: Brunner/Mazel, pp. 5–20.

Wacker, D, Berg, WK, Asmus, JM, Harding, JW, & Cooper, LJ (1998) Experimental analysis of antecedent influences on challenging behaviours. In Luiselli, JK & Cameron, MJ (Eds.) *Antecedent Control: Innovative approaches to behavioural support*. Baltimore: Paul H. Brookes, pp. 67–86.

Webster, CD, Harris, GT, Rice, ME, Cormier. C & Quinsey, VL (1994) *The Violence Prediction Scheme. Assessing Dangerousness in High Risk Men*. Centre of Criminology: University of Toronto.

# Chapter 6

# Counter-intuitive strategies for crisis management within a non-aversive framework

Gary W LaVigna and Thomas J Willis

## Introduction

A values-based approach to people with intellectual disabilities and challenging behaviour is not new. The Social Role Valorization movement has caused us all to focus on helping the people we serve to achieve valued and valuable outcomes. Unfortunately, an artifact of this values-based approach for many has been the unnecessary rejection of behavioural technology.

Behavioural technology, however, can be used in support of and in subordination to values. As we have described elsewhere (LaVigna & Willis, 1996), our values were strongly influenced by Wolfensberger (1983). We value community presence and participation, in ways that are age appropriate and valued by society; autonomy and self-determination, through the exercise of increasingly informed choice; continuous involvement in the ongoing process of becoming; increasing independence and productivity to the point of economic self-sufficiency; and the opportunity to develop a full range of social relationships and friendships.

These values serve as a foundation for the work we do with the people at the Institute for Applied Behaviour Analysis. With these values in mind, we have developed a model (LaVigna & Willis, 1995) for supporting people with challenging behaviour which is designed to produce the following outcomes:

- First, when the behaviour concerned is very dangerous, we need to be concerned about achieving rapid change. So, *speed and degree of effects* is one of the outcomes we are interested in producing.

- Second, we want *durability*. We want lasting change.

- Third, we want those changes to *generalize* to other settings, particularly to the community and the other natural settings that others have an opportunity to access and enjoy.

- Fourth, we want to *minimize the development of negative side effects*. Accordingly, we track collateral behaviours.

- Fifth, we want to use strategies that have *social validity*, that is, those strategies that are acceptable to our client, our client's family, support staff, and the community.

- Finally, we need to demonstrate that what we do has *educational and clinical validity*. This means that as a result of what we have done, we can show that the person has a better quality of life; the person is happier, has greater access, greater opportunity, greater control, etc. That is, we have achieved our *valued outcomes*.

When we are designing our support strategies, it is this entire breadth of these desired outcomes that we focus on. No one of these dictates what we do at any given time. We discipline ourselves to stay focused on the entire range of needs.

## The Multi-Element Model

To achieve all of these outcomes, we begin with a person-centered assessment aimed at understanding the meaning of the behaviour (Willis & LaVigna, 1996a; b). This involves a broad look at the person's life situation, and not just the immediate antecedents and consequences of their behaviour, his or her skills, family, history, health, environments, etc. This is an effort to get a very broad understanding of the meaning of the behaviour for that individual. On the basis of this broad understanding, we design a multi-element support plan. These plans include *proactive strategies*, including ecological changes, positive programming and focused support, designed to *produce changes over time* and, where necessary, *reactive strategies*, to *deal with situations* when they occur. The plan is then implemented by a support team using effective management systems that help ensure consistency (LaVigna et al, 1994). This is the multi-element model that integrates our effort to produce the full range of outcomes, guided by the values described above (LaVigna & Willis, 1995).

One of the significant concerns in working with people who have severe and challenging behaviour is in dealing with crisis situations when they occur. The person is breaking windows *now*, the person is starting to bite himself *now*, the person is throwing furniture at other people *now*, the person is biting, kicking or scratching others *now*. It is relatively easy for us to agree to use strictly positive, non-aversive strategies in the proactive mode, but we tend to get more challenged in coming up with strategies in the reactive mode that are equally positive.

The multi-element model can help liberate some very creative, equally positive, reactive strategies. It provides access to reactive strategies that we previously never thought we had. Using the multi-element approach, we construct our proactive plans to produce certain changes over time. Accordingly, when we are planning what to do about a behaviour when it occurs, we are liberated from needing to address the issue of the future. Our sole agenda becomes situational management. This gives us options that in other contexts might produce counter-therapeutic effects.

Here is one brief example of an early experience of ours that led us to become aware of the new options that might be available to us in using the multi-element approach. We were asked to carry out an assessment for a man a number of years ago who had a very serious form of self-injury that involved him tugging at his lip to the point where he had separated it from his face on a number of occasions, necessitating surgical re-attachment. The doctor was saying that we could not let it happen anymore because he did not know how many more times he could successfully reconstruct the lip. We carried out our assessment and we designed a multi-element plan. Eighteen different proactive strategies were included (ie, 18 different ecological, positive programming and focused support strategies).

The question, of course, was what were we going to do when he started engaging in this form of self-injurious behaviour? In designing a support plan, in many cases, we may need to anticipate some level of occurrence of the challenging behaviour. The best we could come up with to keep him safe when he started tugging at his lip was to put our arms around him and hold him. You might expect that holding him was an aversive event. However, the problem was just the opposite, since being held in this manner was a reinforcing event for this person. The position that this person put us in therefore was that what we were doing to keep him physically safe was potentially reinforcing the problem behaviour. This could have produced a counter-therapeutic effect, which would have made the behaviour more likely to happen in the future.

Using the multi-element model, there was a certain logic in holding the person when he engaged in self injurious behaviour. This logic was that the reactive strategy was used to get the most rapid and safest control over the crisis situation. If this reactive strategy had potentially reinforcing properties, the counter-therapeutic effect could be prevented by including certain additional strategies in the proactive plan. Specifically, this would include the independent and non-contingent availability of the event used as a reactive strategy, supplied at frequent levels. By taking these proactive steps, the reactive strategy provided a very effective means of dealing with the situation without producing a counter-therapeutic effect.

In the case at hand, to assure the proactive, non-contingent availability of the event, five minutes every half hour was scheduled to ensure that staff provided him with a deep muscle massage. The reason for this was that we did not want his intense physical contact with staff to be accessible to him only through the problem behaviour. *We want you to be very aware of this safety valve built into the proactive plan.* What happened over time was that years later, the person has retained their lip. Further, because of the proactive plan, he no longer engages in any level of self-injurious behaviour. In this example, a reactive strategy that was actually a reinforcing event that was made more neutral via the provision of the same reinforcer on a proactive and non-contingent basis. This provided a very effective situational management strategy when the target behaviour occurred and yet was able to do so without producing a counter-therapeutic effect. The multi-element model allows these kinds of options.

We want to discuss how we address this need for management strategies in situations that might be considered to be of a *crisis* nature. This is important since many carers are working with people whose behaviours can occur at crisis levels, and where health and/or safety are at immediate and serious risk. There are many reactive strategies that could be employed which are not particularly counter-intuitive or which are perhaps more appropriate for more innocuous non-crisis problem behaviour. These are discussed fully elsewhere (Willis and LaVigna, in press). Within this chapter, we shall discuss strategies that may appear extremely strange until they are seen within the context of the multi-element model. The first reaction to them may be *"that sounds absolutely crazy."* Hence the term 'counter-intuitive' – at first glance the strategies just do not seem to make sense.

Since the best crisis management strategy is one that prevents crises to begin with, we will start with some counter-intuitive strategies for preventing crises, and then turn to some counter-intuitive strategies that are remarkably effective in getting rapid control over crises when they are actually occurring.


## Preventing Behavioural Crises

### Introducing and Maintaining a High Density of Non-contingent Reinforcement

One counter-intuitive strategy for preventing behavioural crises is introducing and maintaining a high density of non-contingent (ie, time-based) reinforcement. This is worth considering because what we do intuitively if a problem behaviour occurs is to cancel all activities that we feel might inadvertently reinforce the problem behaviour.

> *He had an extreme temper tantrum this afternoon! He broke furniture! He hurt somebody! We better cancel taking him out to dinner because we wouldn't want to reinforce the problem behaviour.*

Consider the following situation however. It is the end of a hard working day, your child comes up to you and makes a perfectly reasonable request. Because you have had a lousy day, instead of making a reasonable response, you snap and snarl and are mean to her. Even as you are acting in this way, you are thinking to yourself *"She doesn't deserve this."* You know full well that your child is totally innocent, and that your behaviour has nothing to do with your child, and everything to do with the work pressures that you are under. In such situations, how many of you react to your inappropriate behaviour by canceling your plans for the evening, calling up your friends and saying: *"Sorry, I can't go to the film tonight"* or *"I know we were supposed to come over for dinner tonight, but I'm afraid that if I go over and enjoy myself, I am going to inadvertently reinforce this terrible parenting behaviour"*? None of you did that. Why didn't you become a terrible parent? Why wasn't your problem behaviour reinforced and strengthened? There are two reasons. First, the reinforcing event was not a contingent event. It is not as if *"I'm going out to dinner tonight because I was mean to my child."* Second, there was a delay between the event that happened in the afternoon (your behaviour) and the (reinforcing) event that happened in the evening.

We know that for reinforcement to strengthen behaviour, it has to be immediate *and* contingent. As long as there is a sufficient delay and/or if there is no contingency relationship, then we should not have to worry about going ahead with an independently scheduled, non-contingent reinforcement. Such a reinforcing event should not strengthen problem behaviour, even if the behaviour occurred earlier in the day.

There are many reasons for maintaining a high-density of time-based reinforcement. Firstly, a high density of reinforcement may be a setting event for the low rate of challenging behaviour, whereas a low density of reinforcement may be a setting event for a higher rate of problem behaviour. So, by initiating, or by introducing, a high density of reinforcement, we are creating a pervasive setting event which by itself should reduce the level of challenging behaviour and behavioural crises.

Furthermore, when we cancel the evening's plans because we are afraid that the problem behaviour is going to be reinforced, we introduce an aversive event; namely, the withdrawal of a reinforcing activity or reinforcing event. This withdrawal can in itself trigger a crisis situation. Rather than acting in a way which minimizes the likelihood of a crisis, we have immediately done something that makes a crisis more likely. This is not just because a low density of reinforcement is a setting event for a higher probability of challenging behaviour, but also because the withdrawal of the reinforcing event itself is a type two punisher and can very likely elicit a problem behaviour.

Perhaps the greatest reason for maintaining a high-density of time-based reinforcement is its impact on the quality of life of the individual. Consider the quality of life of the people we serve who also have challenging behaviours. It does not approximate ours. Surely, setting the conditions for a low-density of reinforcement does not improve a person's quality of life. If one of our goals is to give people a better quality of life, one of the most direct ways of doing this is to introduce a higher density of time-based reinforcement that just improves the quality of life generally. It is our contention that in whatever we are doing to support a person, we should be able to demonstrate that the person is experiencing a higher density of reinforcement than before our intervention. A high density of reinforcement should be non-contingently available to a person before we even consider any contingencies in which the person has to earn reinforcement. We don't have to "earn" most of our pleasures in life – why should the people we support?

Consider this example. We were working recently with a 14 year-old girl whom we had just helped move home after being in a 24-hour residential school, where she had been for the previous four years. She moved home on her parents' initiative because what they were using in the 24-hour facility, among other things, was a restraint procedure. Now that she had become an older and big 14-year-old as opposed to a young and small 10-year-old, the kind of restraint procedure they were using was leading to injury. Furthermore, it was no longer acceptable to the funding educational authority.

She came home and we established a multi-element support plan. One of the things we knew about her was that she had very poor impulse control and, for that and a variety of other reasons, we recommended that we introduce and maintain a high level of time-based reinforcement, independent of what she did or didn't do. One of the things she did right from the very beginning was to not go to school every day. When she would stay home from school, how would we spend the day? We didn't insist that she stay home as you might with a typical child. You might say, "If you don't *go to school today, then you can't go out and play.*" With her, we got out of the house; we went into the community; we did a variety of things, including on one occasion stopping and buying a snack.

The question to us could be *"Why weren't you concerned that you would be reinforcing her refusal to go to school?"* That's a legitimate question to ask. We had reason to think that we would not be differentially reinforcing that behaviour because community access was something she was enjoying every day anyhow, as was buying snacks in the community. These were not contingent events. Further, we knew that when she got to school, she really enjoyed the activities that were there and even though we might be out in the community doing things, what she was not getting access to were some of the activities she really enjoyed at school. It may be a high density of reinforcement should she choose not to go to school, but we believed it would be an even higher one if she chose to go.

Part of the monitoring system here was not just to determine whether or not we were avoiding severe property destruction and aggressive behaviour, her target behaviours. One of the things we were also tracking in our evaluation system was time spent in school. Sure enough, over time she spent more and more time in school. Obviously this needed to be tracked and we needed to plan these things with care, based on all the information that we had gathered in our assessment process.

To summarize, introducing and maintaining a high density of time-based reinforcement can help prevent behavioural crises. The avoidance of a behavioural crisis can be made more likely since a high density of reinforcement is a setting event for a lower probability of problem behaviour. Further, not canceling a reinforcing event avoids an aversive event which itself can increase the likelihood of target behaviour and/or escalation to a behavioural crisis. This recommendation also normalizes the density of reinforcement experienced by the people we support by providing a density closer to the norm and by removing artificial contingencies. This recognizes that most of our day-to-day reinforcers are also non-contingent. Possible counter-therapeutic effects can be prevented by assuring the non-contingency of the reinforcing events, making sure to schedule their occurrence independent of the occurrence of target behaviour. Other concerns about counter-therapeutic effects can also be addressed through the proactive plan in a multi-element approach.

## Avoiding Natural Consequences

Another counter-intuitive strategy for preventing a behavioural crisis is to avoid some natural consequences. This suggestion may sound strange to many of you.

It may even be objectionable for people who take an explicitly values-based approach who may rely heavily on natural consequences to promote the quality of the lives of the people they serve. But, we feel there are a number of good reasons for avoiding **some** naturally occurring consequences. Consider this, if the natural consequence is aversive for the person, it may escalate the person's behaviour to a potentially crisis level. In addition, consider that the natural consequence can itself lead to further exclusion and devaluation. When natural consequences have the potential for causing crisis level escalation, and when they further stigmatize the person, we suggest that maybe we should avoid the natural consequence.

Here is an example of the problem. We were supporting a woman in her job and we knew she was on the verge of getting fired. Her manager was not happy with her work. He found her lazy, disrespectful, and unresponsive. This was not a sheltered workshop. This was a real job situation. We knew it was coming. It was a natural consequence to her behaviour. At the same time we knew enough about her to know that if she was fired, that experience would be likely to cycle her into a two-week period of hell where she may have had to be hospitalized in a psychiatric unit.

What did we do in this case? We talked to her. We established that from her point of view she was not happy with her job. From her point of view, she would rather look for a different job. We established with her that she did not have much time to do that, given that she had this other job that she didn't like. Our suggestion to her was the following: *"Why don't you resign? Why don't you just go in this afternoon and quit?"* She said, *"That's a terrific idea. I wish I had thought of that."* We did a little role-play with her about how she should submit her resignation. She went in and she quit. Fortunately, her boss didn't say, *"You can't quit. You're fired."* She had a chance to *avoid* being fired with our guidance. This is counter-intuitive since many of us would say *"Let her experience the natural consequence. That is how she'll learn."*

The proponents of natural consequences argue that the people we serve have the right to these consequences and that we devalue them by not providing them. They ask, "What is wrong with natural consequences? I experienced them and I turned out OK." If there is one thing that characterizes the people we are discussing here, it is that they are not likely to learn from natural consequences. If they were going to learn from natural consequences, the field of challenging behaviour would not exist. We would all be working in a different field. We are talking about people who characteristically have not and will not learn from natural consequences. It seems to us that the proponents of natural consequences are arguing two points. First, they seem to be saying that the people we serve would be OK today if people would have "just used natural consequences from the outset". Second, they seem to be saying that parents and teachers **failed** to use natural consequences, and that is why their adult children misbehave. That is just not the case. Parents and teachers usually began trying natural consequences. That did not work, so they got a little more contrived in what they did. That did not work either, so they called in a consultant and it got even more contrived. As they got more and more contrived, they probably got more and more punitive and more and more segregated and isolated. So, by the time that child was an adult, she was in a strict program, isolated and segregated from the rest of society.

For the past fifty plus years, all of us have been striving to liberate the people we serve from the degradation, isolation and abuse they experienced in segregated places. The proponents of natural consequences seem to be saying, "Now that they have been liberated, let's use natural consequences to manage their behaviour." It seems that they are suggesting that we go back to square one, back to the ineffective things that were tried by parents and teachers when their children and students were very young. Unfortunately, it seems to us that this would be just starting the "cycle of escalation" all over again.

We caution you, be careful of natural consequences and avoid them where they may lead to crisis situations or to further exclusion and/or devaluation. In any event, do not expect the occurrence of natural consequences to be an effective teaching strategy for many of the people we are concerned about. It is the people who do not have severe and challenging behaviour who may have learned from natural consequences, not the people whom we are concerned about here.

## Don't Ignore Behaviour Under Certain Conditions

Guido Sarducci established a 20 minute university in which he teaches in twenty minutes what the typical university student remembers five years after they have graduated. His idea is: why teach all that other stuff if all they are going to remember is 20 minutes' worth of information. That is all he teaches them to begin with. So in economics, he teaches *"supply and demand"* because that is all we remember from economics class five years after we have graduated.

What do we remember from our 'Introduction to Behaviour Modification' course? What we remember is that when a person acts inappropriately, we should "ignore." How many of you have ever heard this phrase? *Ignore her – she is doing that for attention.* We will bet you that this phrase was not used with reference to a peer or a colleague, but that it was used with reference to one of our clients.

Many of us believe there is something to the idea that aberrant behaviours communicate legitimate messages. If that is true, what is worse than to advise somebody to ignore the behaviour? What you would be saying functionally is to ignore their efforts to communicate. What happens if you ignore a person's communication? The person's behaviour escalates.

We have talked about precursor behaviours before; you know, those minor behaviour problems, those low levels of agitation that may signal that the person is preparing to engage in something serious. These precursors might be understood as the *whispers* of behaviour. Because of what we remember from the Sarducci school, we ignore them. Consequently, what are we requiring of the person? It seems to us that we are requiring that the person not whisper to us, but *shout* at us; and it is the "shout" we then call *severe and challenging behaviour.*

The consultant you are likely to hire off the street for advice on what to do with problem behaviour is likely to say '*Ignore it*'. However, if you want to avoid crises, good advice may be '*Don't ignore* it'. But there are some qualifications to this advice. In the first place, ignoring does not always equate to extinction, and it is really the extinction event that causes the escalation (the opposite effect we look for in a reactive strategy in a multi-element approach). Extinction is the withholding of a previously available reinforcer, whereas ignoring may be defined as continuing with what you were doing as if the behaviour had not occurred. The following examples illustrate when ignoring represents extinction and when it does not.

### When ignoring is extinction

**Scenario** – A teacher has been reprimanding the student and sending her to the vice-principal's office whenever she uses profanity in the classroom. He observes that the behaviour is getting worse and not better and concludes that contrary to his intentions he has been reinforcing this behaviour. For one thing, the student seems to enjoy getting the teacher upset. Secondly, the student seems to like missing class. Accordingly, the teacher plans to start ignoring this behaviour, thereby withholding the previously available reinforcers.

Immediate likely effect on behaviour – Escalation.

Advice when using a multi-element approach – Don't ignore.

### When ignoring is not extinction

**Scenario** – During class time, a nine-year-old student challenged with problems associated with autism, frequently holds his open hand between his eyes and the lights on the ceiling and moves his hand back and forth. The teacher believes that it is the visual stimulation that is reinforcing the stereotypic behaviour. She decides to ignore it when it occurs and simply continue with her instructional program as if it had not occurred.

Immediate likely effect on behaviour – Ignoring the behaviour will not escalate it and continuing with the instructional program may naturally redirect the student to engage in the instructional activity.

Advice when using a multi-element approach – Since ignoring the behaviour will not lead to an escalation in the behaviour, this may be an option to consider. However, other reactive strategies may be necessary to get rapid and safe control over the situation.

## Don't Punish

This is our final counter-intuitive strategy for preventing behavioural crises. We have worked with a number of large service delivery agencies over the past 20 or so years. During that time, we have seen two very large agencies simply abandon punishment altogether after our training; overnight, by policy. No more punishment allowed! You might expect that once the punishment was stopped so quickly, there would be a tremendous "recovery after punishment" phenomenon. You might expect that all of a sudden high rates of challenging behaviour would begin to occur. Yet when these agencies said "no more punishment allowed", the overall level of behaviour problems decreased immediately and what remained were less serious problems.

Consider why that may be. A person acts in a way that is considered inappropriate. Let us say there is a low level punisher available, loss of tokens, loss of privileges, cancellation of an event, etc. The person reacts to that with some agitation, some acting out, which gets another level of punishment. Now we might provide for an over-correction procedure or some kind of time-out procedure. Let us say the person is not so happy about the over-correction procedure or does not want to be escorted to the time-out room, and now starts to physically resist the effort to put them into that situation. What happens is that now staff are having to use physical management, restraint and other very extremely aversive procedures in order to finally control the behaviour. While it is true that if you do not punish that very first behaviour in the sequence, that behaviour may increase in its frequency, what we *may* have avoided are the more serious behaviour problems, the behavioural crises that result purely from our use of punishment.

One way to avoid crises is to eliminate punishment from our support plans. This is counter-intuitive, since we think of punishment as a strategy for suppressing problem behaviour. The suppressive effects of punishment, however, are *future* effects. In the context of situational management, punishment can escalate the situation, producing the opposite effect that we look for in a reactive strategy in a multi-element approach.

## Resolving Behavioural Crises

So far, we have discussed how introducing and maintaining a high density of non-contingent reinforcement, being very careful with our use of natural consequences, not ignoring behaviour under certain circumstances, and avoiding punishment, while counter-intuitive, may be very helpful in preventing behavioural crises.

Despite the potential usefulness of the strategies, a key question remains: '*What about the crisis that you can't prevent? What about 2 o'clock Saturday afternoon when he starts to break every piece of furniture in the house? What can you do?*' Let us now introduce two counter-intuitive strategies for resolving behavioural crises.

### Diversion to a Reinforcing or Compelling Event or Activity

The first is diversion to a powerfully reinforcing or compelling event or activity. That is, when the person is starting to act up, divert him or her with the most powerful reinforcing or compelling activity or event you can identify. For example, in the above case of the person who was engaging in the lip pulling behaviour, our holding him was an inadvertent reinforcing event. We did not design it to be reinforcing, but it certainly had the potential to produce a counter-therapeutic effect. As you will recall, to prevent this, we had to balance this reactive strategy by including certain features in our proactive plan.

Let us point out the intuitive part of this approach. What is intuitive is that if you introduce a dramatically reinforcing or compelling activity or event, it is not surprising that it can divert the person from whatever he is doing. What is counter-intuitive about it is that this would appear to result in the potential reinforcement of the problem behaviour. This is the part that is counter-intuitive and appears, therefore, to contraindicate it as a useful reactive strategy.

If we didn't have the multi-element model, there would be no hope of using this strategy as part of a rational support plan. With the multi-element approach, however, we end up with a proactive plan that compensates for the potential counter-therapeutic effects of the reactive strategy. This leaves us with a reactive strategy that does not produce any unwanted changes over time, but which instead gives us a very effective way of dealing with a crisis situation when it occurs.

We want to give you a further example of this. In one of our training programs, we were guiding a teacher who had selected one of her students to provide a focus for her practical assignments. Her recommended proactive plan included, among other things, changing her curriculum and reorganizing her educational space so it was less distracting. In terms of positive programming, her support staff were teaching her to use a picture communication board with which, for example, she could point to a picture of a glass of water if she wanted something to drink. She could also ask to go to the girls' room, ask for a magazine, and ask for break time by pointing to associated pictures. They were also teaching her the relaxation response, that is that when she was getting upset, to take a deep breath, hold it and relax. As a focused support strategy to produce rapid change in her problem behaviour, they had also designed a particular schedule of reinforcement.

Then the question came up: "What do we do when she engages in the target behaviour of screaming and scratching her own face?" Staff wanted to continue to use "corner time out," but we pointed out to them that this appeared to be an ineffective reactive strategy insofar as they had been using it with little result. They were still getting an average of 40 minutes a day of the screaming and scratching behaviour after 18 months of trying to solve this problem. We invited them to go back to their assessment information and identify, if they could, a behaviour that was reinforcing or compelling enough that it would interrupt almost anything. What they realized was that if they handed her a magazine, what she "needed" to do was open it and take the staples out. At the moment, that seemed to override everything else in her life. So the recommendation was that the minute staff saw the tantrum coming, they should hand her a magazine.

You would be concerned about two things in following such advice. First, you would be concerned that you would just be reinforcing tantrum behaviour and increasing its future occurrence. The other thing you would be concerned about is that she would be with her magazines all day long and would not participate in any educational activities. So to make a long story short, the results were that from day one, no day had more than five minutes of screaming and tantrums, representing an immediate and significant reduction in duration. We also tracked her on-task educational time. That also started increasing from day one. There was never a reduction in time spent in productive education. Furthermore, the frequency of tantrums gradually decreased and by the end of the school year tantrums were no longer occurring. Therefore, it was no longer necessary for staff to hand her a magazine as a reactive strategy, since, with the elimination of the target behaviour, a reactive strategy was no longer necessary. The last report we had was that it had been two years since there had been any tantrums.

Notice the safety valves included in the support plan. She could ask for a magazine using the communication board. Therefore, having a tantrum was not the only way to get access to a magazine. Further, in the play area, where she was at least twice a day, was a stack of magazines, with which she could do anything she wanted. Such safety valves (eg, independent, non-contingent access) allow using reinforcing and/or compelling activities and events to divert a person and interrupt a problem behaviour, perhaps even at a crisis level, as a reactive strategy, without producing a counter-therapeutic effect.

Perhaps a little more should be said here about such strategies for minimizing the potential for a counter therapeutic effect. Above, we suggested that one such strategy could be to provide independent, non-contingent access. A possibility could be raised that such non-contingent access could reduce the distracting qualities of the event as a reactive strategy. However, this approach suggests using a previously unused band within the satiation-deprivation continuum.

Most commonly, we use the satiation end of the continuum when we want to reduce the motivation to engage in the target behaviour to achieve a certain outcome, and we use the deprivation end of the continuum when we want the person to be motivated to meet the criterion established in a formal schedule of reinforcement. In the present approach, quite uniquely, we are suggesting that some mid-level between deprivation and satiation may be clinically useful as well, ie, enough satiation to prevent the counter-therapeutic effect but enough deprivation to cause its sudden presentation to divert the person from the current behaviour.

It may be of interest to note that we have not seen the counter-therapeutic effect, although we frequently use diversion as a common reactive strategy in our practice. On the other hand, the context for most of our work is one in which we have tried to ensure that the people we work with have a very good quality of life, with rich access to a variety of contingent and non-contingent reinforcement. In such situations, the person does not seem to be driven to acquire the specific reinforcing event or item we are using in the reactive strategy. The potential for producing a counter-therapeutic effect may be greater when there is very limited access to a variety of reinforcers and may be less when there is a high density of reinforcement in the person's life.

## Strategic capitulation

Last, and perhaps most counter-intuitive of all reactive strategies, is what we call *strategic capitulation*. Many times we know what the message is. We know what the person is asking for. We know what the person wants. When you know what the person wants, it is obvious that the quickest way to get him to stop asking for it is to give it to him. Capitulation!

Let us give you a very dramatic example of this involving a man on whose behalf we provided some consultation (LaVigna, 1989). His behaviours were quite serious. His aggression was so severe that his staff were often out on sickness leave due to the injuries they had incurred. His self-injury was so severe because of his banging his head into the corners of walls and furniture; they were afraid he was going to be permanently blind, suffer severe neurological damage or possibly even kill himself. After a year of using a non-aversive approach, he was still considered to be an extreme risk to himself, so much so that the clinical supervisor thought contingent shock was necessary.

To make sure that they had their strategy right, they brought in an independent behavioural consultant with excellent credentials. After he did his assessment, he concluded the following that, in spite of the fact that "state of the art" non-aversive procedures had been used, this person remained a serious danger to himself and others. He suggested that not only were staff ethically justified in using contingent shock to treat this behaviour, they were ethically required to use contingent shock to treat this behaviour because this person has the right to effective treatment.

We were also asked to carry out an independent assessment. We concluded quite differently, and felt that his behaviour served a very obvious function. One of his precursor behaviours was to say "ba ba ba ba," along with a backward swaying motion of his hand as he turned away from you. We also asked the staff, "In your experience, is there anything you can do when he is hitting you or hurting himself that if you do it he stops?" Their answer was "Yes, when we walk away he stops." We concluded that the meaning of the behaviour was "Leave me alone!"

The clinical supervisor had told them not to walk away or back off when target behaviour occurred, since that would (negatively) reinforce the problem behaviour. In fact, outside of the context of a well-balanced multi-element support plan, counter-therapeutic effects (ie, the reinforcement and strengthening of the target behaviour) this might very well have been the result. However, in this case, we recommended that capitulation be used as a reactive strategy as a strategic element in a comprehensive multi-element plan. Along with the reactive use of capitulation we also recommended a variety of proactive environmental, positive programming, and focused support strategies, which among other things involved teaching him to tolerate performing non-preferred activities, teaching him to tolerate the presence of others, and teaching him to access the community. What we asked staff to do when he started hitting them or himself was to turn and walk away. The end result was that from that day forward, injuries stopped occurring. Staff were not longer hurt. He was no longer hurt. Furthermore, beyond the dramatic reductions in the rate and severity of his self-injury and aggression, his quality of life was also greatly improved.

The following guidelines indicate how strategic capitulation can be used as a reactive strategy for target behaviour to avoid escalation to crisis levels and/or getting a crisis under rapid and safe control (Willis & LaVigna, in press). In these guidelines we also include some advice for using some of the other counter-intuitive strategies:

1. If you are going to use capitulation, the earlier you use it the better. Ideally, this would even be in response to precursor behaviour.

2. Whether the reinforcement that you have identified as operative is positive or negative, it should be made freely available to the person, simply for the asking.

3. Have a fully developed proactive plan which, among other things, is aimed at: a) improving the person's overall quality of life; b) giving the person more control over her or his life; c) teaching the person how to communicate; d) teaching the person how to cope; e) preventing negative side effects of reactive strategies; and f) reducing the need for any reactive strategies by using focused support strategies.

4. Design an adequate and accurate data system to measure effects on both target behaviour and relevant collateral behaviour.

5. Address social validity issues, including obtaining the collaboration and consent of the individual and all those who will be affected by the capitulation.

## Conclusions

The toughest part of using counter-intuitive strategies to avoid and/or resolve crises is the social validity of those strategies. As effective as strategies such as these may be in establishing rapid and safe control in a crisis situation, getting people to accept them can sometimes be difficult. There may be many reasons for this resistance but we believe that one of them is that these strategies do not meet one of the needs that the use of punishment often meets so well. Whether punishment sufficiently changes the person's behaviour or not, the use of punishment meets our own emotional needs in many situations. Recognizing and dealing with this issue may end up being the biggest challenge in adopting a strictly non-aversive approach. Certainly, our experience tells us that counter-intuitive strategies such as we have described here can prevent behavioural crises or get them under rapid and safe control within a strictly non-aversive, multi-element approach. Physical management strategies inherently increase the risks of injury, both for the staff person and the client, and, in our opinion should only be considered as a last resort, after strategies, including the counterintuitive strategies described above, have been fully considered and explored.

# References

LaVigna, GW (1989) *A model for multi-element treatment planning and outcome measurement.* National Institutes of Health Consensus Development Conference, Washington DC, September 11–13.

LaVigna, G W & Willis, T J (1995) Challenging behaviour: A model for breaking the barriers to social and community integration. *Positive Practices,* 1, 1, 8–15.

LaVigna, G W & Willis, T J (1996) Behavioural technology in support of values. *Positive Practices,* 1, 4, 7–16.

LaVigna, G W, Willis, T J, Shaull, J F, Abedi, M, & Sweitzer, M (1994) *The Periodic Service Review: A total quality assurance system for human services and education.* Baltimore: Paul Brookes H. Publishing Co.

Willis, T J & LaVigna, G W, (1996a) Behavioural assessment: an overview. *Positive Practices,* 1, 2, 8–15.

Willis, T J & LaVigna, G W, (1996b) Behavioural assessment: an overview part 2. *Positive Practices,* 1, 3, 11–19.

Willis, T J & LaVigna, G W (in press) *Challenging behaviour: Crisis management guidelines.* Los Angeles: Institute for Applied Behaviour Analysis.

Wolfensberger, W (1983) Social role valorization: A proposed new term for the principle of normalization. *Mental Retardation,* 21, 234–239.

# Chapter 7

# Low arousal approaches in the management of challenging behaviours

Andrew McDonnell, Tony Waters and David Jones

## Introduction

Aggressive behaviour in people with intellectual disabilities is a major concern for service providers (Allen, 2000). Many of these behaviours are likely to be long-term, and often it is not possible to completely eliminate them from behavioural repertoires (Reiss & Havercamp, 1997). It has therefore been suggested that successful non-aversive intervention should contain long-term pro-active intervention strategies combined with short-term reactive strategies (Donnellan et al, 1988; Horner et al, 1990; LaVigna & Donnellan, 1986). Although LaVigna et al. (1989) recognised that 'a major goal of research should be to develop reactive strategies that minimize the potential of either reinforcing or aversive qualities' (p.62), it remains the case that little information exists about the content of effective behaviour management strategies (McDonnell & Sturmey, 1993).

## Strategies for defusing incidents

While there are numerous outcome studies on long-term non-aversive interventions (eg, Ager & O'May, 2001; Emerson, 1993; Whitaker, 1993), there appears to be no coherent theoretical model or rationale for the content of non-aversive short-term behaviour management strategies (McDonnell & Sturmey, 1993), and no equivalent supporting evidence base (Allen, 2001). Anecdotal evidence would suggest that the two most common strategies advocated in clinical practice involve stimulus change and ignoring behaviours. These will be discussed in turn.

Stimulus change has been defined as 'the sudden and non-contingent introduction of a new stimulus or the dramatic alteration of stimulus conditions resulting in a temporary period of target response reduction' (Donnellan et al, 1988, p 128). This can involve doing something 'odd or bizarre' to interrupt a behaviour. Suggested strategies can include 'singing, jumping up and down, giving a ridiculous instruction, telling the other clients to jump up and down, laughing hysterically' (Willis & LaVigna, 1985, p 12).

While this may be a theoretically valid strategy, practical applications of stimulus change could be potentially quite dangerous if utilised with high-risk behaviours. There is very little research conducted into the effectiveness of these types of procedures, and the social validity of some of these strategies must also be questioned (McDonnell & Sturmey, 1993). Even if a strategy of this type was effective, it is still important to consider how other people might perceive its use. What would a lay observer think, for example, if they saw a member of staff apparently laughing hysterically in the company of a person with an intellectual disability who appeared to be in distress?

Ignoring behaviours as a strategy generally occurs as a component of a more general behavioural intervention. In differential reinforcement programmes, for example, appropriate behaviours are reinforced and inappropriate behaviours are effectively ignored (Donnellan et al, 1988). Proponents of gentle teaching also advocate ignoring behaviour in conjunction with other strategies, such as redirection and reward (McGee, et al, 1987).

Ignoring a person who is being verbally abusive may be a sound behaviour treatment objective. However, there are a number of reasons why ignoring behaviours may be unwise from a behaviour management viewpoint:

- Consistently ignoring behaviours could theoretically lead to increases in the behaviour via 'extinction bursts' (Iwata, et al, 1994; Ducharme & Van Houten, 1994).

- As LaVigna & Willis suggest in chapter 6, it is very likely that service users will tend to get more aroused and angry if they are trying to communicate something to a person who is ignoring them.

- Ignoring an adult with challenges may be impractical in many community settings.

- Behaviours that threaten the physical safety of people are almost impossible to ignore.

If the main objective of behaviour management is the rapid reduction of target behaviours, strategies that involve ignoring behaviours must be viewed with some degree of scepticism.

## Low arousal approaches

McDonnell et al (1994) reviewed a number of defusion strategies and recommended the adoption of low arousal approaches as a first option when designing reactive strategies. A low arousal approach:

*" attempts to alter staff behaviour by avoiding confrontational situations and seeking the least line of resistance."*

(McDonnell, Reeves, Johnson & Lane, 1998, p 164)

In recognition of the potential role of cognitive behavioural frameworks in shaping staff behaviour (Kushlick, Trower & Dagnan, 1997), the approach has now been expanded to include cognitive as well as behavioural elements. Four key components are now considered central to low arousal approaches:

- The reduction of potential points of conflict around an individual by decreasing staff demands and requests.

- The adoption of verbal and non-verbal strategies that avoid potentially arousing triggers (direct eye contact, touch, avoidance of non-verbal behaviours that may lead to conflict, aggressive postures and stances).

- The exploration of staff beliefs about the short-term management of challenging behaviours.

- The provision of emotional support to staff working with challenging individuals.

In most low arousal behaviour management plans, all four components will be required. In some plans specific aspects may take precedence. The remainder of this chapter will attempt to examine each of these behavioural, cognitive and emotional elements in turn.

## Reducing staff demands/requests

Staff behaviour has become a major focus of recent research (Hastings & Brown, 2001). It has also been reported that staff demands often precede incidents of challenging behaviour (McDonnell et al, 2001), and that placing demands on a person who is probably already upset can lead to escalations in behaviour (Carr & Newsom, 1985; Carr et al, 1980). Much of this behaviour may well operate on negative reinforcement principles (Taylor & Carr, 1992; Cipani & Spooner, 1997) in that it appears to serve the function of removing aversive stimuli.

In a recent review of strategies to enhance compliance (Cipani & Spooner, 1997), four approaches were suggested as being appropriate: errorless learning, differential reinforcement of alternate escape behaviour, behavioural momentum (Mace et al, 1988) and functional communication training strategies (Carr & Durand, 1985; Durand, 1990; Durand & Carr, 1991). These strategies may help an individual comply and cope with demands and requests. However, it is interesting to note that the reduction of demands per se was not even suggested as an option. A behaviour management strategy might consider the reduction of demands to low rates as a viable option in itself. This is especially true when the consequence of placing a demand may increase the likelihood of physical assault or other severe behavioural challenges.

Engaging people in purposeful activities can also reduce the frequency of challenging behaviours (Hill & Chamberlain, 1987). However, this process can produce the opposite effect and trigger challenging behaviours (Weld & Evans, 1990).

A low arousal approach suggests that staff demands and requests should be minimised as a short-term goal. From a behaviour analytic perspective, an appropriate question to pose would be 'Under what conditions and circumstances should a demand be made?'. Carers should attempt to be flexible in how they introduce activities to people who present with challenges. The fact that a person is scheduled to go swimming at 10am does not necessarily mean that the activity should take place at that specified time. If the person appears to be upset, then the opportunity to go swimming could be re-presented gently every 10 or 15 minutes.

> **Case example:** *Peter was a young person with intellectual disabilities who presented with high frequency aggressive behaviours when requested by staff to get up and go to work. A wide range of day activities and positive incentives were tried to encourage him to get up with little success. Care staff had also attempted a number of strategies to get him out of bed in the morning. These included: being more assertive, offering him incentives, getting him up first in the morning, and alternatively getting him up last, all with limited success. A low arousal approach was adopted (given that he could not stay in bed all day). Every 20 minutes starting from approximately 7.00am, a member of staff would knock on his door and ask him to get up (he would usually swear at them). They were told not to argue with him under any circumstances. These polite requests were repeated calmly every 20 minutes. On average he would usually get up after 90 minutes, although there were still some days where he still refused to get up or became aggressive. On these 'bad days' staff were encouraged to 'give in'.*

The staff in effect learned to manage his behaviour more appropriately in the short term. They did not change him as a person, but merely reduced the frequency and intensity of the request.

## Avoidance of provocative verbal and non-verbal behaviours

Heightened physiological arousal is often associated with aggression (McDonnell et al, 1994). The development of self-control procedures offers promise as a therapeutic intervention in such circumstances (Benson et al, 1986; Black et al, 1988), but these approaches do not provide any significant advice as to what carers should do when confronted with an angry and highly aroused individual. There are a number of interpersonal factors to consider when attempting to avoid increasing the physiological arousal of people with intellectual disabilities.

## Non-verbal communication

While direct eye contact clearly has a communicative function (Argyle, 1988), it is also a highly physiologically arousing phenomenon (Mehrabian, 1972). For this reason, it may not be advisable to maintain eye contact with a person who is already aroused and/or angry.

Similarly, while touch is a sign of warmth and dominance in the animal kingdom (Major & Heslin, 1982), it is also a sign of hostility, (McDonnell & Sturmey, 1993). Touch may also have paradoxical effects particularly among people with autism (O'Neill & Jones, 1997). While some research has suggested that touch can have a positive therapeutic effect on people who present with challenges (Hegarty & Gale, 1996), it has to be perceived by the person as comforting, and this is cannot be assumed to be a universal reaction. While the authors would not advocate that carers never touch somebody who is angry or upset, they must be very wary of doing so when an individual is clearly in an aroused state.

Research has also demonstrated that individuals are often provoked by people invading their personal space (Hayduk, 1983). Invading a person's space can lead to increased physiological arousal and, in some circumstances, assault (Kinzel, 1970). Again, a low arousal approach would suggest that when a person is upset we should be wary about invading their space.

## Verbal communication

High speech volumes have been shown to be physiologically arousing (Argyle, 1986). People with autism can have marked sensitivity to sounds that can cause distress reactions (Bettison, 1994). Indeed, Temple Grandin (1995) reported that "loud noises were a problem often feeling like a dentist's drill hitting a nerve" (p 67). In addition, receptive and expressive language problems are common place in individuals with intellectual disabilities. Carers should therefore be even more sensitive about how they speak to people, especially when they appear to be upset. They should be aware of the tone of their voices. Speaking slowly and calmly may be useful and most importantly of all they should try to avoid raising their voice.

## Changing belief systems

Staff beliefs about challenging behaviours can have a strong influence on their actions (Hastings & Remington, 1994 a,b; Hastings & Brown 2000). Low arousal approaches can involve challenging such beliefs when they clearly work against successful intervention.

For example, the low arousal approach is often criticised by carers for encouraging them to 'give in' (McDonnell et al, 1998). This usually occurs because there is often a failure to appreciate the difference between managing and changing challenging behaviours, and can sometimes result in staff becoming locked in a 'battle of wills' with service users. The following example illustrates this point.

**Case example:** *A young person with intellectual disabilities was taken out on a day trip that he appeared to enjoy. When the members of staff asked him to return to their car so he could go home he sat on the ground saying 'No!'. A crowd began to gather with the young man refusing to move from the spot. Both members of staff knew that he really liked ice cream. One member of staff bought him an ice cream and then asked him to move, which he duly did. After the person returned home the two staff members began to argue. One person felt that giving him an ice cream was 'reinforcing bad behaviour'. However, the second member of staff asked the question: what would they be reinforcing by grappling and wrestling with the person?*

This example illustrates quite neatly that people often fail to understand the distinction between avoiding conflict in the short-term and long-term behaviour change goals. There is often an underlying fear about 'giving in' to demands and requests that is termed *'catastrophic thinking'*. In the above example catastrophic thinking would lead to a number of assumptions. First, once the person has learned to get an ice cream in this manner they will sit on the ground *every time* they go out until they get one (see chapter 6 for a discussion of this issue). Second, the client will run out of money and the staff will have to use theirs to satisfy this need. Third, the client will become so overweight that they will become ill. Fourth, this strategy will generalise to every aspect of the person's life, he literally will not do anything unless he gets an ice cream. The outcomes described could happen, but how likely is this to be the case in reality? The only way to examine these assumptions is to gently test them out over time. The goal of short-term management is to keep all people involved safe and to avoid unnecessary conflict. Long-term goals involve changing a person's lifestyle and removing the need for the person to present challenges. Thus, to *'give in'* occasionally may seem a problem, but in reality it is a step towards developing a behaviour change programme.

Low arousal approaches may also involve exploring more fundamental beliefs. A number of studies suggest that staff attribute the challenging behaviours of people with intellectual disabilities to a variety of causes (McDonnell, et al, 1997; Watts, et al, 1997; Hastings, 1996). Weiner (1980, 1986) proposed an attributional model of helping behaviour. In this model, the perceived control-lability and the stability of the attributions are critical in carer decisions to help individuals. Challenging behaviours should be viewed more positively if the behaviour is perceived to be outside the person's control and stable (eg, a person had epilepsy), whereas a carer may be more angry and negative towards a person if they perceive the person to be in control of their behaviour (Dagnan et al, 1998). It is the authors' experience that many staff tend to perceive service users as attempting to assert control by employing challenging behaviours in a purposeful and deliberate manner. Low arousal methods, when successfully employed, can at times make carers feel that they are 'giving in' (McDonnell et al, 1998) and consequently, that service users are 'controlling' them.

In accordance with the general principles of applied behaviour analysis, low arousal approaches encourage staff to explore the role of external and unstable causes of challenging behaviour. There is some evidence that suggests that staff who attribute the cause of behaviours to unstable factors tend to report higher levels of optimism and helping behaviour (Sharrock et al, 1990). While research has yet to empirically demonstrate that externalising the causes of challenging behaviours may affect staff interactions with people with intellectual disabilities (Hastings, 1996), it would seem logical that staff beliefs need to be addressed if their own behaviour is to change.

> **Case example:** *A person with intellectual disabilities presented with both physically aggressive behaviours and verbal threats on a daily basis. After an initial assessment it was discovered that staff attributed causes to stable dispositional characteristics of the person. The negative attributions were summarised by one member of staff: 'The verbal threats are methods (disposition) he has always (stable) used to control others. He will never change (stable). That's the way he always behaves when he does not get what he wants (controllability).'*
>
> *It was found on analysis that the person was sensitive to noise, heat and mood swings which were not always under his control. He also had problems controlling his anger. A rationale was presented to his carers which argued that the person was rarely in control of his behaviours. At one year follow up it was found that the frequency of behaviours had not radically altered. However, the majority of staff felt that these same behaviours were less problematic as they understood that there were many times where the person 'just loses control'.*

## Emotional factors

Aggressive behaviours can evoke powerful emotions in carers (Bromley & Emerson, 1997). In some cases it may not always be possible to directly modify behaviour for technological and ethical reasons. Under such circumstances, providing support to care staff that helps them to deal positively with the stresses of continuing behavioural challenges may be the primary objective. Indeed, successfully achieving this objective may be central to our ability to provide high-quality support for this group of service users. Although Kushlick et al (1997) provide some illustrations of how this support can be implemented with carers, this is an area of intervention requiring much more work. As with positive behavioural interventions, emotional support to staff is likely to involve pro-active (eg, instruction in stress management techniques) and reactive (eg, post-incident support) elements.

## Conclusions

Low arousal approaches should not be viewed as a panacea. However, further developing this short-term technology could potentially make significant changes for both carers and people with intellectual disabilities. While the low arousal approaches described in this chapter may have some face validity, care should be taken when interpreting their utility as much more controlled research is needed into their efficacy. It remains disconcerting that the majority of behaviour management advice given to carers would appear to be anecdotal in nature (McDonnell & Sturmey, 1993). If the same standards were applied to behavioural interventions we would have no empirical basis to design such plans, and significant criticisms would arise as a result. Finally, low arousal approaches are as much a philosophy as well as a set of behaviour management techniques. Whilst they do not represent a panacea for challenging behaviours, they may increase the possibility that less fearful staff may adopt more proactive behavioural supports.

## References

Ager, A & O'May, F (2001) Issues in the definition and implementation of 'best practice' for staff delivery of interventions for challenging behaviour. *Journal of Intellectual and Developmental disability*, 26, 243–256.

Allen, D (2000) Recent research on physical aggression in persons with intellectual disabilities: An overview. *Journal of Intellectual and Developmental Disability*, 25, 41–57.

Allen, D (2001) *Training carers in physical interventions: Research towards evidence based practice.* Kidderminster: BILD publications.

Argyle, M (1986) *Social Interaction.* London: Methuen.

Benson, BA, Rice, CJ, & Miranti, SV (1986) Effects of anger management training with mentally retarded adults in group treatment. *Journal of Consulting and Clinical Psychology*, 54, 728–729.

Bettinson, S. (1994) 'Auditory Training' as a treatment for sound sensitivity in autism: preliminary results. *Special Education Perspectives*, 13, 1.

Black, L, Cullen, C, Dickens, P, & Turnbull, J (1988) Anger control. *British Journal of Hospital Medicine*, 20, 325–329.

Bromley, J & Emerson, E (1995) Beliefs and emotional reactions of care staff working with people who challenge. *Journal of Intellectual Disability Research*, 39, 341–52.

Carr, EG & Durrand, VM (1985) Reducing behavior problems through functional communication training. *Journal of Applied Behavioral Analysis*, 18, 111–126.

Carr, EG & Newsom, CD (1985) Demand related tantrums: conceptualization and treatment. *Behavior Modification*, 9, 403–426.

Carr, EG, Newsom, CD & Binkoff, JA (1980) Escape as a factor in the aggressive behaviour of two retarded children. *Journal of Applied Behaviour Analysis*, 13, 101–117.

Cipani, E & Spooner, F (1997) Treating problem behaviors maintained by negative reinforcement. *Research in Developmental Disabilities*, 18, 329–342.

Dagnan, D, Trower, P & Smith, R (1998) Care staff responses to people with learning disabilities and challenging behaviour: A cognitive-behavioural analysis. *British Journal of Clinical Psychology*, 37, 59–68.

Donnellan, AM, LaVigna, GW, Negri-Schoulz, N & Fassbender, L.L. (1988) *Progress without punishment: Effective approaches for learners with behavior problems.* New York: Teachers College Press.

Ducharme, JM & Van Houten, R (1994) Operant extinction in the treatment of severe maladaptive behavior. *Behaviour Modification,* 18, 139–170.

Durand, V M (1990) *Severe behaviour problems: A functional communication training approach.* New York: Guilford Press.

Durand, VM & Carr, EG (1991) Functional communication training to reduce challenging behaviors, maintenance and applications in new settings. *Journal of Applied Behavior Analysis,* 24, 251–264.

Emerson, E (1993) Challenging behaviours and severe learning disabilities: Recent developments in behavioural analysis and intervention. *Behavioural and Cognitive Psychotherapy,* 21, 171–198.

Grandin, T (1995) *Thinking in pictures and other reports from my life with autism.* New York: Random House.

Hastings, RP (1996) Staff strategies and explanations for intervening with challenging behaviours. *Journal of Intellectual Disability Research,* 40, 166–175.

Hastings, RP & Brown, T (2000) Functional assessment and challenging behaviors: Some future directions. *Journal of the Association for Persons with Severe Handicaps,* 25, 229–240.

Hastings, RP & Remington, B (1994a) Rules of engagement: Towards an analysis of staff responses to challenging behaviours. *Research in Developmental Disabilities,* 15, 279–298.

Hastings, RP & Remington, B (1994b) Staff behaviour and its implications for people with learning disabilities and challenging behaviours. *British Journal of Clinical Psychology,* 33, 423–438.

Hayduk, LA (1983) Personal Space: Where we stand now? *Psychological Bulletin,* 94, 293–335.

Hegarty, JR & Gale, E (1996) Touch as a therapeutic medium for people with challenging behaviours. *British Journal of Learning Disabilities,* 24, 26–32.

Hill, P & Chamberlain, P (1987) Managing difficult and disruptive behaviour in residential settings: The use of room management. *Behavioural Psychotherapy,* 15, 337–349.

Horner, RH, Dunlap, G, Koegel, RL, Carr, EG, Sailor, W, Anderson, J, Albin, RW & O'Neill, RE (1990) Towards a technology of 'Nonaversive' behavioral support. *Journal of the Association for Persons with Severe Handicaps,* 15, 125–132.

Iwata, BA, Pace, GM, Cowdery, GS, & Miltenberger, RG (1994) What makes extinction work: An analysis of procedural form and functions. *Journal of Applied Behavior Analysis,* 27, 133–144.

Kinzel, AF (1970) Body buffer zones in violent persons. *American Journal of Psychiatry,* 127, 59–64.

Kushlick, A,Trower, P, & Dagnan, D (1997) Applying cognitive behavioural approaches to the carers of people with learning disabilities who display challenging behaviours. In Stenfert Kroese, B, Dagnan, D & Loumidis, K (Eds) *Cognitive-Behaviour Therapy for People with Learning Disabilities.* London: Routledge, pp. 141–161.

LaVigna, GW & Donnellan, AM (1986) *Alternatives to punishment: solving behaviour problems with non-aversive strategies.* New York: Irvington.

LaVigna, GW, Willis, TJ & Donnellan, AM (1989) The role of positive programming in behavioral treatment. In Cipani, E. (Ed) *The Treatment of Severe Behaviour Disorders.* Washington: AAMR, pp.59–83.

Mace, FC, Lalli, ML, West, BJ, Belifore, P, Pinter, E, & Brown, DK (1988) Behavioral momentum in the treatment of noncompliance. *Journal of Applied Behavior Analysis*, 21, 123–142.

Major, B & Heslin, N (1982) Perceptions of same sex and cross sex touching: it's better to give than to receive. *Journal of Nonverbal Behaviour*, 6, 148–162.

McDonnell, AA & Sturmey, P (1993) Managing violent and aggressive behaviour: towards better practice. In Jones, RSP & Eayrs, CB (Eds) *Challenging Behaviour and Intellectual Disability: A Psychological perspective.* Clevedon: BILD, pp. 148–172.

McDonnell, AA, McEvoy, J & Dearden, R (1994) Coping with violent situations in the caring environment. In Wykes, T (Ed) *Violence and Healthcare Professionals*, London: Chapman & Hall.

McDonnell, AA, Cleary, A, Reeves, Hardman, J & King, S (1997) What is a non aversive approach ? A bit of gentle preaching. *Clinical Psychology Forum*, No. 106, 4–7.

McDonnell, AA, Reeves, S, Johnson, A & Lane, A (1998) Managing challenging behaviours in an adult with learning disabilities: The use of a low arousal approach. *Cognitive and Behavioural Psychotherapy*, 26, 163–171.

McDonnell, AA, Johnson, A & Allen, J (2001) *Care staff perceptions of aggressive behaviours.* (manuscript submitted for publication).

McGee, JJ, Menolascino, FJ, Hobbs, D.C., & Menousek, PE (1987) *Gentle Teaching: A non aversive approach to helping persons with learning disabilities.* Human Sciences Press: New York.

Mehrabian, A (1972) *Nonverbal Communications.* Chicago: Aldune, Atherton.

O'Neill, M & Jones RSP (1997) Sensory perceptual abnormalities in autism: A case for more research. *Journal of Autism and Developmental Disorders*, 27, 283–293.

Reiss, S & Havercamp, SM (1997) Sensitivity theory and mental retardation: Why functional analysis is not enough. *American Journal on Mental Retardation*, 101, 553–566.

Sharrock, R, Day, A, Qazi, F, & Brewin, C (1990) Explanations by professional care staff, optimism and helping behaviour: an application of attribution theory. *Psychological Medicine*, 20, 849–855.

Taylor, JC & Carr, EG (1992) Severe problem behaviors related to social interaction 2: A systems analysis. *Behavior Modification*, 16, 336–371.

Watts, MJ, Reed, TS, & Hastings, RP (1997) Staff strategies and explanations for intervening with challenging behaviours: a replication in a community sample. *Journal of Intellectual Disability Research*, 41, 258–263.

Weiner, B (1980) A cognitive (attribution)- emotion action model of helping behaviour: an analysis of judgements of help giving. *Journal of Personality and Social Psychology*, 39, 1142–1162.

Weiner, B (1986) *An Attributional Theory of Motivation and Emotion.* Berlin: Springer-Verlag.

Weld, E & Evans, I (1990) The effects of part versus whole teaching strategies on skill acquisition and excess behaviour. *American Journal on Mental Retardation*, 94, 377–386.

Whitaker, S (1993) The reduction of aggression in people with learning disabilities: A review of psychological methods. *British Journal of Clinical Psychology*, 32, 1–37.

Willis, T J & LaVigna, G W (1985) *Emergency Management Guidelines.* Los Angeles: IABA.

# Chapter 8

# Good practice in physical interventions

David Leadbetter

## Introduction

> 'If all you have in your tool box is a hammer, all the world looks like
> a nail'
>
> (Abraham Maslow)

The very existence of a book on physical interventions in the care sector in itself reflects a significant change in the professional climate. Until recently, practitioners asking "What constitutes good practice in physical restraint?" risked being stereotyped either as "macho" interventionists promoting unethical practice, or as "soft hearted liberals" seeking to rock the boat by questioning prevailing staff practices. Although the use of physical interventions in appropriate circumstances has become accepted as a legitimate, albeit unpleasant, element of practice in many health and social care services, defining what methods are "acceptable" remains a nettle which no one in an executive role seems willing, or able, to grasp.

The emergent research base suggests that several current physical intervention practices are associated with injuries and fatalities. Such methods continue to be widely used and promoted nevertheless. The balance between "risk" and "acceptability" however remains a crucial dichotomy, and the issue of physical intervention therefore continues to be something of a political, commercial and, ultimately, legal battleground with the welfare of staff and service users as the ultimate casualty.

## Physical Restraint – A Short History

> 'Every man may also take his kinsman that is mad, and may put him in a
> house, and bind him and beat him with rods, without breach of the peace'
> (Lambard, 1581; cited in Murray & Turner, 1990)

Earlier in the century, serious academic papers were written on a condition known as "Insane Ear" (Murray & Turner, 1990). Associated with a propensity for fractured ribs, this affliction was primarily restricted to persons with schizophrenia in mental health institutions and involved the enlargement of the ear, invariably the left. Many causal theories were advanced, until a worldlier investigator pointed out that most male nursing staff were predominantly right handed!

Historically, the actual or threatened use of physical force has been commonly used, both as a deterrent and as a means of crisis intervention in many services in the UK and USA. For instance the Skinner Report (HMSO, 1992) suggested that restraint was used in 74% of Scottish children's homes. As Baker describes in chapter 10, the use of physical restraint in health and care sector services often has a lasting emotional impact on recipients. Historically, such interventions have habitually involved the use of "ad hoc" techniques and a lack of formal policy structures and accountability. In many services staff groups have relied on the intervention of specific, invariably male, colleagues to implement physical interventions, a collusive practice with clear negative implications for teamwork, individual reputations and differential staff authority. Fuelled by successive revelations of unacceptable practice, a body of guidance, policy and authoritative advice has gradually developed which outlines the circumstances in which physical intervention may be appropriate in specific service sectors in the UK. Whilst dealing with the "when" of restraint, and indeed often mandating training, a black hole often exists in relation to the question of the "how" in the advice handed down by most official bodies, thus leaving clear tensions between best practice and the actual care provided in many services. For example:

> "Each establishment should have a clear written policy on the management of challenging behaviour, including the use of restraint, and staff should have appropriate training"
>
> (Scottish Office, 1997, p 78)

> "The issue of physical restraint has been taboo in many agencies but the lack of practical guidance and training is damaging"
>
> (HMSO, 1997, p 45)

Despite the requirement that employing agencies adopt a more pro-active approach, the legacy of the historical vacuum of research and official advice on safe, legally defensible methods, has been the perpetuation of a market economy of training. Consequently agency managers wishing to develop training strategies have faced enormous difficulties in identifying appropriate methods and training programmes. Within this market place, many claims are made about the safety and effectiveness of various proprietary approaches, techniques or training systems, often from partisan or commercial perspectives. A wide variety of systems have been adopted, frequently based on the unsupported claims and/or reputations of training providers. Concerns have been expressed about the lack of a free, evidence-based debate on effective practice and 'the defensive cult mentality' (Allan, 1998, p 13) and restrictive role played by some 'guru trainers' (ibid). However, against a background of continuing revelations of abusive practice and an increasing catalogue of fatalities incurred during restraints, a growing constituency has questioned such claims and demanded a more systematic, evidence based debate (eg Paterson & Leadbetter, 1996). However, the continuing inadequacy of the practice research base has made for difficulties in separating the 'safe' from the merely 'available'.

## The Emergence of Systematic Approaches to Physical Intervention

Although the term physical intervention can be used to cover a broad range of interventions that restrict personal liberty, physical restraint usually implies exerting control against a degree of resistance. For example:

*"Physical restraint is the positive application of force with the intention of overpowering the child"*

(DoH, 1993, p 9)

*"Physical intervention implies the restriction of a person's movement which is maintained against resistance. It is, therefore, qualitatively different from other forms of physical contact such as manual prompting, physical guidance or simply support which might be used in teaching or therapy."*

(Harris et al, 1996, p 6)

The technical principles underpinning physical restraint techniques can be located within four broad categories (Leadbetter, 1995):

- *The immobilisation of the subject by the use of weight or strength.*

- *The restriction of movement of the long bones by some form of hold or lock.*

- *Maintaining the subject in an off balanced position.*

- *The use of pain to promote compliance.*

### Adult Care

The first systematic approach to the physical management of violence in any occupational sector in Britain was Control and Restraint (or as it has become almost universally known, 'C & R'), a system developed in the early 1980s for use in the Prison service. The impetus for its development was concerns over a perceived high injury rate affecting both staff and prisoners. A number of benefits have been reported subsequent to its implementation including:

- *Reductions in injuries to both staff and prisoners.*

- *Reductions in staff sick leave.*

- *Increased staff use of verbal interventions, due to increased confidence.*

- *Erosion of discriminatory attitudes.*

(Healey, 1990)

These claims are not however supported by systematic published research and must therefore be viewed with caution. C & R was heavily dependent on "pain compliance" techniques in which pressure is applied against wrists or across joints to gain control. Such practices, based on hyper-flexion, have considerable implications for the welfare and safety of specific vulnerable groups (see below).

There are currently at least three primary versions and numerous other variants of C & R between which there are significant differences. The three main variants are:

- *The approach used within the prison services (which in itself varies to some extent across the countries of the UK)*

- *The physical control skills element that forms one part of the Care and Control programmes offered by the English Special hospitals who themselves no longer use the term 'C & R'.*

- *Control and Restraint General Services (CRGS), an adapted version of C & R developed for use in health and social services contexts by the originators of C & R, Aiden Healy and Keith Mann.*

Under its various brands and acronyms, C & R has been adopted by agencies in the criminal justice, social care, health and educational services. Due to the wide number of trainers offering a multiplicity of C & R variations, the term can no longer be regarded as representing a homogenous training model. Consequently "Control and Restraint" has become simply a misleading and, therefore, unhelpful, euphemism for training in the physical management of violence. It is now increasingly recognised that this confusing situation has serious implications for staff and service user welfare. A recent United Kingdom Central Council for Nursing Midwifery and Health Visiting research report has called for urgent action to develop and standardise good practice in this area (SNMAC, 1999; see also UKCC, 1999).

The initial and continuing association of C & R with the Special Hospitals has led to suggestions that its value base reflects a culture of control and coercion that is wholly inappropriate for broader health and social care settings (Paterson & Leadbetter, 1999). This underpinning culture may partly explain the reported high levels of significant injury to both service users (11%) and staff both in the work place (19%), and to staff during training (27%) (SNMAC, 1999; see also Parkes, 1996). A 1995 report by the Royal College of Psychiatrists expressed a number of anxieties regarding these issues:

> *"There must be grave concern that the widespread and deliberate use of pain, whether actual or threatened, has become part of the management of patients without consideration as to the moral and ethical issues involved. There is no evidence in the literature that the use of pain in Control and Restraint has been examined to determine its relevance. Its role becomes particularly problematic and hazardous where the patient's perception of pain is altered (as might occur with learning disability, autism or various psychiatric states)."*
>
> (RCP, 1995, p 6)

The BBC documentary "MacIntyre Under Cover" (MacIntyre, 1999) vividly illustrated the potential abuses of a pain-based system. Given the increasing evidence for the efficacy of non-aversive methods in a number of sectors (eg Allen et al, 1997; Baker & Bissimire, 2000; Gallon & McDonnell, 2000; Kaye & Allen, in press; McDonnell, 1997; McDonnell & Reeves, 1996; Perkins & Leadbetter, in press; Stirling & McHugh, 1998), some commentators have suggested that the use of "pain compliance" techniques may be inherently unlawful (eg Allen et al, 1997).

## Child Care

The guidance issued by the Department of Health for residential childcare services in England and Wales (DOH, 1993) employed the term "control and restraint" in its discussion of suitable restraint training. It also advised that "managers should seek advice from colleagues in the psychiatric services", a sector where C & R training was commonly employed. It was widely, and incorrectly, assumed that the guidance therefore endorsed the use of C & R in childcare services. Following injuries to children at Ayecliffe secure unit, concerns were raised around the use of such methods. While the subsequent report (Social Services Inspectorate, 1993) did not establish a specific link between the injuries and the use of C & R, it concluded that:

> "Concerns remain, however, about methods which depend on the application of pain to joints for their effectiveness and are derived from those originally devised for use with adults in different circumstances."
>
> (SSI, 1993, p 20)

The other early system widely utilised in UK childcare has been the Therapeutic Crisis Intervention model (TCI). Developed by Cornell University in New York, the first UK Trainers programme was offered in 1992 (Bell & Mollinson, 1995). In the context of heavy marketing as a proven approach and claims with regard to its effectiveness, TCI was widely adopted across UK childcare agencies. However TCI has also been the subject of concerns with regard to its safety, ethics and defensibility in the context of the UK legal framework (eg CRC, 1995: Paterson & Leadbetter 1996; Heron 1996). These concerns include:

- *The routine use of prone restraints and the straddling of young people*

- *The use of basket holds*

- *The silent application of restraint*

- *Staff safety*

- *The restricted inventory of physical techniques and reactive strategies*

- *A reductionist perspective which emphasises individual skills and secondary prevention.*

Given its academic origins, the comparative lack of published research on this model is surprising. Although available studies include a range of positive findings, negative outcomes and indicators have also been identified (Titus,

1989; CRC, 1995; Bell & Mollinson, 1995; Bell & Stark 1998; Chadwick, 1995; Heron, 1996). For example, one independent report concluded that "using the TCI restraint methods may put staff and the young persons involved at risk of serious injury" (Central Region Council, 1995, p 18).

Partially in response to such concerns, a range of "second generation" models of generic and service user group specific restraint training programmes have now emerged. These include Moran; Studio III; Crisis Aggression Limitation and Management (CALM); Strategies for Crisis Intervention and Prevention (SCIP); Teamteach; Positive Behaviour Management; PRICE etc. Some, but not all, are based on specific criteria or principles. Some contextualise restraint training by underpinning it with teaching on de-escalation and organisational preventative measures etc, whilst others do not (see Paterson & Leadbetter, 1999). Many systems "borrow" techniques from other systems or re-brand existing approaches. A number of specific techniques are also common to various systems. Regrettably, instead of focusing on an evidence-based analysis of safety and effectiveness, the debate concerning these models has often been limited to anecdotal claims about the relative merits of one proprietary system over another.

A further concern is that, in addition to several large training organisations, instruction in physical interventions is also offered by a plethora of small organisations and/or single trainers. Many of these have martial arts, army, security or police backgrounds, and do not have any direct experience in the care field, share its value base or have any understanding of related practice, research, or underpinning law and guidance.


## What is Safe Practice?

The lack of reliable, systematically obtained evidence remains a crucial impediment to an empirical evaluation of safe practice. What therefore is the state of our current knowledge? There are presently four potential sources of data on restraint safety:

### Reports on Restraint Injuries and Fatalities

Centralised data on restraint-related injuries and fatalities collated within a consistent framework is conspicuous by its absence. No provisions exist for such centralised reporting either in the UK or the USA (at a Federal level) for any practice sector, thereby making it impossible to derive accurate incidence rates.

In the USA, restraint related fatalities are estimated to run at 150 per year (St. Louis Post Dispatch, 2001). However, New York is the only state which has a comprehensive, long standing reporting system for restraint-related fatalities in the Mental Health & Intellectual Disability sector (General Accounting Office, 1999). New York accounted for almost a third of all the death investigations. One study (Sundram et al, 1994) reported 111 restraint and seclusion related deaths in this state between 1984 – 1993, whilst four other agencies investigated had a combined total of 107 deaths.

The other major source of North American data is the Hartford Courant database (Hartford Courant, 1998) which was collated by investigative reporters concerned at the increasing, yet invisible, number of restraint related fatalities in the USA. This lists a total of 142 deaths from 1988 to 1998, with the ages of the deceased ranging from 6 to 84 years. Although the database lacks detail, and further analysis therefore presents problems, it is possible to identify certain trends. Around 54% of the cases cited contain no information on the method/type or position of restraint. Of the remainder, 50% were associated with a wide variety of factors in which the mechanical restraint of elderly people featured prominently. However, 31% involved restraint in a prone position, a further 7% involved some kind of floor restraint, 11% involved "take downs" to the floor, and 3% involved basket holds. In all, taking the restrained person to the floor was implicated in around 49% of cases.

A subsequent summary of reports collated by the National Alliance for the Mentally Ill (NAMI, 2000) provided a further source of information on abuses and fatalities incurred during restraint in the USA. Of the 58 recorded incidents from October 1998 to the time of writing, 13 resulted in fatalities. Of these 31% involved prone restraint, 15% taking to the floor, 15% basket holds; the methods used were unknown in 39% of cases.

The lack of a centralised cross sector reporting system for restraint related injuries in the UK remains the focus of concern and criticism, and has been the subject of recommendations in a recent large scale evaluative study on restraint training (Lindsay et al, 2000).

## Coroner's Inquests

It is thought that at least 27 people have died in restraint-related incidents in the UK over the last 10 years. These fatalities occurred in the context of detention and intervention by the police, within the prison service and/or care services. Twelve of the deaths occurred in health or social care; four fatalities (those concerning Freda Latham, Michael Craig, Zoe Fairley and John Patterson) involved people with intellectual disabilities (Paterson, 2001).

Home Office research has shown that detainees of Afro-Caribbean ethnic origin are more likely to be linked to police action than those involving Caucasian suspects (Naidoo, 1999). Coroners' inquests into sudden deaths have established that at least 7 people of Afro- Caribbean ethnic origin have died in prison service custody over the last 10 years, and that at least 8 of the 10 unlawful killings in police and prison service custody over the last two decades were restraint related (ibid).

## Evaluative Research

As a research question, the safety of physical interventions presents complex problems when it comes to identifying and isolating the active variables. Even where research is genuinely independent, it largely employs post hoc qualitative approaches.

There are currently three exhaustive overviews of available research. The Royal College of Psychiatrists (1998) conducted a meta-analysis using the Cochrane methodology, a systematic approach to the analysis of research literature, involving the rating of identified studies against specific validity criteria. The work group encountered a lack of systematic data and acknowledged that the subsequent guidelines relied on the opinion of experts and respected authorities rather than on robust research evidence. The study concluded that there was weak quantitative evidence that training and experience in coping with aggression reduced injuries to staff. However, it was not clear whether incidents of violence were actually reduced.

Sailas & Fenton (1999) undertook a similar Cochrane analysis of the effects of seclusion and restraint in the mental health sector. Although the analysis yielded 2,155 studies, none met the minimum inclusion criteria.

Finally, a review produced by the British Institute of Learning Disabilities (BILD) (Allen, 2001) concluded that training programmes can achieve a range of positive outcomes in terms of participant knowledge, and a reduction in challenging behaviour and injuries to both staff and service users. However, such outcomes were not guaranteed and training can achieve the opposite result. Again, the quality of the research data was acknowledged to be poor.

The most recent, and potentially the most rigorous, independent evaluation of any restraint system (Lindsay et al, 2000) was undertaken as a consequence of the Marshall inquiry into unrelated abuse within residential child care units run by City of Edinburgh Council (Marshall, 1999). The subsequent independent inquiry on the effectiveness of the system employed cited various positive results and supported the use of the system. The study provides a constructive exploration of the crucial importance of a "whole organisation" approach (Cox & Cox, 1993; Leadbetter & Trewartha, 1996; Braverman, 2000) and adequate quality assurance procedures in the development and maintenance of safe practice. This conclusion was echoed by a similar recent study on training in special education (Perkins & Leadbetter, 2001).

These conclusions suggest that some training programmes may reduce overall risk whilst other programmes may increase it. Determining the key independent variables that promote constructive outcomes is a major problem.

## Expert Opinion

In the absence of research data, expert opinion remains central to the debate on safe practice in this highly specialist area. Again the difficulty lies in determining the criteria and qualifications that confer "expert" status (see Bell & Stark, 1998).

Regrettably, many training providers seem to regard safe practice and the methods employed by their specific system as synonymous without regard to any external criteria. The recent quality assurance initiatives under the auspices of BILD, involving representatives from a number of the major training providers, have however produced a remarkable and constructive degree of consensus on safe practice that upholds the main tenets of available authoritative advice.

In summary, the current state of the debate on safe restraint remains polarised. On the one hand, advocates of "high tariff" or "aversive interventions" argue that the inadequacy of the data precludes regulation. On the other, many leading commentators argue that, although inadequate, the available aggregated data unequivocally suggests that specific techniques are associated with fatalities and injuries and that others (notably pain compliance procedures) are ethically unacceptable. At the present time, high-risk techniques appear to include:

- *Restraint in a prone position*
- *Techniques which restrict breathing*
- *Taking to the floor*
- *"Basket holds"*
- *Locks across joints (eg straight arms).*

This inventory broadly corresponds to the advice contained in the various documents on acceptable practice issued by, or on behalf of, Government Departments responsible for Health and Social Care (e.g. DoH/Scottish Office, 1996; HMSO, 1996: Royal College of Psychiatrists, 1998; HMSO, 1997; Centre for Residential Child care, 1997; Department for Education and Skills and Department of Health, 2002).

## What is "Acceptable" Practice?

Whilst "safety" may ultimately be determined by objective empirical research, "acceptability" is a concept influenced by more subjective social, legal, political and commercial processes. "Acceptability" implies a judgement in which staff action is measured against specified authoritative criteria.

### Issues of Defensibility

In a judicial context, "reasonable" force will be judged against the standard of peer performance. What would the average reasonable worker have done in a comparable situation? The courts will examine any authoritative advice or guidance and also consider "expert" testimony, which contesting lawyers will inevitably ensure conflicts. The fact that a practice is in common use does not, in itself, justify it per se, given the court's power to judge its acceptability under the "Bolam Test" (see Watson, 1995).

A crucial question will centre on whether the technique employed conformed to the principal of "least restriction". Defenders of high-risk techniques invariably argue that the use of such techniques is necessary, either because alternatives are ineffective, or because a greater harm would have resulted had they not been used. Whether such assertions represent subjective post hoc justifications or are the product of valid, systematic risk assessments will determine their legitimacy.

Leadbetter (1995) suggests 5 key criteria which influence the validity of a technique:

## Compatibility with professional values

The rights accorded to all individuals are enshrined in various codes and statutes, the most recent of which is the Human Rights Act (1998) (see Schedule 1, Articles 2,3,4,5). Similarly, most professions operate within a codified set of values (eg BASW 1975; UKCC 1992). Above all, in the context of a legal duty of care, the application of physical restraint must be aimed at preserving the service user's best interests and their physical, emotional, material and social well being (Harris et al, 1996, p.15). Although the application of physical interventions in crisis situations requires complex and often instant judgements by staff, some techniques (particularly prone restraints and pain compliance methods) carry considerable potential for humiliating and degrading the service user. These are widely viewed as morally abhorrent.

*"Young people suspect that advantage may be taken of their helplessness when they are being restrained, so that they may be sexually harassed. They feel very exposed. This is particularly difficult for children who have in the past been sexually abused for whom the restraint may stir up appalling memories."*

(HMSO, 1997, p 11)

McDonnell et al (1993) and McDonnell & Sturmey (2000) provide data that suggest that restraint in a seated position is perceived as more socially acceptable by observers. Given clear available alternatives for many forms of aggressive behaviour, it is hard to square the routine use of aversive techniques with a professional value base.

## Are the techniques effective?

Judgements of effectiveness are complex. Even with a technically sound technique a range of variables potentially impact on successful application. Obvious factors include:

- *Assailant: Size, strength, endurance, weight, severity of assaultive behaviour, degree of arousal etc.*

- *Staff: Numbers, competence, training, relationships, self-control, co-ordination, fear, attitude etc.*

- *Team: Co ordination, communication, leadership, numbers etc.*

- *Environment: Space, obstacles, risks, exits, bystanders, weapons, ability to summon help etc.*

- *Organisation: Culture, expectations, opportunity for practice, policy, management support etc.*

The position of staff unable or unwilling to attain the necessary standard of competence due to medical or other factors presents a potential morass of legal implications. Given the prevailing workforce profile, the perception that all staff groups can be equipped with the requisite skills for the physical management of extreme behaviour must be viewed with scepticism. It is both undesirable and impracticable to staff health and care sector services exclusively with young, athletic males. It must therefore be accepted that even effective training programmes will have their limits, and that the unrealistic expectations which invariably increase the pressure on staff trained in physical intervention are avoided (see Lindsay et al, 2000; Perkins & Leadbetter, 2002).

A further determinant of effectiveness concerns quality assurance, the ability of a training provider to ensure consistent outcomes across all training programmes. The principal extant study on the development of competence in physical interventions questioned the expertise of the expert group nominated by the training provider, and raised concerns about the resulting legal implications (Bell & Stark 1998). The BILD Code of Practice (BILD, 2001) will provide a crucial standards framework that should ensure the quality of training of those providers subscribing to it, and enhance the safety and defensibility of those agencies employing such accredited training (see Paterson & Leadbetter, 2000).

## Do they comply with the principal of "reasonable/minimum force"?

Whilst the determination of what is reasonable will be dealt with retrospectively and individually by the courts, a key implication for restraint training is the requirement for a clear hierarchy of techniques which allows the practitioner to demonstrate the matching of the level of intervention to the presenting behaviour. Training systems comprised of a disparate collection of unconnected techniques are likely to reduce the ability of practitioners to offer a robust defence based on a "least restrictive" intervention argument, a disadvantage shared by systems which contain only "high tariff" or aversive techniques.

## Are the methods employed "safe in themselves"?

The argument that aversive or high-risk techniques are justified on the basis of the prevention of a greater and significant harm is commonly made. There is however no systematically generated body of data to support this argument, and the onus of proof resides with those advocating the routine and/or specific use of such approaches. Such assertions may however be valid, when based on a process of systematic risk assessment. The presence or otherwise of such risk assessments is likely to be a significant element in the determination of liability in the event of injury. There is a potentially crucial distinction between an injury caused by the employment of an ad hoc or unsafe technique by naive or untrained staff in the heat of the moment, and a similar injury involving an unsafe technique taught as part of an agency approved training programme.

In the context of litigation following an injury to a service user or staff member, the question of whether the techniques taught to staff a) conformed to any prevailing authoritative advice and b) were safe in themselves, is likely to be a crucial determinant of liability. The safety of specific techniques can be potentially established by a process of independent bio-mechanical and medical assessment.

It is important to recognise that single person interventions offer potentially the greatest risk. Many training programmes include one on one techniques. Such interventions will not only require high levels of individual competence, confidence and fitness to accomplish successfully, but also raise implications for ongoing relationships. Significantly, in situations where solo interventions are attempted, the absence of a witness to corroborate the appropriateness of the intervention may be a crucial factor that exposes staff to accusations. It is unwise for training providers to collude with agencies whose priority is the provision of minimal staffing levels by teaching solo intervention techniques. Safe application invariably requires adequate staff numbers, and in the face of foreseeable risk, the absence of adequate resources is not a credible defence under the Health & Safety legislation.

The most controversial debate at present concerning the safety of specific intervention techniques relates to positional or restraint asphyxia. This was first described by Reay (1992), and refers to situations when restraint impairs the free action of the diaphragm and intercostal muscles, and respiration is compromised as a consequence, thereby causing hypoxia, disturbed heart rhythm and death:

> *"Restraint asphyxia is similar to suffocation, if oxygen demand is high and your ability to breathe is restricted, you fall down the slippery slope very quickly."*
>
> (Cary in Naidoo, 1999, p 16)

Positional asphyxia has been implicated in a number of fatalities involving both mechanical and personal restraint techniques (Paterson & Leadbetter, 1998).

Given the liability implications, the underpinning mechanisms of death have become the focus of competing claims and studies. The seminal experimental studies (Reay et al, 1992; Roggla et al, 1997) demonstrated that prone restraint reduces available oxygen levels and cardio-pulmonary function and impairs the heart's ability to recover in healthy adults, a conclusion supported by a number of other studies (Kumar, 1997; O' Halloran & Lewman, 1993; Pollanen, 1998). These conclusions were in turn refuted, principally by Chan et al (1997). Chan's study has in turn been extensively criticised however (Miller, 1998) and, in a later paper, Chan (Chan et al, 1998) appears to acknowledge that prone restraint is associated with increased risk to some degree.

Although the clinical debate continues, it is now generally accepted that a combination of factors are implicated in fatalities, of which the actual position in which restraint is applied, notably prone, is crucial. The contributing medical or physiological factors identified to date include prolonged struggle, drug and alcohol intoxication (especially cocaine), exposure to CS gas, cardio-vascular disorders, mental health problems (notably psychosis and mania), respiratory disease (asthma, emphysema, bronchitis etc), prescription drugs, and excited delirium.

Obesity is a particular focus of concern. In restrictive positions, such as prone restraints, excess adipose tissue will tend to be forced upwards into the abdominal cavity, compressing the diaphragm and compounding any hypoxia resulting from the subjects' exertions. Acidosis, the inability to clear lactic acid production due to severe exertion and leading to cardio-vascular collapse, has also been suggested as a possible mechanism. This may be compounded by psychosis, delirium or drug use. Citing a 20% reduction in maximal ventilatory volume between a prone restrained and a seated position, Hick et al (1999) state:

*"Though restraints may not have significant impact on healthy people even post exercise, reduction in ventilatory volume by 20% may significantly impact the ability of an acidotic patient to develop a compensatory respiratory alkalosis. The restraint process itself may increase mortality, possibly because efforts at physical restraint often provoke still further struggle, increasing acid production in already compromised patients."*

(Hick et al, 1999, p 242)

There have also been more controversial suggestions (eg, Williams, 1998) that positional asphyxia fatalities in the prison service have involved a disproportionate number of black Afro Caribbean prisoners, and with the raised incidence of sickle cell anaemia being proposed as a potential pre-disposing risk factor.

Despite a plethora of contradictory opinions, the risks of specific procedures have been sufficiently widely recognised to bring about changes in physical intervention practice in some areas. An audit of the data from the New York State led to a ban on two previously authorised restraints that became linked with injuries and deaths throughout the region. These were described as the "prone wrap up", thought to involve a prone "basket hold" (in which the arms are pulled across the front of the chest and held from behind), and the use of a towel to prevent biting or spitting.

Other US States are issuing 'wake up' calls on the dangers of specific restraint practices. For example, following the deaths of young people in 1998 and 1999, officials in North Carolina have called for a ban on basket holds. The Chicago Police Department advise against such positions as:

- Tying the hands and feet together

- Hog tying (where the hands are tied behind the back whilst in a prone position)

- Prolonged restraint in a prone position (back or stomach)

- Sitting forward with hands and feet tied together

- Pressure on the back.

(*Chicago Reporter*, March 1999)

### Are the techniques appropriate for a specific individual and/or service user group?

Whether techniques are appropriate again may depend on a range of factors relating to the individual needs, vulnerabilities and the predisposing risk factors of individual service users. Some groups may well have a predisposition to certain health risks, whilst others may find specific techniques particularly aversive. The social validity of specific techniques must also be considered. It is essential that the appropriateness of any given technique employed in the context of foreseeable risk is determined through the process of individual risk assessment and any 'one size fits all' claims by training providers rejected.

Specific risk factors may be inherent in different settings and service user populations that increase the risk of positional asphyxia. Recreational drug use may be prevalent in criminal justice and/or childcare services, and prescription drugs in mental health settings. Childcare settings may also have to consider developmental issues such as brittle bones, prevalence of asthma, developmental issues etc. Services for people with intellectual disability in particular may have to consider a complex range of factors that substantially elevate risk levels (Biersdorff, 1994; Clark, 1997; Welsh Health Planning Forum, 1992). These include an increased prevalence of:

- Orthopaedic deformities and consequent breathing disorders
- Predisposition to epileptic seizures
- Cardiac abnormalities
- Obesity
- Risk of fractures
- Spinal instability (in people with Down syndrome)
- Respiratory problems
- Mental health problems
- Elevated pain thresholds
- Anti-psychotic drugs use (the possible side effects of which include a range of cardio-pulmonary complications).

Either singly or in combination, pre-existing health problems and the side effects of remedial medication may significantly increase the risk of injury, particularly where specific high-risk techniques impose further stresses on vulnerable physiological processes. It is thus ironic that the very service user groups whose behaviour is potentially most likely to initiate the reactive use of restraint, are also those who are the most vulnerable to its most damaging effects. This fact is often lost in the technical debates about the safety of specific restraint techniques that fail to consider the context of their use.

## Conclusions

What then is the status of our knowledge of safe restraint and best practice? Clearly there is an urgent need for research initiatives into current approaches and the mechanisms of injury. Few definitive conclusions will be reached until a body of data on injuries and fatalities, collated on a consistent basis, is generated. The ongoing absence of a national, cross-sectoral requirement for the centralised reporting of restraint use and resulting injuries in the public sector and care services is viewed by many as a national disgrace. The continuing paradox of a framework of legal expectations which mandate the provision of training, in the continuing absence of adequate mechanisms for auditing, regulating and promoting safe practice, is anomalous. Guidance from central government confirms the heightened risk of specific techniques. Whilst congruent with conclusions from available research, it falls short of proscription or regulation. This effectively abrogates responsibility and potential liability to individual employers. It is also to be anticipated that challenges will emerge under recent Human Rights legislation in due course.

Whilst the specification of safe and/or approved techniques has, to date, been the missing piece of the good practice jigsaw, even the use of such techniques will not improve safety or the quality of life unless they are supported by a whole organisation approach in which the welfare of all parties is considered. Staff will only feel confident in the use of physical interventions if they are clear about the parameters of acceptable practice and are held accountable for their actions. They must also be supported in their use by agency management (see Paterson & Leadbetter, 1999).

A "safe system" for the use of physical interventions will include:

- Clear agency policies and protocols.

- Specification of and training in, methods which conform to "best practice" for the specific service sector

- Skill maintenance through practice, regular update and re-accreditation training

- Pro-active risk assessment

- Individual care planning and specification of techniques based on the assessed needs of individuals

- Assessment of potential risk factors (medical; psychological etc)

- Accurate reporting

- Routine post incident de briefing for staff and service users

- Effective complaints procedures

- Effective occupational health structures.

"Blame cultures", in which the main post-incident agency imperative is the allocation of liability, only serve to block the necessary development of an open climate of discussion and clear accountability through consistent incident reporting (see Rowett, 1986; Leadbetter, 1993; Leadbetter & Trewartha, 1996).

Clearly specific techniques have become identified with heightened risk, and their use has been widely criticised as a result. Such criticisms have, in turn, triggered a heated, often partisan response from training providers and user agencies, who are concerned at the emerging perception of the unacceptability of their current practices. Defensive arguments which stress that such techniques are necessary to contain high risk behaviours, and thus avoid a greater and significant harm, may well be valid, but only in specific, systematically assessed circumstances. This is an issue which is open to empirical scrutiny. It is the routine, rather than the absolute use of such methods, which must be questioned.

Where they are employed they should be subject to safeguards which include:

- Formal written endorsement by senior agency management

- Explicit specification of the reasons why non aversive techniques are inappropriate

- Specification of the circumstances and/or behaviours which require the employment of aversive methods

- Description of any aversive techniques approved for use and the likely risks.

The process of validation is however the key issue. More adequately funded and conducted research is vital. Rather than continuing the current reactive debate, based on the post-hoc analysis of actual injury statistics, the safety of specific techniques could then be effectively determined pro-actively by a process of independent bio-mechanical and medical analysis. The probability of injury associated with specific techniques when applied to specific populations could then be determined. This would provide a basis for regulation which, in conjunction with procedures for independent assessment and adequate monitoring, would make a hugely significant difference to this area of work.

In the meantime however, the exact nature of "good practice" is still unclear, and the welfare of all those involved in the delivery and receipt of care services remains the principal victim of this enduring ambiguity.

## References

Allan, B (1998) *Holding Back, restraint rarely & safely*. Bristol: Lucky Duck Publishing.

Allen, D (2000) *Training Carers in Physical Interventions: Research Towards Evidence Based Practice*. Kidderminster: British Institute for Learning Disabilities.

Allen, D McDonald, L, Dunn, C & Doyle, T (1997) Changing care staff approaches to the management of aggressive behaviour in a residential treatment unit for people with mental retardation and challenging behaviour. *Research in Developmental Disabilities*, 18, 101–112.

Baker, PA & Bissimire, D (2000) A pilot study on the use of physical intervention in the crisis management of people with intellectual disabilities who present challenging behaviour. *Journal of Applied Research in Intellectual Disabilities*, 13, 38–45.

Bell, L, & Mollinson, A (1995) *An evaluation of Therapeutic Crisis Intervention Training in Grampian Region*. Stirling: Stirling University.

Bell, L, & Stark, C (1998) *Measuring Competence in Physical Restraint Skills in Residential Child Care*, Edinburgh: Scottish Office Central Research Unit.

Biersdorff, KK (1994) Incidence of significantly altered pain experience among individuals with developmental disabilities. *American Journal on Mental Retardation*, 98, 5, 619–631.

Braverman, M (2000) The prevention of violence affecting workers: a systems perspective. In Gill, M., Fisher, B., & Bowie, V. ( Eds) *Violence at Work, Causes patterns and prevention*. Devon: Willan Publishing

British Institute for Learning Disabilities (2001) *Code of Practice for Trainers in the use of Physical Interventions*. Kidderminster: BILD.

British Association of Social Workers ( 1975) *A Code of Ethics for Social Workers*. Birmingham: BASW.

Central Region Council (1995) *Safety Audit of TCI at Brodie Youth Care Centre, Central Region Council*. Unpublished internal report: CRC.

Centre for Residential Child Care (1997) *Clear Expectations, Consistent Limits - Good Practice in the Care and Control of Children and Young People in Residential Care*. Glasgow: CRCC.

Chan, TC, Vilke, GM, Neuman, T, & Clausen, JL (1997) Restraint position and positional asphyxia. *Annals of Emergency Medicine*, 30, 578–586

Chan, TC, Vilke, GM, & Neuman, T (1998) Re-examination of custody restraint position and positional asphyxia. *American Journal of Forensic Medical Pathology*, 19, 3, 201–5.

Chicago Reporter March (1999) Chicago Police Training Bulletin on Positional Asphyxia. *http://www.chicagoreporetr.com/03–99/0399postion.htm*

Clark, DJ (1997) Towards Rational Psychotropic Prescribing for People with Learning Disability. *British Journal of Learning Disabilities*, 25, 2, 46–52.

Cox, T, and Cox, S (1993) *Psychosocial and organisational hazards: Control and Monitoring. Occupational Health Series, no 5*. Copenhagen: World Health Organisation (Europe).

Chadwick, J (1995) *Restraint Monitoring August 1994 to 28 February 1995. Children & Families Services-Community Services Devon*. Exeter: Devon Social Services

Department of Health (1993) *Guidance on Permissible Forms of Control in Children's Residential Care*. London: DoH.

Department for Education and Skills, and Department of Health (2002) *Guidance for Restrictive Physical Interventions: How to Provide Safe Services for People with Learning Disabilities and Autistic Spectrum Disorder*. London: Department of Health.

Department of Health/Scottish Office (1996) *"Taking Care/Taking Control"*. London: HMSO.

Gallon, I, & McDonnell, A (2000) *The development and evaluation of a staff training package in non-aversive behaviour management: An alternative to control and restraint?* Bath: Studio III Training Systems.

General Accounting Office (1999) *Mental Health: Improper Restraint or Seclusion Use Places People at Risk*. Washington: GAO.

Harris, J, Allen, D, Cornick, M, Jefferson, A, & Mills, R (1996) *Physical Interventions. A Policy Framework*. Kidderminster:BILD.

Hartford Courant (1998) Deadly Restraint – A Hartford Courant Investigative Report. *http://www.courant.com/nesw/special/restraint/index.stm*

Healey, A (1990) *Control & Restraint.* Course Support Material.

Hick, JL, Smith, SW, & Lynch, MT (1999) Metabolic Acidosis in Restraint – Associated Cardiac Arrest: A Case Series. A*cademic Emergency Medicine, 6,* 3, 239- 243.

HMSO (1996) *The Prevention and Management of Aggression, A Good Practice Statement, CRAG Working Group on Mental Illness.* Edinburgh: HMSO Scotland.

HMSO (1992) *Another Kind of Home, a review of residential child care (The Skinner Report).* Edinburgh: Social Work Services Inspectorate for Scotland.

HMSO (1997) *Children's Safeguards Review (The Kent Report).* Edinburgh: Social Work Services Inspectorate for Scotland.

Heron, G (1996) *An analysis of the Effectiveness of Therapeutic Crisis Intervention (TCI) within Social Work Residential Child Care.* Unpublished MSc Thesis: Jordan Hill College.

Home Office (1998) *Human Rights Act* (1998) London: HMSO.

Kaye, N, & Allen, D (In press) Over the top? Reducing staff training in physical interventions. *British Journal of Learning Disabilities.*

Kumar, A (1997) Sudden Unexplained Death in a Psychiatric Patient: A Case Report: the role of phenothiazines and physical restraint. *Medicine Science and the Law,* 37,2, 170 – 175.

Leadbetter, D (1993) Trends in Assaults on Social Work Staff, the experience of one Scottish Authority. *British Journal of Social Work,* 23, 6, 613–628.

Leadbetter, D (1995) Technical Aspects of Physical Restraint. In – Lindsay, M. (Ed) *Physical Restraint; Practice, Legal, Medical & Technical Considerations. Practice Paper No 2.* Strathclyde: The Centre for Residential Child Care, University of Strathclyde, pp. 33 – 48

Leadbetter, D & Trewartha, R (1996) *Managing Violence at Work, a Training Manual.* Lyme Regis: Russell House.

Lindsay, M, & Hosie, A (2000) *The Edinburgh Inquiry. The Independent Evaluation Report.* Strathclyde: The University of Strathclyde and the former Centre for Residential Child Care.

Marshall, K, Jamieson, K, & Finlayson, A (1999) *Enquiry into abuse and protection of children in the care of Edinburgh City Council.* Unpublished Report.

Miller, CD (1998) Chan et al's study, as published in the November 1997 issue of Annals of Emergency Medicine is found to be seriously flawed! *http://www.angelfire.com/co/charlyDMiller/ chanflaw.html*

McDonnell, A (1997) Training Care Staff to Manage Challenging Behaviour: An Evaluation of a Three Day Training Course. *The British Journal of Developmental Disabilities,* 43, 2, 156–162.

McDonnell, A, & Reeves, S (1996) Phasing out seclusion through staff training and support. *Nursing Times,* 92, 32, 43–44.

McDonnell, AA, Sturmey, PS, & Dearden, RL (1993) The acceptability of physical restraint procedures. *Behavioural and Cognitive Psychotherapy,* 23, 3, 255–64.

McDonnell, A, & Sturmey, P (2000) The social validation of physical restraint procedures with people with developmental disabilities: a comparison of young people and professional groups. *Research in Developmental Disabilities,* 21, 85–92.

Murray, RM, & Turner, TH (Eds) (1990) Lectures on the History of Psychiatry. London: Gaskell.

National Alliance for the Mentally Ill (2000) A Summary of Reports of Restraints & Seclusion Abuse Received Since the October 1998 Investigation by The Hartford Courant. *http://nami.org/update/hartford.html*

Naidoo, S (1999) A Death Less Ordinary. *The Big Issue, May 10–16,* 16–17.

O'Halloran, RL, & Lewman, LV (1993) Restraint Asphyxiation in Excited Delirium. *American Journal of Forensic Medical Pathology,* 14, 289–295.

Parkes, J (1996) Control and Restraint training: a study of its effectiveness in a medium secure psychiatric unit. *Journal of Forensic Psychiatry,* 7,3, 525–534.

Paterson, B (2001) *Deaths associated with restraint use in health and social care within the United Kingdom.* Unpublished paper.

Paterson, B, & Leadbetter, D (1996) Pressing need for physical restraint evaluation. *Professional Social Work, Feb, p.5.*

Paterson, B, & Leadbetter, D (1998) Restraint & Sudden Death from Asphyxia. *Nursing Times,* 94, 44, 62–64.

Paterson, B, & Leadbetter, D (1999) Managing Physical Violence. In Turnbull, J & Paterson, B (Eds) *Aggression and Violence: Approaches to Effective Management.* Basingstoke: MacMillan.

Paterson, B, & Leadbetter, D (2001) Zero in on Violence. *Nursing Management,* 8, 1, 16–22.

Paterson, B & Leadbetter, D (2000) Standards for Violence Management Training. In Gill, M, Fisher, B & Bowie, V (Eds) *Violence at Work, Causes patterns and prevention.* Devon: Willan Publishing

Perkins, J, & Leadbetter, D (In press) An Evaluation of Aggression Management Training in a Special Educational Setting. *Emotional & Behavioural Management.*

Pollanen, MS, Chiason, DA, Cairns, JT, & Young, JG (1998) Unexpected death related to restraint for excited delirium: A retrospective study of deaths in police custody and in the community. *Canadian Medical Association Journal,* 158, 12, 1603 – 1607.

Reay, DT, Stilwell, AD, & Arnold, J (1992) Asphyxia during law enforcement transport. *American Journal of Forensic Medical Pathology,* 13, 90–97.

Roggla, M, Wagner, A, Muellner, M, Bur, A, Hirschl, MM, Laggner, AN, & Roggla, G (1997) Cardio respiratory consequences to hobble restraint. *Wein Wochenser,* 109, 10, 359–361.

Royal College of Psychiatrists (1995) *Strategies for the Management of Disturbed and Violent Patients in Psychiatric Units.* Council Report CR41. London: Gaskell.

Royal College of Psychiatrists (1998) *The Management of Violence in Clinical Settings: An Evidence-Based Guideline.* London: Gaskell.

Rowett, C (1986) *Violence to Social Work Staff.* Cambridge: Cambridge Institute of Criminology.

Sailas, E, & Fenton, M (1999) Seclusion and restraint as a method of treatment for people with serious mental illness. *The Cochrane Library, Issue 3. Oxford: Update Software. Cochrane Library number CD001163.*

Stirling, C & McHugh, A (1998) Developing a non-aversive intervention strategy in the management of aggression and violence for people with learning disabilities using natural therapeutic holding. *Journal of Advanced Nursing,* 27, 724–727.

The Scottish Office (1997) *Scotland's Children. The Children (Scotland) Act 1995. Regulations and Guidance.* Edinburgh: HMSO Scotland.

Social Services Inspectorate (1993) *A Place Apart, An investigation into the handling of serious injuries to children and other matters at Ayecliffe, Centre for Children, County Durham.* London: SSI/Department of Health.

Standing Nursing and Midwifery Committee (1999) *Mental Health Nursing: Addressing Acute Concerns.* London: SNMAC

Sundram, C, Stack, EW, & Benjamin, WP (1994) *Restraint and Seclusion Practices within New York State Psychiatric Facilities.* Schenectady, N.Y.: New York State Commission on Quality of care for the Mentally Disabled.

St Louis Post Dispatch (2001) Training Could Prevent Tragedy. *St.Louis Post Dispatch Editorial*, March 4.

Titus, R (1989) Therapeutic Crisis Intervention Training at Kinark Child and Family Services: Assessing the Impact. *Journal of Child and Youth Care*, 4, 3, 61 – 71.

UKCC (1992) *Code of Professional Conduct, 3rd Edition.* London: United Kingdom Central Council for Nursing, Midwifery and Health Visiting.

UKCC (1999) Nursing in a Secure Environment. London: United Kingdom Central Council for Nursing, Midwifery and Health Visiting.

Watson, D (1995) Legal Aspects of Restraint. In Lindsay, M., ( Ed) *Physical Restraint – Practice, Legal, Medical & Technical Considerations.* Glasgow: The Centre for Residential Child Care.

Welsh Health Planning Forum (1992) *Protocol for Investment in Health Gain: Mental Handicap (Learning Disabilities).* Welsh Office NHS Directorate: The Welsh Planning Forum.

Williams (Lord Williams of Mostyn) (1998) Positional Asphyxia, *Hansard* 20th April, column WA 192.

## Chapter 9

# Training on physical interventions: Making sense of the market

John Harris

## Introduction

It is generally accepted that staff perform more effectively if they receive training. Notwithstanding the limited evidence to support this assertion (Allen, 2001), in most services a significant amount of staff time and a considerable proportion of the revenue budget is applied to staff training. For staff working in schools for pupils with special educational needs or services for people with an intellectual disability, it is reasonable to assume that training will be based upon a rational appraisal of the match between existing staff competencies and the knowledge, skills and attitudes required to deliver the service objectives. To the extent that staff often lack knowledge, are deficient in skills or display inappropriate attitudes, there appears to be a clear case for supporting training.

However, this is not to argue that training is a panacea for all service deficits. Not is it true that training is in itself *sufficient* to bring about required changes in staff performance. Other factors over and above training will also need to be in place, in order that training can improve staff performance.

Training is not a homogenous product like a vitamin pill, which can be distributed easily and uniformly to any number of people. Rather, it is one of several inter-connecting processes that are required for optimal organisational effectiveness. These processes operate, either singly or in combination, to reinforce or neutralise the potentially beneficial outcomes of training. They include internal psychological systems, the social interactions by which individuals relate to each other and, finally, the organisational culture which sets the context for individual action and inter-personal collaboration.

Given the dearth of research based evidence to guide any planning on staff training in the use of physical interventions, and the complexity of the relationships between training and subsequent performance, how might a well intentioned head teacher or service manager approach the task of organising staff training on the subject of physical interventions?

When looking around for expertise or 'sources of best current knowledge', anyone wishing to commission training will sooner or later make contact with a training provider. Irrespective of whether the training provider is a salaried member of staff or an independent practitioner, he or she will have a number of characteristics in common with other providers. First, trainers must appear to believe in both the competencies they seek to promote among those who attend their courses and in their own ability to create the conditions that enable others to learn. Like sales staff and ministers of religion, trainers who do not appear to have convinced themselves of the validity of their message will have an uphill struggle in winning new converts. Secondly, all trainers, whether salaried or self-employed, have a strong financial interest in convincing people that their training is effective. Thirdly, good trainers genuinely want to achieve positive outcomes for exactly the same reasons as anyone else who has a strong commitment to working with children with special educational needs or people with an intellectual disability. It is perhaps this capacity of gifted trainers to ally themselves to the values and aspirations of their customers that presents the greatest risk to objective assessments of training outcomes.

## Background to the BILD Code of Practice

Following the publication of the Policy Framework described in chapter 3, BILD received many enquiries from services that had introduced policies on physical interventions, or were in the process of developing policies, and wanted advice on staff training. The following are typical of the questions asked:

- Can you recommend a good trainer?

- What is the right kind of training for the children/adults who use my service?

- How can I be sure that any trainer will deliver what my staff need?

- What techniques are approved by BILD?

In the absence of research evidence or objective criteria against which to evaluate training or trainers (Allen 2001), these questions were impossible to answer. And yet the frequency and urgency with which these questions were asked indicated a deep-seated concern among service providers that revolved around two related issues:

- the belief that staff training is an essential pre-requisite for delivering high quality care to service users who may need physical interventions

- the recognition that poor quality or inappropriate training might involve significant amounts of money being wasted, the safety of staff and service users being compromised, and the legal responsibilities of managers and employers being exposed to challenge.

More than anything else, it has been the realisation by service managers and employers of the huge legal and financial consequences of *not* training staff (or providing training which failed to deliver competency based outcomes), which has generated the momentum for the work described in this chapter. In a very short period of time, physical intervention was highlighted as being among those elite topics in special education and intellectual disability services where the provision of training per se was not enough. What matters is *quality assured training* which can be used to provide legal protection for staff and employers.

The demands for some form of quality assurance were given additional encouragement with the publication of guidance on the use of physical interventions by the Department for Education and Skills and the Department of Health, which emphasised the importance of staff training by approved trainers offering recognised courses.

## Making the market more effective

The problems surrounding the provision of training on physical interventions do not arise as a direct result of the commercial interests of buyers (those responsible for commissioning training) and sellers (the trainers), but rather because the market operates imperfectly. While there are few, if any, artificial restrictions on either the supply or demand for training, the availability of different kinds of important market information is extremely limited. First, relatively few service managers or training officers have experience in the use of physical interventions. The most accessible people with a claim to have such expertise are those who deliver staff training and, not surprisingly, commissioners are somewhat sceptical of the impartiality of advice that comes from sources which have a strong commercial interest in their own recommendations. Secondly, it is often difficult for commissioners to identify independent experts, or even other trainers, who can offer separate advice and/or competing quotations for the provision of training. Thirdly, in the absence of any agreed protocol for the delivery of training, anyone who is not an expert in the use of physical interventions will find difficulty in comparing training specifications offered by different training providers.

The strategy adopted by BILD has been to increase the amount of relevant information available to those responsible for commissioning training. The strategy comprises three elements, each of which is described below. The final section of this chapter provides a more detailed discussion regarding specific training issues addressed by the second of these elements, the Code of Practice.

### A 'Yellow Pages' for training

Anyone wishing to purchase a service in the market place is advised to consult at least two separate vendors in order to compare differences in cost and quality of independent quotations. This is, of course, only possible if purchasers have easy access to a number of potential providers.

Like the Yellow Pages, the *BILD Directory of Physical Interventions Training Organisations* was compiled to meet the needs of both purchasers and providers. Those responsible for delivering training are encouraged to think of the directory as a way of marketing their services, while those interested in commissioning training are invited to use the directory to obtain advice and training specifications from several different trainers.

In developing the directory, training providers were invited to complete a short pro-forma describing the courses they delivered, their main areas of expertise and their contact details. Further assistance was offered to commissioners in the form of questions to ask potential training providers. The directory includes explicit statements from BILD disclaiming any responsibility for factual accuracy of the printed material or for the quality of the training which might be delivered.

## A Code of Practice

The Code of Practice is designed to establish minimum requirements for the provision of training on physical interventions for staff working in schools or in other services for adults or children with an intellectual disability. Building on the principles set out in the earlier BILD publication, *Physical Interventions: A Policy Framework* (Harris et al, 1996), it describes how training should be integrated with existing policies and practices within a service environment and adapted to address the needs of service users and staff. In terms of improved communication in the market place, it provides both buyers and sellers of training with agreed criteria to evaluate the quality of a training programme.

To help commissioners to identify trainers who are most likely to meet the quality standards set out in the Code, BILD invited trainers to submit written documentation which states that they have voluntarily decided to abide by the Code of Practice. Those trainers who have adopted the Code will in future be clearly labelled in the BILD data base. For their part, commissioners are invited to evaluate whether or not trainers conform to the Code and to contact BILD if they become aware that the Code is being disregarded by trainers identified on the BILD data base as working in compliance with the Code. BILD has reserved the right to remove trainers from the data base if there is evidence that, after voluntarily adopting the Code, they have failed to implement it.

The Code covers the following topics:

- Links with organisational policies and procedures regarding the management of challenging behaviour
- Promoting the best interests of service users
- Techniques for physical interventions
- Health and safety during training
- Course organisation
- Monitoring performance of training participants
- Evaluating and recording participants' performance
- Professional conduct of trainers.

## Accreditation

An important limitation of the Code of Practice is that it depends on voluntary agreement and an informal system of monitoring. Work recently undertaken to establish an accreditation scheme to regulate the provision of training on physical interventions will help to address both of these concerns. To the extent that the scheme is based on the Code of Practice, it represents a further development of the voluntary approach to quality assurance described in the previous section.

Support from the Department of Health and the Department for Education and Skills has been important, not merely in terms of funding the development of the scheme, but perhaps more crucially, in giving official endorsement to the status of training accredited by BILD. Following a pilot exercise, the scheme was launched in 2002.

The scheme has been designed so that both training organisations and individual trainers (operating as salaried employees or as independent practitioners) can be included. Training organisations submit documentation setting out how they ensure that their trainers comply with the Code of Practice while sole practitioners are required to submit less detailed documentation. All trainers are required to demonstrate appropriate continuous professional development and their performance is monitored using routine reports from those who commission training and by random visits to training courses by an independent verifier. An Accreditation Panel has been convened to adjudicate on all aspects of accreditation and ensure that the scheme operates effectively to maintain high standards of training.

## Developing the BILD Code of Practice on Physical Interventions

The Code of Practice is the outcome of close collaboration between BILD and an extensive network of trainers with experience of delivering courses of physical interventions to staff working with children and adults with intellectual difficulties. It describes what services might reasonably be expected from a trainer and how trainers should seek to engage with service managers and employers. Above all, it seeks to promote the principle that the main purpose of training staff is to raise the standard of care available to those who use the service.

The Code was developed in draft form by a working group comprising representatives of six different training organisations (Positive Response Training; Price; SCIP; Studio 3; Team Teach; Timian) and circulated for comment to representatives of government department and professional organisations. A revised draft was sent to several hundred trainers and service providers with an invitation to submit comments using a short questionnaire attached to the document. A total of 136 completed questionnaires were returned together with several longer written responses. BILD also organised five consultation workshops in England and Scotland, hosted by members of the working group and attended by over 130 participants. Finally, one service user who had personal experience of receiving physical interventions was able to provide additional comments during an informal one-to-one interview.

**Table 9.1:** Service roles of those who submitted questionnaires on the BILD Code of Practice

| Role of respondents who completed the questionnaire | Number of questionnaires |
|---|---|
| Trainer | 90 |
| Service provider | 59 |
| Service commissioner | 3 |
| Parent/family carer | 3 |
| Service user* | 1 |
| Local authority inspector | 2 |
| Health and safety officer | 1 |
| College development officer | 1 |
| Representative of English Nursing Board | 1 |

*\* interview*

**Table 9.2:** Main client group supported by those who submitted questionnaires on the BILD Code of Practice

| Client group | Number of questionnaires |
|---|---|
| Adults with an intellectual disability | 85 |
| Adults with autism | 45 |
| Adults with mental illness | 37 |
| Children with intellectual difficulties | 36 |
| Children with emotional and behavioural difficulties | 30 |
| Children with autism | 28 |
| Children with acquired brain injury | 2 |

**Table 9.3:** Country in which respondents are currently working

| Country | Number of questionnaires |
|---------|--------------------------|
| England | 96 |
| Ireland | 5 |
| Scotland | 24 |
| Wales | 11 |

The questionnaire invited respondents to indicate their main areas of responsibility and the country in which they worked. Inevitably, the categories described above are not mutually exclusive, and for this reason the sum of responses across categories exceeds the total number of responses received.

Written feedback from each of the workshops was prepared and circulated to members of the working group together with all the questionnaire responses.

The full array of responses was then reviewed and organised under three headings:

● Non-contentious changes to correct errors, increase clarity and minimise ambiguities;

● Substantive issues raised by several respondents;

● Comments made by only one or two respondents and requests for changes which fell outside the remit of the Code.

**Table 9.4:** Support for the Code

| Question | 'Yes' | 'No' | 'Missing' |
|----------|-------|------|-----------|
| Is the Code easy to understand? | 86% | 1% | 13% |
| In your experience, is the Code relevant to training practice? | 85% | 1% | 14% |
| If the Code were to be widely adopted, would it help you to monitor the quality of training? | 78% | 3% | 19% |
| If the Code were to be widely adopted, do you think it would lead to improvements in the overall quality of training? | 79% | 2% | 19% |
| Is there anything which the draft Code has omitted which should be included? | 37% | 31% | 32% |

All but one of the questionnaire responses expressed strong support for the Code although many went on to make suggestions for additions and improvements. The responses to four general questions about the potential benefits of the Code are summarised in table 9.4.

Below is a sample of general comments submitted by those who completed questionnaires:

*'Extremely well written, easy to read, very clear and concise'*

*'It gives a clear framework which can be shared with service providers re expectations from both parties'*

*'It is the kind of practice that I would adopt already but reference to this kind of document with a national acceptance will help to resist pressure from organisational management to cut corners'*

*'Provides clear guidelines and expectations'*

*'Hopefully everyone will be working to the same criteria'*

*'Very structured approach covering all aspects of identified needs'*

*'Very clearly states what is and is not acceptable'*

Following the consultation, all the non-contentious changes were implemented. Since the bulk of the draft Code had been endorsed by those who participated in the consultation, it was decided not to make changes on the basis of only one or two adverse comments or where only one or two respondents suggested additions. Issues which fell into the remaining category – substantive issues raised by several respondents – were taken forward for further consideration by the working group. The remainder of this chapter provides an overview of the main areas of concern, the different views expressed, and the way these were resolved to achieve an agreed text for the Code.

## Areas of concern identified during the consultation

### Who is the Code for?

Implicit in the content of the Code is the expectation that trainers will work closely with service providers to develop courses to meet the needs of particular groups of staff and service users. Similarly, the strategy of encouraging service providers to take responsibility for monitoring the standards of training provided implied that the Code needed to be useful and relevant to both commissioners and providers of training. A number of comments suggested that the requirements of these two separate audiences were not fully addressed in the draft Code:

*'I feel each section as a whole confuses the responsibilities between trainers and commissioners/employers. I feel it would be easier to follow if the Code were in two separate formats – a code for trainers and a code for commissioners, each identifying specific responsibilities.'*

*'I feel it would be clearer if the Code was separated into issues only pertinent to training organisations and then issues relevant to provider agency/in-house trainers.'*

These comments lead to further clarification regarding the respective roles of trainers and commissioners of training, both in the body of the Code and in a new introductory section.

## Pain based compliance

The earlier BILD publication 'Physical Interventions: A Policy Framework' (Harris et al, 1996) set out the principle that physical interventions should not cause pain. However, there are two ways in which this principle might be undermined in practice.

First, it might be claimed that techniques which, in reality, depend upon pain to achieve compliance are 'pain free'. Typically, this claim is made on behalf of physical interventions which involve the service user being held in a 'lock' whereby movement at a joint (usually a finger, wrist or elbow) is restricted by

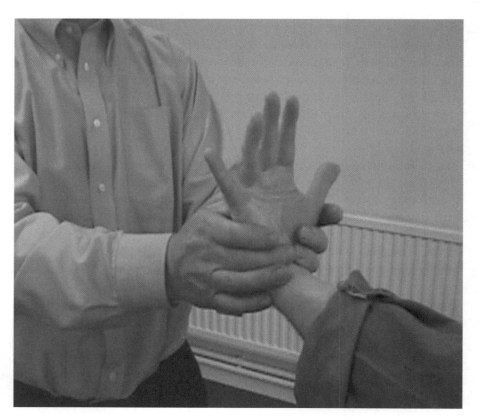

**Figure 9.1:** Application of a 'goose neck' hold

**Figure 9.2:** Application of a 'goose neck' hold

opposing pressure. The 'goose-neck' hold is a good example (See figures 9.1 & 9.2 above). Compliance is achieved because the level of discomfort and pain for the service user increases in direct proportion to the amount of pressure applied. Somewhat surprisingly, it has been suggested that these techniques are not 'pain based' because they only result in pain if the service user struggles thereby increasing the pressure on the joint.

Secondly, it has been suggested that in some situations there is no safe alternative to pain based interventions. For example, 'Breakaway' techniques are designed to help a member of staff disengage from an aggressive service user. When a service user grabs someone's hair or takes hold of soft tissue (for example around the face or a woman's breasts) a variety of widely used techniques for releasing the hold involve inflicting short-term pain on the assailant.

The draft Code included two lengthy statements designed to deter trainers from using pain based techniques, and to encourage them to indicate appropriate safeguards to protect service users if such methods were to be taught on a course:

3.7 Techniques that cause pain or discomfort pose major ethical, legal and moral difficulties. For this reason they should never be taught where an alternative pain free method can achieve the desired outcome. Teaching one or more pain based methods of physical intervention must only be carried out after the following procedures have been followed:

- A detailed assessment of the service user and his or her circumstances, which demonstrates that non-pain based methods have not achieved the desired effect and the likely reasons for this

- Preparation of a written statement which describes the particular behaviours under consideration, why non aversive methods are inappropriate and a description of the specific methods which are being proposed including how they might cause pain or discomfort. The information should be included in the service user's support or care plan

- The trainer and the senior managers of the service agency formally endorse the methods of physical intervention and specify which members of staff will be trained to use it.

3.8 Where physical interventions that cause pain or discomfort are taught, they should be designed to address specific behaviours presented by individual service users. They should only be introduced where there is clear documented evidence that other less intrusive procedures have been systematically implemented without addressing the specific risks associated with these behaviours. Such procedures should be individually prescribed, time limited, subject to detailed recording and reviewed by a multidisciplinary team at regular intervals, not exceeding 6 weeks.

This attempt to acknowledge the practical difficulties which might arise when translating the 'no pain' principle into practice, and to establish procedures which safeguarded the interests of service users, was supported by some of those who participated in the consultation exercise but was criticised by others.

There were several supportive comments:

**Para 3.7**
  'Good point well made'

  'A good attempt at introducing appropriate checks/controls to the generally abhorrent practice of pain compliance'

**Para 3.8**
  'Very comprehensive guidance given in this area'

  'This is prescriptive and I like it because it tightens up the system and usage'

  'Both these sections say all the right things'

However, the majority of responses took the view that this section of the Code was an implicit endorsement of pain based methods and would encourage, rather than reduce the extent to which they were employed. Many respondents wanted all pain-based methods to be prohibited.

**Para 3.7**

*'Couldn't see our organisation ever referring to any techniques that specifically cause pain'*

*'No techniques which cause pain to control should be used at all'*

*'This is totally unacceptable...The very notion of teaching such techniques seems to validate their use...'*

*'I am totally against this section'*

*'I could not endorse any method that includes pain'*

*'We don't teach pain based techniques!'*

**Para 3.8**

*'Not happy with this. Very difficult to find justification for ever using pain-compliant techniques – think again!'*

*'I cannot see why techniques that cause pain or discomfort should ever be taught – pain free is possible'*

*'I do not feel that BILD should approve pain based techniques'*

In the light of this feedback, paragraphs 3.7 and 3.8 were carefully reviewed. It was recognised that the provision of detailed advice regarding the administrative procedures to be put in place prior to the teaching of pain based techniques may have inadvertently implied that these techniques would be widely used. Doubts about the feasibility of introducing and monitoring such procedures were also raised. It was therefore decided to delete paragraph 3.8 and all but the first two sentences of paragraph 3.7 from the final version of the Code.

## Course numbers and ratio of trainers to course participants

Courses on the use of physical interventions are designed to teach participants how to use practical techniques in 'real life' settings. In addition to verbal instruction, this usually involves practical demonstrations of 'moves' and 'holds' by the trainers followed by rehearsal by the participants while being observed by the trainer. This emphasis on the acquisition of practical skills places constraints on the maximum number of participants which can be safely supervised on a single course and the minimum ratio of trainers to course participants.

Under Section 4 of the draft Code, which addressed relevant health and safety issues, was the following statements:

4.8 It is good practice for trainers to work in pairs. The ratio of trainers to course participants shall not be less than one trainer to 12 participants. Best practice requires that training groups are considerably smaller than this, ie, one trainer to eight participants (ie, the largest group for two trainers is 16)

**4.9** In very exceptional circumstances, for example, where there are overriding concerns for the safety of staff or service users, larger groups may be taught. Where this happens, there should be a written agreement that sets out:

- The reasons for working with a large group

- The limitations this imposes on the teaching programme

- The additional concerns regarding health and safety during training and how these risks will be managed

- Limitations on group management and assessment of performance arising from the larger group

- Additional further training which is required to ensure appropriate levels of competence among course participants.

The comments from the consultation indicated strong support for restrictions on both the total number of participants to be included on one course and the ratio of trainers to course participants.

Many respondents argued for lower limits:

*'Would prefer ratio to be no more than 1:6 for C&R and 1:8 for breakaway.'*

*'I would suggest a minimum of two trainers per twelve participants. I personally would not like to take 12–1 ratio for safety of the group'*

*'Ratio of 1–12 is too large in our opinion 2–16 should be the maximum group size ratio allowed'*

*'. . . I and my colleagues work to a ratio of 1 trainer to 4 participants and max groups of 12 are the norm'*

Other respondents recognised the importance of maintaining some degree of flexibility:

*'The cost implications of trainers always working in pairs is restrictive'*

*'Good idea to include this (proviso for larger groups in para 4.9) – as large groups do pose specific problems '*

*'(para 4.9) offers an exception which hopefully will never be needed.'*

The working group was mindful that requirements set out in the Code should describe best practice in ideal circumstances and take account of practical constraints which might argue in favour of somewhat more lenient requirements. For the final version of the Code, the text was revised to improve clarity, but the recommendations on the maximum number of course participants and the ratio of trainers to course participants were left unchanged.

# Summary

The provision of training on the use of physical interventions for staff in schools and intellectual disability services is a relatively new phenomenon. It has grown rapidly over the last 20 or 30 years in response to a number of developments affecting service provision for children with special educational needs and adults with intellectual disabilities. The resettlement of adults and children previously cared for in segregated institutions has brought many people who present various forms of challenging behaviour into what are loosely referred to as 'mainstream services'. Here the design of buildings, the proximity of the public, the limited qualifications and experience of front line staff and the restricted availability of medical interventions contribute to a burgeoning demand for training in safe and effective strategies for managing dangerous behaviours.

Employers and managers have become increasingly aware of their obligations to their staff under health and safety legislation and the severe financial penalties that can be imposed if they are found negligent (see chapter 5). To the extent that staff have been trained in the use of physical interventions, managers and employers will be able to offer a defence in the event of injury arising from challenging behaviour by a pupil or service user.

UK legislation (for example the Children Act and the Human Rights Act), together with international agreements (for example, UN Convention on Human Rights), has emphasised the rights of pupils in schools, and people using other services, to be treated in a fair and reasonable way, even when their own behaviour may appear irresponsible and unreasonable. Where it is foreseeable that a pupil or an adult service user will present dangerous or violent behaviour, staff should be trained to respond in ways which both minimise the risk of injury or psychological distress.

These pressures have lead to the creation of a market place in which courses on physical intervention are 'traded' between service providers and trainers. In the absence of external interference, the laws of economics will ensure that the supply of training will sooner or later increase to meet rising demand. Left unchecked the same laws also predict that, as resources (ie trainers with appropriate experience and expertise) are depleted the quality of the goods and services available in the market place will deteriorate. In other words, as more training becomes available, the standard of training will decline. Consumers will have to be increasingly vigilant if they wish to purchase high quality training and avoid inept, inappropriate or sub-standard training.

If one assumes that purchasers would prefer to buy high quality rather than poor quality training, one strategy to encourage high standards among training providers is to increase the availability of accurate and relevant information within the market place. This chapter has described three specific initiatives to achieve this.

- First, the compilation of a list of trainers so that those purchasing training have an opportunity to draw comparisons between different training products.

- Secondly, publication of a Code of Practice which sets the criteria against which the quality of training can be measured.

- Thirdly the development of an independent accreditation scheme which will enable purchasers of training to quickly and easily identify those organisations which conform to the standards set out in the Code of Practice.

It is worth noting that while helpful, the availability of accurate and relevant information will not, on its own, prevent a reduction in quality as the supply of training is increased to meet demand. The other crucial requirement is regulation to discourage the sale or purchase of sub-standard goods or services. Chapter three in this volume considers the role of organisational policies and government guidelines in raising standards of practice and training in the use of physical interventions.

The Code of Practice was developed through a process of consultation involving trainers, service providers, representatives from government departments and professional bodies and one service user. The draft version of the Code received widespread support. The most contentious topics concerned the most appropriate way of limiting the use of pain based techniques and recommendations regarding the maximum number of participants who should attend a single course and the minimum ratio of trainers to course participants. A scheme to accredit training on the use of physical interventions has recently been launched by BILD.

## Acknowledgements

The work described in this chapter was made possible by grant funding from the Department of Health and the Department for Education and Skills. I am indebted to a great many people who contributed to the development and publication of the BILD Data Base and the BILD Code of Practice, particularly all those who responded to the consultation on the Code by completing a questionnaire or by attending a workshop. Special thanks are due to David Allen, Catherine Allsopp, Lucy Bennett, Ros Blackburn, Marion Cornick, David Ellis, Danielle Epps, James Hourihan, Allen Jefferson, David Leadbetter, George Matthews, Richard McElheren, Andy McDonnell, Brian Nicholson, Sharon Powell, Suzi Stevens and Alison Wall.

## References

Allen, D (2001) *Training Carers in Physical Interventions: Research Towards Evidence Based Practice*. Kidderminster: BILD Publications

BILD (2001) *Code of Practice for Trainers in the Use of Physical Interventions*. Kidderminster: BILD Publications

BILD (2003) *BILD Directory of Physical Interventions Training Organisations.* Kidderminster: BILD.

Department for Education and Skills and Department of Health (2002) *Guidance for Restrictive Physical Interventions. How to provide safe services for people with learning disabilities and autistic spectrum disorders.* London: Department of Health.

Harris, J, Allen, D, Cornick, M, Jefferson, A, & Mills, R (1996) *Physical Interventions: A Policy Framework.* Kidderminster: BILD Publications.

# SECTION IV:

**The Thin Line – Physical Intervention and Abusive Practice**

# Chapter 10

# Best interest? Seeking the views of service users

Peter Baker

## Introduction

It is only relatively recently that a debate has taken place regarding the issues surrounding the use of physical interventions in the management of challenging behaviour presented by people with intellectual disabilities. A consensus appears to have arisen, even from the most critical of opponents, that the occasional use of physical intervention is justified (eg, Penhale & Brown, 2001).

As reported in chapter 2, there is an increasing body of evidence to suggest that the use of physical intervention as a response to challenging behaviour in this user group is a very frequent occurrence. It is likely that the frequency of use of physical procedures has contributed to a situation whereby such practices are justified by an argument of proven necessity. The debate has then shifted to consider training provided to care staff in physical intervention and further, to define the content of this training.

A similar process occurred in adult mental health services where there was a general recognition that reliance on such procedures was an unfortunate necessity for people who present severe challenging behaviour (eg, Hopton, 1995). In the main, there was an assumption that their use should be 'as a last resort' to prevent imminent harm to self and others. However, it should be noted that the caveat of last resort was not a universally held position, and that some authors suggested that restraint or seclusion be used in situations other than emergencies, for example, to prevent damage to property, protection of the ward milieu from socially unacceptable behaviours, to decrease stimulation and at the patient's request (Fisher, 1994).

Although generally widely accepted, the notion that the use of physical intervention is a proven necessity has been subject to some scrutiny. Sundram et al (1994a) carried out a major survey of over 1,000 former inpatients of New York State's psychiatric facilities. They found substantial variations in the use of restraint and seclusion between facilities. These variations were not accounted for by client characteristics, but rather were a result of attitudes and treatment philosophies of administrative and clinical leaders. Furthermore, Rangecroft et al. (1997) examined incidents requiring emergency medication or seclusion in a large hospital for people with intellectual disabilities. Simply overtly monitoring the use of these practices resulted in a significant reduction in use of restraint and emergency drugs given. These two studies would suggest that, at least on some occasions, the use of these practices is determined by factors other than clinical need.

Fisher (op.cit) went on to predict that as, the consumer empowerment movement in relation to mental health services grew, there would be a marked difference in the viewpoints of those who have experienced physical intervention and those who feel obliged to use it. This has been seen by some as a positive tension and a fundamental pre-requisite to the establishment of good practice. There can be little argument that a parallel debate is required between people with intellectual disabilities and those who manage their care. However, there are significant obstacles to this process that, unless overcome, cast doubt over whether this debate can be realised.

## Eliciting the views of people with intellectual disabilities

The publication of the White Paper 'Valuing People' (DoH 2001) marked a distinct change in the way in which the views of people with intellectual disabilities are perceived. Choice, control and advocacy were key themes and people with intellectual disabilities themselves played a direct part in formulating government policy and were explicitly included as part of the consultation process.

However, the difficulties involved in ascertaining the views of people with intellectual disabilities are also well documented. Historically, individuals with intellectual disabilities have not had a voice and have, at best, been planned for in a spirit of benign paternalism (Chapman & Oaks, 1995). As a result of a combination of cognitive limitations and limited experience of involvement in decision making, individuals with intellectual disabilities may have problems understanding questions, relating to their own experience, or accurately articulating their own views (Witts & Gibson, 1977). There is evidence that they are prone to certain response effects that have been shown to systematically bias any information gleaned. For example:

- People with intellectual disabilities have been shown to acquiesce (ie respond by saying yes) in response to yes/no questions (Sigelman & Budd, 1986).

- The tendency of consumers of public services to be over generous in their praise of these services is exaggerated in people with intellectual disabilities (Flynn, 1986).

- Clare & Gudjonsson (1993) found that people with mild intellectual disabilities were more vulnerable to leading questions than their non-intellectually disabled counterparts. There is evidence that suggestibility may be a very common phenomenon experienced when interviewing people with intellectual disabilities.

Since the late 1980s, major efforts have been made to overcome these difficulties and to establish a technology for gaining effective service user feedback (Kroese et al. 1998; Prosser & Bromley, 1998). This has led to claims by some authors (eg Wadsworth & Harper, 1991) that the literature supports the notion that adults with moderate to severe intellectual disabilities can provide accurate and reliable information about most aspects of their service provision, providing the questions are presented in a structured and supportive format. This appears to be ambitiously premature however. Particular problems are likely to arise with the population of individuals who are likely to experience physical intervention. Both the presentation of challenging behaviour itself and the probability of higher levels of intellectual disability (Emerson, 1995), would appear to present significant obstacles to those wishing to seek feedback from these individuals. Indeed, people who are least likely to be involved in evaluation of services are the ones most likely to be receiving the worst services (Ritchie, 1996).

## Studies of the views of service users with intellectual disabilities on their experiences of physical intervention

Only two studies that commented on the views of service users with intellectual disabilities who had experienced physical intervention during the emergency management of their challenging behaviour could be identified.

Sequeira & Halstead (2001) examined the personal experiences of 5 women with intellectual disabilities who were inpatients in a secure independent sector hospital. They used semi-structured interviews to elicit themes relevant to understanding psychological responses to emergency management (including physical restraint, seclusion and rapid tranquillisation).

Four themes emerged:

- Physical pain or discomfort – for example:

  *'It really hurts'*

  *'It bloody hurts'*

- Anxiety, mental distress – for example:

  *'Me don't know how me feel. Sometimes me keep dreaming these things having nightmares. Don't know why. I do worry about it a bit'*

  *'It's awful, when they restrain you it's awful. Nurses and doctors they say you're awful and they give you one of these' (mimes giving self an injection).*

- Perception of staff using emergency management to punish, control. Attributions of anger, hatred and enjoyment to the staff – for example:

  *'The staff are angry with me. Is it meant to hurt, is it?'*

  *'They were laughing about it … those lot in there – the staff in there.'*

- Angry feelings and urge to express aggression whilst experiencing the intervention – for example:

*'Angry – makes (me) more angry.'*

*'When you have got people holding you, you kick off more than you have done. "Smash up". That's what I feel like.'*

Murphy et al (1996), as part of a wider evaluation of a service for people with mild intellectual disabilities and challenging behaviour who had committed criminal offences, asked twenty six service users their views on their treatment in a specialist, hospital-based unit. Sixteen of these people had been restrained, with the majority stating that they felt angry about the experience. A similar number had been secluded and again, the majority reported negative feelings regarding this experience. However, two of these individuals reported 'happy or ok' feelings about their experience.

## Studies of service users with mental health problems

Slightly more evidence on user views concerning behaviour management is available from the field of mental health. Research from this speciality has not reported a total rejection of physical interventions by service users. Sundram et al's (1994b) postal survey, for example, found both positive and negative views expressed. A small percentage of respondents offered positive comments about their placement in restraint or seclusion. Common themes were that their behaviour was dangerous, that they had been treated fairly and that they benefited from the use of the interventions. However, nearly all those placed in restraint or seclusion cited at least one complaint. Whether the individual had been placed in restraint or seclusion appeared to have considerable influence over their rating their overall care as negative. This was especially so if the person reported that staff had made no effort to calm them down or resolve their problems prior to the use of restraint or seclusion. Specific complaints included that staff had:

- Used unnecessary force (50%)

- Psychologically abused, ridiculed or threatened them (40%)

- Physically abused them or physically injured them (29%)

- Sexually abused them (29%).

Sheridan et al (1990) detailed similar findings, with the majority of respondents on a psychiatric ward reporting a negative response to being restrained, and describing feelings of fear and anger. However, 41% of participants expressed positive responses with some suggesting that the restraint had a calming effect.

Only a limited number of studies have attempted to identify emotional responses associated with particular characteristics of the intervention. Sequeira & Halstead (unpublished) obtained similar feedback from service users of a secure psychiatric facility, all of whom had experienced physical intervention. The dominant response to restraint was anger. This was often related to perceptions of 'injustice' and the feeling that the restraint had been used as a punishment. In particular some felt extremely angry when staff were talking and laughing during the procedures. This makes salient the scenes in the 'MacIntyre Undercover' documentary (MacIntyre, 1999), where staff were laughing as they restrained a woman in an attempt to force her to take medication. Experiencing the intervention as painful was also associated with anger as well as removal of personal control. Contrary to the idea of the intervention bringing about resolution to the incident, this elicitation of anger often contributed to further behavioural escalation and violent behaviour. This study also identified a sub-group of individuals who described desirable or sought after aspects of restraint. Two themes emerged, containment and release of feelings. Containment appeared to be important for individuals who felt out of control and those who wished to relinquish responsibility for their behaviour. Additionally, the release of feelings experienced through the struggle was an important cathartic experience for some participants.

Several studies have concentrated solely on the use of seclusion in the emergency management of challenging behaviour. Seclusion has been considered conceptually different from restraint, as the secluded individual continues to have freedom to move within a confined area. However, some sort of physical intervention would invariably be required to escort the individual to the seclusion area. These studies have indicated consistently negative responses to seclusion.

Two relatively recent British studies indicated that the use of seclusion may have a negative impact on relationships between service users and staff (Mason, 1995; Meehan et al, 2000). Seclusion was associated with feelings of powerlessness, fear, humiliation and worsening mental states. Meehan et al, in particular noted the importance of poor communication between staff and service users and how this fed perceptions of abandonment and punishment. This is particularly apt within this discussion, as Mason found that people with intellectual disabilities were nearly twice as likely to be secluded as individuals with other diagnoses. Way & Banks (1990) reported similar findings in a mental health facility in the USA.

Various authors have commented on the potential of restraint re-traumatising individuals who had previously suffered abuse. Emotions of fear, anxiety and rage were reported with associated feelings of vulnerability, helplessness, powerlessness and loss of dignity (Braise-Smith, 1995; Gallop et al, 1999; Johnson, 1998; Sequeira & Halstead, unpublished). Many of these feelings were associated with the use of leather straps as a restraining device, a practice relatively common in the United States (see Sundram et al 1994b).

## Lessons to be learned from studies of service user views

The available literature concerning the experience of people with intellectual disabilities and emergency behavioural management is clearly not sufficient to enable any definitive judgements to be made. The literature relating to people with mental health problems is potentially of some use, although caution should be exercised when making generalisations from one population to another. In addition, much of the available research is North American, and practices in the USA and the UK appear to have some important essential differences. Sundram et al (1994a), in their study of New York psychiatric facilities, indicated that the majority of restraint incidents involved mechanical restraints. The use of mechanical restraint, particularly as an emergency management procedure, is relatively rare in the UK. However, in spite of the inadequacies of the available literature, it is possible to establish a preliminary view as to service user feedback of their experience of physical intervention and use this feedback to make some recommendations as to what would constitute good practice:

- The voice of the service user, particularly those with intellectual disabilities, has not been adequately researched.

- Nevertheless, the overwhelming amount and the nature of negative feedback regarding people's experience of physical intervention indicates that there is justifiable cause for concern regarding such practices. In particular, reports that the use of physical intervention can lead to escalation of aggression are particularly concerning.

- A significant minority of individuals recognised that physical intervention was necessary and justified.

- The physical interventions employed were regularly reported as causing pain. This is clearly unacceptable.

- The demeanour and behaviour of staff whilst implementing the intervention is critical. Especially problematic is staff laughing whilst intervening.

- The use of physical intervention has the potential to damage relationships between service users and staff.

- Particular care and attention needs to be paid to individuals who have previously experienced physical or sexual abuse.

- Active attempts to calm the individual and to solve their problems should be attempted before consideration of physical intervention.

- Physical intervention should only be used as a last resort.

- The purpose of and reasons for the intervention need to be clearly communicated to the individual and the individual should be enabled to indicate their preference as to how their challenging behaviour can be reasonably managed.

- The interventions should be used only for purposes of safety and not to punish or to demonstrate staff control.

## Issues for future research

Whist there is no doubt that there is a considerable amount that can be learned from mental health studies, immediate and urgent action is required in order to address the near absence of research involving people with intellectual disabilities. There are some areas where the potential views of the two groups of service users may diverge. Some evidence, albeit anecdotal, exists that people who have been diagnosed as autistic have an increased likelihood of suffering from abnormalities of sensory sensitivity. For example, Grandin (1989), herself diagnosed as suffering from autism, reported

> 'I pulled away when people tried to hug me, because being touched sent an overwhelming tidal wave of stimulation through my body',

She went on to say

> 'I wanted to feel the comforting feeling of being held but then when somebody held me the effect on my nervous system was overwhelming. It was an approach – avoid situation … '.

There is also evidence of this paradoxical effect of touch with less able people with autism (O'Neill & Jones, 1997). Secondly, there is some evidence that some people with intellectual disabilities may have substantially altered pain thresholds (Biersdorff, 1994). This raises serious concerns regarding the amount of force that may be required for the intervention to be effective. Finally McDonnell et al (1991) suggested that the aggressive incidents encountered in services for people with intellectual disabilities were sufficiently different from those presented by people who do not have an intellectual disability. This has major implications for reactive interventions.

Considerable debate has surrounded the use and teaching of specific physical intervention techniques. In particular, the use of pain-compliance techniques (techniques that involve the deliberate infliction of discomfort, pain or injury) in the management of challenging behaviour has attracted much controversy (Allen et al, 1997; Baker & Allen, 2001; Hopton, 1995; LaVigna et al, 1989). Regretfully, no research appears to have actively and systematically sought the views of the people with intellectual disabilities who are experiencing such interventions.

## Planning for individuals

As previously highlighted, the available service user feedback gives a very clear message that individuals should have involvement in planning their own behavioural management strategies. Indeed, the imposition of a physical intervention against a person's wishes could well constitute an unlawful act (Harris et al, 1996). However, in spite of the best intentions of carers, a significant group of people with intellectual disabilities who present challenging behaviour and experience physical interventions, will be unable to give informed consent to such procedures (Arscott et al, 1999). Legally there is no one who can give consent to treatment on behalf of adults with intellectual disabilities. However, they may be treated without their consent providing such treatment is deemed to be in their best interest. The Law Commission has suggested that the following criteria be used when making a judgement of best interest:

- the past and present wishes and feelings of the person

- the availability of less intrusive/restrictive alternatives

- the effect on life expectancy, health, happiness, freedom and dignity (Based upon Lyon 1994a, cited in Harris et al 1996).

At present, it would be ill-advised for any single individual to make judgements concerning the best interest of another. It is an imperative to conduct widespread consultation, in order that the nearest approximation of what the individual would consider to be in their best interest can be achieved. However, *Making Decisions* (Lord Chancellor's Dept, 1999) has recommended that one person should have Continued Power of Attorney in situations where an individual does not have the Capacity to consent to treatment. It should be noted that this does not reflect current legislation.

This legal framework should provide sufficient safeguards to promote good practice. However, recent British research gives significant cause for concern. Dowson et al (1999) evaluated incidents of aggression in service users in intellectual disability units in 10 National Health Service Trusts. No satisfactory written record of physical restraint was found in 87% of the incidents, there were deficiencies in the training of staff, and deficiencies in policies for victim support. It was concluded that Trusts should consider reviewing their policies on the prevention and management of violence, particularly in relation to staff training. Baker & Bissmire (2000), in a study of the use of physical intervention in a non-specialised intellectual disability service, suggested that these interventions may well be taking place in a policy and competence vacuum.

In order to safeguard the rights of the individual and ensure that their needs are paramount, any planning process should include the following steps:

1.  A risk assessment of situations where the management of challenging behaviour might potentially involve physical intervention should be carried out.

2.  Consideration should be given as to whether that individual is capable of consenting to these physical interventions. If so, their consent should be sought. If not, wide-ranging consultation should be conducted, including the individual's advocate, relatives, appropriately qualified and experienced professionals, etc. This consultation should consider the criteria stated previously in relation to best interest.

3.  If the desired outcome for that individual is a reduction in the frequency, duration or impact of their challenging behaviour, an intervention plan should be devised with the appropriate balance between proactive and reactive strategies.

4.  An individualised *written* management plan should be constructed, including steps required to prevent the behaviour from either occurring at all or escalating.

5.  All care staff working with that individual should be trained and *competent* in the execution of this plan.

6. All use of physical intervention should be recorded.

7. The use of physical interventions should be reviewed to ensure that they are not being used to excess and that only those interventions detailed in the written management plan are being used.

## References

Allen, D, McDonald, L, Dunn, C and Doyle, T (1997) Changing care staff approaches to the Prevention and Management of Aggressive Behaviour in a Residential Treatment unit for people with Mental Retardation and Challenging Behaviour. *Research in Developmental disabilities*, 18, 101–112.

Arscott, K, Dagnan, D, Kroese, BS (1999) Assessing the ability of people with a learning disability to give informed consent to treatment. *Psychological-Medicine*, 29, 6, 1367–1375

Baker, PA & Allen, D (2001). Physical Abuse & Physical Interventions in Learning Disabilities: An element of risk? *Journal of Adult Protection*, 3, 2, 25–31.

Baker, PA & Bissmire, D (2000) A Pilot Study of the Use of Physical Intervention in the Crisis Management of People with Intellectual Disabilities who present Challenging Behaviour. *Journal of Applied Research in Intellectual Disabilities*, 13, 1, 38–45.

Biersdorff, KK (1994) Incidence of significantly altered pain experience among individuals with developmental disabilities. *American Journal on Mental Retardation*, 98, 5, 619–631.

Braise-Smith (1995) Restraints: retraumatisation for rape victims? *Journal of Psychosocial Nursing*, 33, 23–28.

Chapman, K & Oakes, P (1995) Asking people with learning disabilities their views on direct psychological intervention. *Clinical Psychology Forum*, 81, 28–33.

Clare, ICH & Gudjonsson, GH (1993) Interrogative suggestibility, confabulation and acquiescence in people with mild learning disabilities (mental handicap): Implications for reliability during police interrogations. *British Journal of Clinical Psychology*, 32, 295–301.

Department of Health (2001) *Valuing People: A New strategy for Learning Disability for the 21st Century.* Norwich: The Stationery Office.

Dowson, JH, Butler, J & Williams, O, (1999) Management of psychiatric in-patient violence in the Anglia region: implications for record-keeping, staff training and victim support. *Psychiatric Bulletin*, 23, 8, 486–9.

Emerson, E (1995) *Challenging Behaviour: Analysis and Intervention in People with Learning Difficulties.* Cambridge: Cambridge University Press.

Fisher, WA (1994) Restraint & Seclusion: A review of the Literature. *American Journal of Psychiatry*, 151, 11, 1584–1591.

Flynn, MC (1986) Adults who are mentally handicapped as consumers: Issues and guidelines for interviewing. *Journal of Mental Deficiency Research*, 30, 369–77.

Gallop, R, McCay, E, Guha, M & Khan, P (1999) The experience of hospitalisation and restraint of women who have a history of childhood sexual abuse. *Health Care for Women International*, 20, 401–416.

Grandin, T (1989) An autistic person's view of holding therapy. *Journal of the National Autistic Society*, 23, 3, 75–78.

Harris, J, Allen, D, Cornick, M, Jefferson, A, & Mills, R (1996) *Physical Interventions: A Policy Framework*. Kidderminster: BILD.

Hegarty, JR & Gale, E (1996) Touch as a therapeutic medium for people with challenging behaviours. *British Journal of Learning Disabilities*, 24, 26–32.

Hopton, J (1995) Control and restraint in contemporary psychiatric nursing: some ethical considerations. *Journal of Advanced Nursing*, 22, 110–115.

Johnson, ME (1998) Being restrained: A Study of Power & Powerlessness. *Journal of Mental Health Nursing*, 19, 191–206.

Kroese BS, Gillot, A & Atkinson, V (1998) Consumers with Intellectual Disabilities as Service Evaluators. *Journal of Applied Research in Intellectual Disabilities*, 2, 116–128.

LaVigna, GW, Willis, TJ and Donnellan, AW (1989) The role of positive programming in behavioral treatment. In Cipani, E (Ed.), The Treatment of Severe Behavior Disorders. Behavior Analysis Approaches. Washington: American Association on Mental Deficiency, pp 59–83.

Lord Chancellor's Office (1999) *Making Decisions. A report issued in the light of responses to the consultation paper 'Who decides?'*. London: Stationery Office.

MacIntyre, D (1999) *MacIntyre Undercover. One Man, Four Lives*. London: BBC.

Mason, T (1996) Seclusion and Learning Disabilities: Research and Deduction. *The British Journal of Developmental Disabilities*, 42, 1, 3–9.

McDonnell, A, Dearden, B and Richens, A (1991) Staff training in the Management of Violence and Aggression, 3. Physical restraint. *Mental Handicap*, 19, 151–154, 148–172.

Meehan, T, Vermeer, C & Windsor, C (2000) Patients' perceptions of seclusion: a qualitative investigation. *Journal of Advanced Nursing*, 31, 2, 370–7.

Murphy, GH, Estien, D & Clare, ICH (1996) Services for People with Mild Intellectual Disabilities and Challenging Behaviour: Service-user Views. *Journal of Applied Research in Intellectual Disabilities*, 9, 3, 256–283.

O'Neill, M & Jones RSP (1997) Sensory perceptual abnormalities in autism: A case for more research. *Journal of Autism and Developmental Disorders*, 27, 283–293.

Penhale, B & Brown, H (2001) Editorial. *Journal of Adult Protection*, 3, 2, 2–7.

Prosser, H, & Bromley, J (1998) Interviewing people with intellectual disabilities. In Emerson, E, Hatton, C, Bromley, J & Caine, A (Eds) Clinical Psychology and People with Intellectual Disabilities. Chichester: Wiley, pp. 99–113.

Rangecroft, MEH, Tyrer, SP, Berney, TP (1997). The use of seclusion and emergency medication in a hospital for people with learning disability. *British Journal of Psychiatry*, 170, 3, 273–277

Ritchie, P (1996) Involving Service Users. In R. McConkey (ed) *Innovations in Evaluating Services for People with Intellectual Disabilities*. Lancashire: Lisieux Hall.

Sequeira, H & Halstead, S (2001) "Is it meant to hurt, is it?" Management of violence in women with developmental disabilities. *Violence against Women*, 7, 4, 462–476.

Sequeira, H & Halstead, S (unpublished) Psychiatric Patient Experienced of Control & Restraint in the UK.

Sheriden, M, Henrion, R, Robinson, L & Baxter, V (1990) Precipitants of violence in a psychiatric hospital setting. *Hospital and Community Psychiatry*, 41, 776–780.

Sigelman, CK, & Budd, EC. Pictures as an aid in questioning mentally retarded persons. *Rehabilitation Counselling Bulletin,* 29, 173–81.

Sundram, C, Stack, EW & Benjamin, WP (1994a*) Restraint and Seclusion Practices in New York State Psychiatric Facilities.* Schenectady, NY: New York State Commission on Quality of Care for the Mentally Disabled.

Sundram, C, Stack, EW & Benjamin, WP (1994b) *Voices from the Front Line: Patients Perspective of Restraint and Seclusion Use.* Schenectady, NY: New York State Commission on Quality of Care for the Mentally Disabled.

Wadsworth, J & Harper, D (1991) Increasing the reliability of self report by adults with moderate mental retardation. *Journal of the Association for People with severe handicaps,* 16, 228–32.

Way, BB & Banks, SM (1990) Use of seclusion and restraint in public psychiatric hospitals: Patient characteristics and facility effects. *Hospital and Community Psychiatry,* 41, 75–81.

Witts, P & Gibson, KP (1997) Satisfaction with an adult learning community support team. *Journal of Applied Research in Intellectual Disabilities,* 10, 1, 41–47.

## Chapter 11

# The risks of getting it wrong: Systems failure
# and the impact of abuse

Paul Cambridge

### Introduction

The aim of this chapter is to review the organisational conditions and processes in services for people with intellectual disabilities in relation to adult protection. Evidence from inquiries suggests that there are intrinsic factors in the ways services are commissioned, organised and managed which contribute to the development of abusive service cultures or to the late recognition and reporting of abuse. These will be discussed in relation to a case study of an abuse inquiry (Cambridge, 1998; 1999a) and with particular reference to issues concerning physical intervention.

#### Categorising abuse by services

An important consideration is the potential relationship between poor quality services and abuse, and one of the first abuse policies in services for people with intellectual disabilities *Recognising and Responding to the Abuse of Adults with Learning Disabilities* (Greenwich Social Services, 1993), considered this. In addition to the well-recognised categories of abuse, such as physical, sexual and financial abuse, categories were included where staff or services had failed in their responsibilities or duty of care:

- physical neglect *'failure to keep the person clean, warm and in good health, to ensure adequate nutrition and health care is available'*

- negligence in the face of unacceptable risk taking behaviour *'the wilful failure to intervene, or consider the implications of non-intervention, in behaviour which is dangerous to the individual concerned or to others. This might include the failure to use agreed risk-taking procedures and consultation processes resulting in the person taking unwarranted and unnecessary risks'*

- unauthorised administration of, or withdrawal of, prescribed medication *'either over-medication, irregular administration of medication or refusal to abide by approved treatment on the part of the staff or carer'*

- unauthorised use of restraint, punishment or seclusion *'the use of arbitrary force, the use of unauthorised or unsupervised time-out, or seclusion procedures, the sabotaging of positive programmes for the management of challenging behaviour on the part of a staff person or carer'.*

## Best practice and abuse

During the 1990s, the trend towards generic vulnerable adult and adult protection policies in local authorities, culminating in *No Secrets* (Department of Health, 2000), tended to deflect attention away from client group specific concerns. A classic high-risk area in intellectual disability is challenging behaviour, because of the vulnerability of the client group and the complexities of technical and other supports required of staff.

The difficulties associated with defining and attributing abuse is illustrated by the conceptual sub-continuum between the active and passive perpetration of abuse. Although punching or kicking a service user is different from not doing something (such as failing to change a continence pad or administer medication), the consequences for the person (such as pain or distress) may be similar. Passive forms of abuse are usually less visible and, therefore, tend to receive less attention. Abuse characterised by inaction is particularly difficult to detect and investigate. Similarly, inflicting unnecessary force and pain when using authorised physical interventions, or bathing someone at a temperature known to cause them distress may be hard to identify.

A more general continuum can be theorised to exist between best management and practice and abusive services, characterised by neglect, negligence or mistreatment. The reality is undoubtedly more complex than a linear relationship between quality and abuse, as numerous intervening and compounding variables determine how, why and when abuse happens. These may include, for example, whether the index incident is part of a wider culture of abuse or a one off incident, its relationship with other forms of abuse, and the level of individual responsibility.

## Conceptual underpinnings

The findings of 'failure of care' type abuse inquiries, in both institutional and community services for people with intellectual disabilities, provide important markers of abuse or failure. Central to most have been the nature of the dependency relationships and power differentials between support staff or carers and people with intellectual disabilities, and their inherent capacity to corrupt the nature of care (Wardhaugh & Wilding, 1993). Wider social inequalities, such as those generated by gender, race, culture, sexuality and age, can magnify such differences. People with intellectual disabilities also remain significantly segregated and isolated in community services, and tend to be politically and economically marginalized. Gender and ethnicity can also influence service support and responses to challenging behaviours (Di Terlizzi et al, 1999).

Wolfensberger (1975) described the production of sub-human language and images associated with infantilisation, depersonalisation, dehumanisation and victimisation. This is mirrored in the use of euphemisms to decriminalise crimes committed against people with intellectual disabilities (Sobsey, 1994). For example, 'restraint' may be used to describe assault or imprisonment, and 'physical intervention' to describe procedures that deliberately inflict pain upon service users (Penhale & Brown, 2001).

### Historical evidence

In addition to the critical analyses (Townsend, 1962; Morris, 1969; Robb, 1967) which fuelled broader disquiet about the role of institutions, a series of exposés and scandals focused public and political attention on abuse within institutions themselves (Department of Health & Social Security, 1969; 1971; 1974). Martin (1984) summarised the ingredients of institutionalised abuse as individual callousness and brutality, low standards and morale, weak and ineffective leadership, pilfering by staff, vindictiveness towards complainants and the failure of management to concern itself with abuse.

Abuse within and by community services has continued to mirror many of these attributes and those identified by wider discourses (Goffman, 1961; Foucault, 1977), suggesting fundamental characteristics of abuse within services. Biggs et al (1995) ask whether residential and institutional care is abusive in itself, looking at who inhabits institutional space, how people are expected to live private lives in public spaces and the contradictions between the open and closed nature of such spaces. Such characteristics are also features of many community services, where abuse has also remained unreported or there has been a reluctance to investigate it properly.

At organisational and systems levels, there have often been attempts to manage abuse internally to avoid the political consequences of disclosure or to ignore warning signs and signals. The Longcare (Buckinghamshire County Council, 1998) scandal centred on independent provisions in Buckinghamshire where residents had been systematically sexually and physically abused or subjected to humiliation by the manager-owner. The inquiry found that social services had continued to purchase care despite various allegations of abuse, and that the inspection service had failed to spot or act on the appalling conditions prevailing in the service. The television exposée of abuse in a private care home in Medway (Macintyre, 1999) demonstrated similar dynamics between commissioning, inspections and registration, and service management. These issues are discussed further in chapter 12.

MacIntyre exposed abuse through inappropriate physical interventions as well as physical abuse per se. In other inquiries (Cambridge, 1999a), the very distance between purchasing and providing and front line support was a contributory factor, but there was also a failure to recognise unexplained increases in the frequency and intensity of challenging behaviours as warning signals. Although in the following case study the principal failure was on the part of the management and individual members of the staff team, wider shortcomings in the service system were also detected and mapped.

## Interpreting the Evidence

Service failures have implications for a wide range of interests in services for people with intellectual disabilities and challenging behaviours beyond the well-being of service users themselves. However, caution is needed in interpreting evidence and reaching conclusions, and a number of important caveats are apparent.

### Individual and ecological fallacies

Attributing 'failings in care' types of abuse to an individual or group of people and their particular actions or inactions, thus suggesting a degree of individual culpability, risks the 'individual fallacy' and distracting attention away from wider systemic causes. Direct sexual or physical abuse perpetrated by a powerful individual against a vulnerable person is clearly one instance where such interpretations are likely to be most valid. Even in such cases however, wider individual and social factors can invariably help explain and locate abuse in a broader social or economic context. Abuse can also be interpreted as a failure in risk management or duty of care on the part of the service.

When a service is under the spotlight in a 'failure in care' type of inquiry, there is a tendency for management and practice to be interpreted outside a normative context. There is likely to be a general trawl of available information and evidence and, however well this is constructed (Cambridge, 2001), there are potential methodological and interpretative pitfalls to consider. Interactions between staff and users or particular interventions can have abuse attributed to them in a simple cause and effect model. This may be despite such behaviours being well established, informally sanctioned, unchallenged or prevalent elsewhere in services. A correlation between say, a physical intervention or an intimate care task and physical abuse or neglect, does not demonstrate cause, effect, intent or experience. Such potentially complex connections require careful exploration and interpretation. Yet the buck frequently stops with staff and managers, despite issues of power and powerlessness applying within such hierarchies.

A second potential pitfall is to assume that having adult protection policies, procedures and systems in place (such as for the use of physical interventions for challenging behaviours) will necessarily have a positive impact on reducing the incidence of abuse. Policies and procedures should impact on the sensitivity of staff, by reducing the tolerance of and thresholds to reporting abuse. Evidence from adult protection policy development (Brown & Stein, 1998) suggests a subsequent increase in adult protection alerts, investigations and subsequent incidence and prevalence figures. However, this is not the same as a real increase in cases due to the high proportion of hidden cases (Brown et al, 1995).

In addition, there is evidence that multiple abuse may be better recognised with generic policies and procedures (Brown & Stein, 1998), but also that reports will mainly concern clients already known to the organisations involved, diverting attention from the risk of abuse in private and unregulated care settings. Policies and procedures also provide the capacity to produce general intelligence on patterns of occurrence in typology, topography and geography. Although such information may have a preventative function, for example in helping detect cases of multiple or serial abuse, it will not prevent the emergence of new cases. Long-running national initiatives such as *No Secrets* and the implementation of local multi-agency adult policies appear to be an essential baseline to making real inroads in tackling abuse.

It is emotionally alluring, but intellectually dangerous, to assume that if a proven case of abuse is thoroughly investigated and lessons constructed and disseminated, then this will help prevent abuse from happening in the future. This 'preventive fallacy' risks ignoring the centrality of unique factors and circumstances in explaining abuse, such as the characteristics of each service user, their support arrangements and immediate social and physical environments. Such variables provide infinitely variable conditions for the potential development and execution of abuse. While descriptions of individual cases of abuse can undoubtedly help increase our accumulated understanding of risk factors and the characteristics of abuse, lessons may not necessarily be transferable and will require careful generalisation. Indeed, inquiries may worryingly give us a sort of voyeuristic gratification that such things could 'never happen here'.

Other conceptual dilemmas exist with adult protection practice. HIV prevention workers, health promotion agencies and safer sex campaigns never receive recognition for HIV infections that do not happen as a consequence of their interventions. For good ethical, moral and methodological reasons, we choose not to use a controlled experimental design to evaluate such interventions. Adult protection faces the same difficulty and it is easier to argue against the costs of implementing new policies and procedures than acknowledge their hidden cost savings.

Inquiries also have a range of benefits or purposes. They can demonstrate that social care organisations really are user centred and concerned for the well-being of relatives and users, public accountability can be maintained in transparent ways and that mistakes or failures can become a positive learning experience. However, to maintain credibility, abuse inquiries must themselves be method-ologically sound and well designed (Cambridge, 2001). This often presents a challenge considering the competing political, management and operational demands made and resource constraints imposed.

## Testing Boundaries

Brown & Stein (1998) identify the tension between formal and informal responses to abuse in relation to thresholds for responding and other workload considerations. The former included *'draconian'* and *'all or nothing'* approaches and the latter *'tea and sympathy'* and *'blind-eye'* approaches. The ability to differentiate between these approaches is seen as key to coherent reporting and effective intervention. This approach recognises the need to ground responses in an understanding of local pressures and demands. Most importantly however, responses should be both informed and value led, with the consequences for service users, services and organisations fully considered. Only by facilitating a paradigm shift from defensive management and practice to openness and accountability can we begin to learn constructive lessons for managing services and supporting people with intellectual disabilities and challenging behaviours.

## How Things Can Go Wrong

Evidence from inquiries suggests action can be taken on a number of fronts in an effort to minimise the conditions under which abuse can happen or become established in services for people with intellectual disabilities. The following section undertakes this task in relation to the evidence from a case study (Cambridge, 1998;1999a). This centred on two people with severely challenging behaviours who were supported by a dedicated service, delivered in their own home. The team of staff and managers delivering the service worked for a small local provider organisation. The service users lived in a detached house, both were Black British/African, and one was female and the other male. Their challenging behaviours included property destruction, aggression towards others, screaming and stereotypies.

The allegations of physical abuse included hitting, kicking and throwing objects at service users. They also included the breaking of care guidelines, which had been designed to reduce the frequency, duration and severity of the challenging behaviours encountered. The guidelines had been developed by a specialist challenging needs team, and much input and advice had been provided on individual interventions based upon applied behaviour analysis.

The abuse had come to light from the non-verbal disclosure of being kicked from one of the service users to a parent (both users had very limited expressive and receptive communication). The inquiry itself also identified intimidation across the staff team.

### A culture of abuse
*'They were like a closed society, a law unto themselves. I got the instant impression of so much that was wrong'.*

The service culture displayed institutional characteristics, in that it was inward looking, the regime was punishing, there was staff intimidation and the response from managers was to distance themselves from any problems. The culture also echoed the features associated with the corruption of care, including the neutralisation of normal moral concerns (Wardhaugh & Wilding, 1993). Isolation, coupled with regimented personal care work and control of private spaces by staff (Lee-Treweek, 1994) combined to create a culture of abuse and exploitation. The development of the culture was aided by low levels of staff competence in responding to challenging behaviour and ineffective management within the service and provider organisation. A number of defining characteristics of the culture of abuse and exploitation were identified:

## Isolation

*'I had no idea of what went on elsewhere. They used to work the shift pattern so they would be on duty at quiet times. They would challenge the manager so he tended to comply with their demands and avoid any confrontation.'*

The service was isolated within the provider organisation and local purchaser-provider system. The provider organisation management was resistant to challenging or engaging service managers who were reluctant or unable to challenge inappropriate staff behaviours. This created critical fractures in management and accountability. In addition, staff were also isolated from other services and without peer scrutiny, and were consequently able to develop and sustain inappropriate individual and team interactions, responses to client behaviours and interactions with clients and care practices.

Staff successfully resisted the input and involvement of outside professionals and purchaser representatives, thus exacerbating this isolation. Behaviours such as working the shift system to be on duty at a certain time or with certain people, as well as a range of avoidance behaviours, also provided indicators of isolation and the reluctance of managers to intervene in what was a failing service. Wardhaugh & Wilding (1993) observed the corruption of care to be more likely in closed, inward-looking organisations, referencing this as a common finding of inquiry reports. Lee-Treweek (1994) also observed that the isolation of services and staff is relevant to the development of abusive staff-user interactions. Williams (1995) demonstrated how abuse against people with intellectual disabilities can remain largely hidden in high dependency care situations. Cambridge & Carnaby (2000b) identified the particular risks of abuse associated with private and hidden tasks such as intimate care.

## Ineffective staff supervision

*'There was no understanding of what was normal or acceptable amongst the staff team. There was no support, no honesty, no trust and no teamwork.'*

Staff supervision was ineffectual or ineffective within the service and provider managers failed to maintain regular contact with the service and staff group. When managers did attempt to intervene and met resistance, they failed to exercise appropriate management control or sanctions. Line management appeared not to recognise or respond to potentially abusive practices and failed to discipline the principal alleged abusers in relation to a number of alleged inappropriate behaviours and care practices outside those immediately related to the allegations of abuse. There were also repeated absences and non co-operation with outside professional input and advice.

Management failures have been observed to be commonly associated with the corruption of care in institutional and community settings (Martin, 1984; Wardhaugh & Wilding, 1993), either because pressures were so great that abuse received a low priority, or that staff were stranded without clear leadership from above. Night shifts and the provision of personal and intimate care is also often provided outside management or peer scrutiny (Lee-Treweek, 1994: Cambridge & Carnaby, 2000a), similarly making service users vulnerable.

## Intimidation

*I was told to say nothing. If I reported anything then it was made clear to me that I would have to take the consequences. It was also made clear that any breach of confidence would be seen as a betrayal of racial identity.'*

The principal alleged abuser appeared to be able to gain control over the staff and service managers via a combination of collusion and intimidation. Race and culture were exploited as an instrument of control through the psychology of group identity and loyalty. Co-workers were prevented from voicing their concerns or disclosing abuse, with verbal and emotional abuse and physical threats to them and their families. Colleagues were reported to have been cross-questioned and managers shouted at by the principal alleged abuser. Accusations of racism were also made towards those who challenged low standards, neighbours who complained to the provider agency about events at the house (including noise), and managers during supervision.

Considerations of staff power and powerlessness are relevant in this regard, as broader society and service management systems reflect structural racism: *'The crucial issue may well be that staff are simultaneously powerless and powerful and that this creates a dangerous ambivalence'* (Wardhaugh & Wilding, 1993, p.12). Intimidation has repeatedly been a feature of abuse in both institutional and community based services (Martin, 1984: Longcare, 1989), making it a potentially powerful indicator of abuse. This observation fits the social learning model of abuse (Sobsey, 1994), but in relation to staff learning abusive behaviours from each other, as graphically illustrated by MacIntyre (1999).

## Institutionalised practice

*'I was told to do the first hit and then it would be OK . . . X never expressed any feelings of liking for the people and had complete control over them. You weren't allowed to show openly that you cared.'*

Newly appointed staff were set up to fail in difficult care situations or one to one encounters with clients. They also often lacked the necessary competence or experience to perform essential care tasks well, let alone to respond appropriately to violent or destructive challenging behaviours. Their abilities were then openly questioned and they were emotionally undermined by the principal alleged abuser, a practice that was sustained by other staff in the core group who had moved from the old institution. The confidence of new staff to challenge inappropriate practices was immediately eroded, especially without management support. Some interviewees reported that they were encouraged to hit service users by both example and deception. They were told that to do *'the first hit'* was important. After *'the first hit'*, the person concerned would respect you and do as they were told. Such behaviours are typical of the ritualised disciplinary techniques associated with institutions, such as humiliation and dispossession (Goffman, 1961) and exclusion and marginalisation (Foucault, 1977).

One of the alleged abusers was reported to have referenced how they had hit their own children when justifying physical assaults against people with intellectual disabilities. This mirrors the neutralisation of normal moral concerns, a phenomenon that may be a product of the infantilisation of people with intellectual disabilities (Wardhaugh & Wilding, 1993; Hollins, 1994).

## Inexperience

*'I was totally inexperienced in this kind of work. I worked there for three months without any form of training and had to sleep in on my own after just two weeks.'*

The relative inexperience of most new team members contributed to the late recognition and reporting of abuse. An example was provided by one relatively new member of staff who had no experience of working in social care services or knowledge of intellectual disability. They also had no notion of the functions of challenging behaviour or appropriate responses. This deficit was compounded by a lack of training on challenging needs, the absence of positive peer learning and review, no scope for reflective practice, the poor development, implementation and monitoring of individual care programmes and the absence of applied behaviour analysis and informed interventions designed to reduce the frequency and duration of challenging behaviours.

Wardhaugh & Wilding (1993) noted the association between the corruption of care and particular pressures and kinds of work and the nature of certain client groups. Lee-Treweek (1994) also referred to the lack of qualifications of many hands-on workers, with low pay, low social status and poor working conditions. In this case study, individuals with challenging behaviours were supported by some inexperienced staff, thus creating a disastrous formula which both reinforced and helped sustain abuse. A similar culture was evident in the Medway case study (MacIntyre, 1999).

## Anti-professionalism

*'If you followed procedures or guidelines there would be hell to pay.'*

*'Everyone was guilty of not following policies because you did not know what else to do. After a while, boundaries became blurred and you began to worry about how far you were going with self defence.'*

The culture of abuse was aided by the absence of procedures and guidelines on abuse and physical interventions within the provider service. This was coupled with a lack of competence for supporting individual communication and positive staff user interactions. At a wider level, there had been no training for staff on abuse or adult protection or physical interventions. Physical interventions are particularly relevant to responding to some people with violent challenging behaviours (Harris, 1996; Harris et al, 1996) and their misuse or non-use can result in serious injury which amounts to physical abuse (Spreat, et al, 1986;

Williams, 1995). Physical abuse may also therefore be closely associated with negligence in the face of unacceptable risk taking (Baker & Allen, 2001). Without clear guidance, inappropriate and abusive staff responses were informally developed and learnt by the staff group.

Such interactions became routine and normalised within the service culture. Staff demonstrated an unwillingness to engage local professionals and take advice from outside the service. They consequently had no shared commitment to implementing favoured philosophies of care or best practice, were unwilling to keep the records and information needed for the development of effective behavioural programmes and had little or no regard for or awareness of the rights of people with intellectual disabilities. Williams (1995) has demonstrated how abuse against people with intellectual disabilities can remain largely hidden in high dependency care situations, and Hollins (1994) has observed that the risk of abuse in dependency relationships is increased by the various gaps between user needs and the meaning of disability and needs for the carer.

## Risk Management in Adult Protection

Risk taking underpins best practice because it is the basis on which service users develop their potential as individuals and lead more independent and meaningful lives. It is also central to some particularly critical areas of practice, such as supporting people with challenging behaviours, including the risks to the person, other service users or staff and the risks associated with physical interventions themselves. Risk assessment is designed to identify the level and nature of risk, whereas risk management looks at the more complex relationships between risk taking and other demands on services, such as duty of care and responsibilities for protection.

In the context of adult protection, it is also helpful to consider the idea of risk management at the macro-level, such as in the review of adult protection policy or physical intervention guidelines. It is particularly important for organisations because of its conceptual links to cost-benefit analysis (Eby, 2000) and the high profile of performance management and best value in social care (Cambridge, 2000). A basic model for risk management and decision-making might include the following criteria or actions (developed from Carson, 1990):

- draw up lists of competing considerations regarding the risk (benefits and costs) to the authority or agency

- consider both the length of the respective lists as well as the relative importance and weighting of the different factors

- identify decision-making models at the various stages of the adult protection process (single worker, team, senior manager, director, specialist advisor)

- define the primary responsibilities of individuals in relation to lead and management roles for adult protection generally and individual cases or stages in particular

- identify any action that could be taken to reduce uncertainty, support the agency or worker or inform decision-making

- consider the steps which could be taken to make the benefits or advantages more likely to occur for the organisation, client, service and staff concerned

- consider long-term gains and risks against short term gains and risks

- record the decisions made, responsibilities for the actions recommended and outcomes for policy and individual cases

- review the content and implementation of policies and guidelines in relation to the above considerations.

In differentiating the immediate circumstances surrounding abuse from wider systems factors within services, a potential framework for undertaking inquiries can be devised (Cambridge, 2001). Such frameworks are helpful for focusing attention beyond simplistic *'bad apple'* interpretations of abuse. They encourage inquiries to look beyond the immediate and obvious to the dynamics of the establishment and its relationship with the outside world (Brown, 1999). Conflicts such as those between the development and policing roles of purchasers and regulators are more readily identified and are fundamental to understanding how abuse is caused or facilitated. The interaction between *'structural'* and *'environmental'* factors and the *'individual characteristics'* of staff and residents will also be made more apparent (Rowlings, 1995; Clough, 1999):

## I. Individual client level

Individual service users, their lives, characteristics, behaviours and experiences form a natural focus and starting point for any abuse inquiry or risk assessment.

**Sources of information:** Engagement with support staff, outside specialists and professionals. Relationships with other service users and family members. Activity records and engagement data. Inputs from activity programmes, keyworkers and behavioural specialists. Individual records, guidelines, case notes, diaries, activity records and observational data. Individual assessments and care plans, including behavioural support plans and any prescribed physical interventions. Interviews with service users or their advocates or family members.

**Key questions:** Are individual guidelines and recording systems for challenging behaviour and physical interventions in place? How are they monitored and reviewed? Is there an individual plan, activity programme and risk assessment for each user? Is there a nominated care manager and are they in regular contact? How are the views of relatives and advocates included? Is there an individualised communication system? What does the individual client file contain and how is it used?

## 2. Staff level

The qualifications, experience, backgrounds and attitudes of individual staff and managers are central to the relationship with service users, interactions, activities and consequently the quality of care.

**Sources of information:** Qualifications, experience and training in challenging needs, physical interventions and adult protection. Numbers of staff receiving induction and refresher training in these topics. Job applications, references, training records and supervision notes. Observations and interviews with staff. Defined individual responsibilities for key-working and individual support. Agreed individual roles and responsibilities in the context of team working.

**Key questions:** Are there explicit job descriptions and person specifications? Do these reference challenging behaviour, physical intervention and adult protection? Are there screening, induction and training programmes and what do these cover? What individual supervision, appraisal and development systems operate? How are rostering and deployment arrangements designed and how are staff involved? What systems for peer review and supervision exist? Is there protected time in team meetings for adult protection or wider practice concerns? Are collective views formed and are actions and responses consistent?

## 3. Service level

The direct support and resources provided for service users, staff and managers, line management and supervision arrangements, providing the basis to sound and supportive services.

**Sources of information:** operational policies concerning physical intervention, risk management and intimate and personal care. The use of local procedures and guidelines. Collective record systems. Planning and staff meetings. Systems for monitoring challenging behaviours, determining their functions and the interventions required. Group activity records. Induction arrangements and service level procedures for adult protection. Training interventions provided and planned, management responsibilities, recording of incidents and responsibilities for developing and implementing policies on physical interventions, employer responsibilities towards safety and well-being of staff (Harris et al, 1996).

**Key questions:** Is there regular staff appraisal and supervision? How are issues of competence and quality addressed? What quality audit and resource management systems exist? What review and line management arrangements exist within the providing agency? How are policies and procedures, such as adult protection, intimate care and physical intervention implemented? Are training interventions designed and targeted at the needs of the service and at the staff group? What training has been received?

## 4. Professional and specialist level

The organisation of human resources provided for service users and the team working in residential or day support settings and the management of outside specialist or professional inputs, providing the basis for effective trans-disciplinary working.

**Sources of information:** Records and notes from different specialists and teams, including social work, specialist challenging needs workers, psychology, psychiatry and a range of therapeutic inputs. Care management records of assessment, individual planning and case review. Allocated and agreed responsibilities and actions. Adult protection risk assessment and risk management records.

**Key questions:** Is care management organised and provided from outside the service? Are responsibilities for the core tasks agreed? Is there an unambiguous lead responsibility for each client? Is there an individual person centred planning system? Do specialists come together for integrated service planning and review? Are inputs from communication, psychiatry, psychology, social work and challenging needs collectively negotiated and agreed? Is the residential team routinely involved and consulted over decisions and the implementation of plans? Are policies on physical intervention shared and owned across different professionals?

## 5. Organisational Level

The visibility of adult protection policy and procedures in organisational systems and cultures and guidelines for using physical interventions are necessary prerequisites to effective adult protection practice.

**Sources of information:** Contracts and inter-agency agreements. Agency responsibilities defined in policies. Lead and co-ordinating responsibilities within purchaser and provider organisations. Job descriptions and person specifications. Agency mission and value statements. Policies and guidelines on high-risk areas of practice such as physical interventions and intimate care. Evidence on performance from Best Value reviews. Agency records on the management and outcomes of abuse alerts, investigations and inquiries.

**Key questions:** How policy and practice varies across provider organisations and the mixed economy of provision. How adult protection policies and procedures vary in coverage and depth. How visible are critical areas of practice such as challenging behaviour in agency policies and procedures? What profile do policies and guidelines on physical intervention have within the organisation? What arrangements exist for reporting and responding to abuse? How abuse policy relates to wider policies and procedures (eg, physical interventions). What are the defined roles and responsibilities for staff and managers? How the agency passes on any allegations, disclosures or concerns. How quality, best practice and accountability are addressed.

## 6. Systems level

Considerations of process and organisation within the lead agencies for adult protection, particularly in relation to policy development, are required for effective policy implementation.

**Sources of information:** Commissioning strategies and community care plans. Arrangements and specifications for care management. Reference to agency responsibilities and co-ordination in adult protection and related policies. Agreed systems for individual and person centred planning. Responsibilities for inspection, registration and quality audit. Specifications for best value, care standards and performance management. Training strategies.

**Key questions:** Is there a multi-agency policy? Are there competent local links with the police and officers specialising in work with vulnerable adults and witnesses? How are adult protection expectations and responsibilities defined through the contract? Is there a local adult protection training strategy? How does the service audit address challenging needs and adult protection? How do policies and training on physical intervention match up to accepted standards (Harris et al, 1996; BILD, 2001)? How do provider organisations and their staff access to such training? How is adult protection and challenging behaviour referenced in the community care plan? Is specialist training available or commissioned on applied behavioural analysis? Are there total and individualised communication systems? Have user advocacy services been commissioned?

## 7. Policy level

The influence of *No Secrets* and other relevant central policy initiatives and the use of research to develop evidence-based practice provide a baseline for assessing local adult protection practice.

**Sources of information:** Recommendations and requirements of *No Secrets*. A range of policy related materials and resources developed by government departments, public agencies and campaigning groups (eg ARC/NAPSAC, 1993; 1997). Academic and research literature on adult protection, the abuse of people with intellectual disabilities, challenging behaviour, physical interventions and intimate care (eg as referenced in this chapter and book). Training initiatives (eg BILD, 2001). Local and national investigations and inquiry reports.

**Key questions:** What is the nature of the implementation gap between national policy and local practice? What are the deficits locally in relation to central policy? Who is the local lead agency for adult protection? Are there allocated or ring fenced adult protection responsibilities and resources across agencies? Are policies and procedures reviewed on this basis of experience? Is intelligence on the types, location, patterns and incidence of abuse collected and analysed and are lessons disseminated?

## Priorities for Reviewing Adult Protection Competence

The case study and above discussion has identified a raft of issues relevant to reviewing the performance of adult protection and to targeting effective management and practice interventions. The following priority areas emerge from the discussion as particularly important markers for reviewing adult protection capacity in services for people with intellectual disabilities and challenging behaviours:

## Support for whistle-blowers

Guidelines for protecting and supporting witnesses who blow the whistle on abusive services or who disclose individual incidents of abuse should be an integral part of adult protection practice and made visible in policies and guidelines. They can help ensure that the emotional and psychological effects of whistle-blowing or disclosing abuse and the social, economic and employment disincentives to disclosure are minimised. Strong disincentives to disclosure often exist within services, particularly if abuse is related to neglect or mistreatment from colleagues, or woven with intimidation and conflict on staff teams or with managers.

Adult protection training often relates experiences of victimisation as a result of raising concerns about care standards or potential abuse or that agencies are sometimes racist or sexist in their responses to disclosures. Strong signals are needed that whistle-blowers will be supported to disclose abuse and helped to navigate any subsequent investigation or inquiry.

## Coherent action in responding

The difficulties experienced in disclosing abuse can be exacerbated by a lack of competence in responding and the management of investigations or inquiries. Critical considerations include confidentiality, safety for the service user, liaison with other interests and agencies, conducting interviews and objectively managing and interpreting the evidence (Cambridge, 2001). These depend on the existence of clear systems for allocating responsibility, information exchange and action and robust methodologies for collecting and interpreting the evidence.

Adult protection responsibilities need clear definition and allocation, using local structures and processes. Multi-disciplinary, inter-agency or specialist care management teams will need to play an important part. Adult protection planning meetings and case conferences are critical junctures in the process from referral, planning, investigation, review and closure (AIMS, 1998; 1999). However, management may be more complex than a linear process, and involve feedback loops and parallel actions. Shared action planning with providers, the police and other interests such as carers will also often be required.

## Scrutiny of service quality

Quality audit, performance management, Best Value and inspection in services for people with intellectual disabilities and challenging behaviours need to be especially robust. These procedures can be designed to address and respond to the recommendations of the Mansell report on *Services for People with Learning Disabilities and Challenging Behaviour or Mental Health Needs* (Mansell, 1993) and the components of a local service strategy for challenging behaviour (Mansell et al, 1994).

Similarly, a pro-active approach is required towards adult protection and related areas of practice, such as physical interventions and intimate care. Explicit reference to abuse, neglect and mistreatment should be routine and any collection of indicators of poor quality or failure should trigger an open and constructive investigation of care practices and standards. Wider consultation and investment in training and care standards should also be initiated between purchasers and providers in order to facilitate longer-term partnerships and agreed goals and outcomes. Communication between adult protection lead and responsibilities and inspection and registration also require tightening, with expectations for sharing information agreed.

## Individual service co-ordination

Although social services have lead agency responsibility for care management (Department of Health, 1989), implementation is left largely to local discretion, (SSI/SWSG, 1991). As a consequence, a wide variety of arrangements have emerged, as have gaps in competence (Cambridge, 1999b). In many care settings, care managers are the only regular and relatively independent advocates for clients. Yet contact may be infrequent and brief. Regular and intensive care management is particularly critical for people with complex needs and where the risks of abuse and mistreatment are highest. People with intellectual disabilities and challenging behaviours are clearly within this group.

The roles of individual service co-ordinators or others working on contracts should be linked with care management or provide an explicit care management function with transparency about roles and process and responsibilities for the core tasks. Many functions can be devolved to multi-disciplinary, inter-agency or specialist team members and the evidence on productive care management points to the need for continuous, single worker lead responsibility, particularly for people with complex and challenging needs (Cambridge, 1999b). Responsibilities across professionals and teams should be reviewed and redefined based on a shared task or lead approach.

## Commissioning and market management

Mansell (1993) recognised that commissioners should take a strategic view of challenging behaviour and purchase services based on individual needs. This requires a strategy which shifts from *'removing'* challenging behaviour by using out of authority placements or *'containing'* challenging behaviour in low cost, poor quality services to *'developing'* local competence through investing in management and staff training. Commitment, individualised services, effective models of support, good management and investing in relationships were seen as pre-requisites for reaching the *'developing'* stage.

The intelligence needed for joint commissioners to develop a comprehensive range of local services for people with intellectual disabilities and challenging behaviours already exists (Mansell et al, 1994; Greig et al, 1996). Such a strategy has been defined as comprising the key components of prevention (aiming to reduce the incidence of challenging behaviour), early intervention (from an awareness of the information required to identify the emergence of challenging behaviour), the provision of technical and practical support (of sufficient intensity to bring about changes in behaviour), placement development (to reflect peoples' special needs) and crisis management (to intervene safely and with minimum force in order to prevent self-injury to the user or violence towards others).

## Maintaining accountability across service systems

Cambridge & Brown (1997) commented on the risks to accountability in social care markets:

*'Management functions located within single hierarchies have been replaced by agreements reached across agency boundaries. Lines of accountability have been extended, important functions have fallen between different agencies and specific knowledge and expertise has been lost or dispersed, creating fractures in user involvement, accountability, information and communication.' (p. 28).*

The joint commissioning models outlined in *Partnership in Action* (Department of Health, 1998) and the Partnership Boards proposed in *Valuing People* (Department of Health, 2001), provide opportunities to close gaps in information and accountability and commission safer services for people with challenging behaviours and specific reference has been made to commissioning and inspection and registration in relation to adult protection (Brown, 1996; Brown et al, 1996).

Best Value, an integral part of the Government's new approach to social services performance and care standards (Department of Health, 1998; 1999), is another example. However, we need to recognise the limits of such generic approaches to cost, quality and market management in areas such as adult protection and challenging behaviour (Cambridge, 2000). Costs may be hidden, and outcomes difficult to define in such areas of support and intervention (Knapp & Cambridge, 1997).

## Opening services to scrutiny

Isolation occurs where individuals are placed in out of authority or private care settings where regular scrutiny from care managers, relatives or advocates may be impossible. Isolation also happens when the person's profound and multiple disabilities or the topography of their challenging behaviour militates against engagement, communication, positive contacts and interactions with other residents and staff. Profound intellectual disability or seriously challenging behaviours are also likely to require regular intimate and personal care conducted in private and isolated care settings (Cambridge & Carnaby, 2000a), or responses and interventions which increase adult protection risks (Harris et al, 1996).

Such isolation can be countered by opening staff and managers to wider peer review and by commissioning independent advocacy. However, working groups comprising a range of interests and people who know the client can be used to help with individual planning and support (Cambridge & Carnaby, 2000b) and with monitoring progress more widely. Specific task and working groups can also be established for staff or particular services to create links and information exchange with other services and encourage reflective practice. They can also be developed around particular themes such as challenging behaviour and physical interventions, bringing together experience and exchanging information and intelligence.

## Concluding Observations

The service culture in the case study displayed institutional characteristics. It was inward looking, punishing and neglectful. It also echoed many of the features associated with the corruption of care, including the neutralisation of normal moral concerns, particular models of work, and the importance of user group characteristics. These combined to create a culture of abuse and exploitation. Management systems, contracts, service audit and care management, and the input of specialist challenging needs workers failed to protect service users from abuse.

At a broader level, the case study and other inquiries point to inherent weaknesses in our care systems. These exist at all levels, but most concerning are those between different professionals involved with individuals or services and those between commissioners and providers of services. Inter-disciplinary working is often fractured by accountability to different agencies and different lines of management and professional accountability. The limits imposed on inspection and registration and also its management distance from social services can create the circumstances under which adult protection concerns remain hidden.

In fighting abuse in services for people with intellectual disabilities we therefore need to consider the wider context to abuse, as much as the individual characteristics of abusive acts or interactions between staff and residents. The argument has been made that abuse can be linked to poor quality services, and that it is possible to identify common failings in services and service systems which contribute to opportunities to abuse or to abuse remaining hidden or unreported. A hierarchical model has been offered to help structure adult protection risk management and for the conduct of abuse inquiries. It also provides a framework for reviewing adult protection competence and navigating the complexities of case investigations.

The resource implications of taking adult protection practice forward in services for people with intellectual disabilities and challenging behaviour is very significant and includes policy development and review, staff training, the pump-priming of specialist services (such as advocacy and individualised communication), workload management across community teams and caseload management for care managers and senior practitioners. The costs attached to individual investigations can also be very significant in terms of administrative support and the professional time taken up with planning, strategy meetings and case conferences.

Lead adult protection agencies, usually social services departments, also need to review the effectiveness of their policies and guidelines through the collection of information on alerts, case conduct and the outcomes of investigations themselves. Local adult protection intelligence requires systems for information recording and analysis. Similarly, the constant scrutiny and review of patterns in the use of physical interventions and their outcomes and effectiveness of training strategies (BILD, 2001) will be required. Such reviews should also examine the quality and effectiveness of individual guidelines targeted at high-risk situations involving particular carers and service users (Baker & Allen, 2001).

Such demands suggest the top slicing of resources for adult protection and development in specialist areas such as physical intervention. Another solution is the demarcation of protected adult protection responsibilities for senior practitioners or specialist teams. Although an alluring panacea for hard-pressed managers, the latter is unlikely to present a durable and robust solution (the Mansell report, 1993, presents a parallel debate about specialist or mainstream competence in challenging behaviour). The reality of functional segregation is likely to be dysfunctional adult protection practice, as specialist workers experience resentment and resistance and mainstream managers, practitioners and front line staff consider adult protection to be someone else's issue.

Failure to act on abuse, such as the misuse or overuse of physical interventions, has potentially very severe implications for services, staff and client care, as has been seen illustrated by the outcomes of the Longcare and MacIntyre cases. Other case studies (Cambridge, 1999a) both have illustrated the wider impact of abuse on a range of parties and interests both within and outside services. In addition to the potential longer-term effects on service users themselves, the anxiety, distress and suffering caused to parents and families is often immense and also long-term.

In our fight against abuse, we also need to recognise the importance of empowering staff and managers. Part of the solution is to effect a conceptual and operational shift from purely punishing responses, which scapegoat individuals, to facilitative and emancipatory responses, which allow people and services to learn from such experiences and progress as workers, professionals, teams and organisations. This needs to go hand in hand with valuing staff and managers.

## References

AIMS for Adult Protection (1998) *The Alerter's Training Pack*. Brighton: Pavilion.

AIMS for Adult Protection (1999) *The Investigator's Guide*. Brighton: Pavilion.

ARC/NAPSAC (1993) *It Could Never Happen Here!* London: Association for Residential Care/ National Association for the Protection from Sexual Abuse of Adults and Children with Learning Disabilities/Department of Health.

ARC/NAPSAC (1997) *There Are No Easy Answers*. London: Association for Residential Care/ National Association for the Protection from Sexual Abuse of Adults and Children with Learning Disabilitie/Department of Health.

Baker, P and Allen, D (2001) Physical abuse and physical interventions in learning disabilities: an element of risk? *Journal of Adult Protection*, 3, 2, 25–31.

Biggs, S, Phillipson, C and Kingston, P (1995) *Elder Abuse in Perspective*. Buckingham: Open University.

BILD (2001) *BILD Code of Practice for Trainers in the Use of Physical Interventions.* Kidderminster: BILD.

Brown, H (1996) *Towards Safer Commissioning: a Handbook for Purchasers and Commissioners.* Nottingham: NAPSAC.

Brown, H (1999) Abuse of people with learning disabilities: layers of concern and analysis. In Stanley, N, Manthorpe, J & Penhale, P (Eds) *Institutional Abuse: Perspectives Across the Life Course.* London: Routledge.

Brown, H, Brammer, A, Craft, A & McKay, C (1996) *Towards Better Safeguards; a Handbook for Inspectors and Registration Officers.* Nottingham: NAPSAC.

Brown, H, Stein, J, & Turk, V (1995) The sexual abuse of adults with learning disabilities: report of a second two year incidence survey. *Mental Handicap Research*, 8, 1, 1–22.

Brown, H and Stein, J (1998) Implementing adult protection policies in Kent and East Sussex. *Journal of Social Policy*, 27, 3, 371–396.

Buckinghamshire County Council (1998) *Independent Longcare Inquiry.* Buckingham: Buckinghamshire County Council.

Cambridge, P (1998) The physical abuse of people with learning disabilities and challenging behaviours: lessons for commissioners and providers. *Tizard Learning Disability Review*, 3, 1, 18–26.

Cambridge, P (1999a) The First Hit: a case study of the physical abuse of people with learning disabilities and challenging behaviours in a residential service. *Disability and Society*, 14, 3, 285–308.

Cambridge, P (1999b) Building care management competence in services for people with learning disabilities. *British Journal of Social Work*, 29, 393–415.

Cambridge, P (2000) Using best value in purchasing and providing services for people with learning disabilities, *British Journal of Learning Disabilities*, 28, 31–37.

Cambridge, P (2001) A framework for managing abuse inquiries: questions of methodology, organisation, process and politics. *Journal of Adult Protection.* 3,3,6–20.

Cambridge, P & Brown, H (1997) Making the market work for people with learning disabilities: an argument for principled contracting. *Critical Social Policy*, 17, 2, 27–52.

Cambridge, P & Carnaby, S (2000a) *Making it Personal: Providing Intimate and Personal Care for People with Learning Disabilities.* Brighton: Pavilion.

Cambridge, P & Carnaby, S (2000b) A personal touch: managing the risks of abuse during intimate and personal care. *Journal of Adult Protection*, 2,4, 4–16.

Carson, D (1990) Taking risks with patients – your assessment strategy, in Professional Nurse, *The Staff Nurse's Survival Guide.* London: Austen Cornish, pp. 83–87.

Clough, R (1999) The abuse of older people in institutional settings: the role of management and regulation. Stanley, N, Manthorpe, J & Penhale, P (Eds) *Institutional Abuse: Perspectives Across the Life Course.* London: Routledge.

Department of Health and Social Security (1969) *Report of the Committee of Inquiry into Allegations of Ill-treatment of Patients and Other Irregularities at the Ely Hospital, Cardiff (Cmnd 3975).* London: HMSO.

Department of Health and Social Security (1971) *Report of the Committee of Inquiry at Farleigh Hospital, Cardiff (Cmnd 4557).* London: HMSO.

Department of Health and Social Security (1974) *Report on the care of Patients at South Ockendon Hospital.* London: HMSO.

Department of Health (1998) *Partnership in Action.* London: HMSO.

Department of Health (1989) *Caring for People: Community Care in the Next Decade and Beyond.* London: HMSO.

Department of Health (2000) *No Secrets: Guidance on Developing and Implementing Multi-Agency Policies and Procedures to Protect Vulnerable Adults from Abuse.* London: HMSO.

Department of Health (2001) *Valuing People: A New Strategy for Learning Disability for the 21st Century.* London: Department of Health.

Di Terlizzi, M, Cambridge, P, & Maras, P (1999) Gender, ethicity and challenging behaviour: a literature review and exploratory study. *Tizard Learning Disability Review*, 4, 33–44.

Eby, M (2000) The challenges of being accountable. In Brechin, A, Brown, H & Eby, M (Eds) *Critical Practice in Health and Social Care.* London: Sage.

Foucault, M (1977) *Discipline and Punishment.* London: Allen Lane.

Goffman, E (1961) *Asylums.* New York: Anchor.

Greenwich Social Services Department (1993) *Recognising and Responding to the Sexual Abuse of Adults with Learning Disabilities.* London: Greenwich Social Services and Greenwich Health Authority.

Greig, R, Cambridge, P & Rucker, L (1996) Care management and joint commissioning. In Harris, J (Ed) *Purchasing Services for People with Learning Disabilities and Challenging Behaviour*, Kidderminster: BILD, pp. 5–20.

Harris, J (1996) Physical restraint procedures for managing challenging behaviours presented by mentally retarded adults and children. *Research in Developmental Disabilities,* 17, 99–134.

Harris, J, Allen, D, Cornick, M, Jefferson, A, and Mills, R (1996) *Physical Interventions: A Policy Framework.* Kidderminster: BILD.

Hollins, S (1994) Relationships between perpetrators and victims of physical and sexual abuse. In Harris, J. & Craft, A. (Eds) *People with Learning Disabilities at Risk of Physical or Sexual Abuse, Seminar Papers No. 4.* Kidderminster, BILD.

Knapp, M & Cambridge, P (1997) The cost dimension in commissioning and providing services for people with learning disabilities. In Bouras, N & Donlan, P (Eds) *Commissioning and Providing Services for People with Learning Disabilities.* Pavilion: Brighton, pp. 71–80.

Lee-Treweek, G (1994) Bedroom abuse: the hidden work in a nursing home. *Generations Review*, 4, 1, 2–4.

MacIntyre, D (1999) *MacIntyre Undercover. One man, four lives.* London: BBC.

Mansell, J (1993) *Services for People with Learning Disabilities and Challenging Behaviour or Mental Health Needs.* London: HMSO.

Mansell, J, McGill, P & Emerson, E (1994) Conceptualising service provision. In Emerson, E, McGill, P & Mansell, J (Eds) *Severe Learning Disabilities and Challenging Behaviours.* London: Chapman Hall.

Martin, J (1984) *Hospitals in Trouble*. Blackwell: Oxford.

Morris, P (1969) *Put Away*. London: Routledge.

Morris, S (1997) Experiences of risk: the role of therapy in sexual health. In Cambridge, P & Brown, H (Eds) *HIV and Learning Disability*. Brighton: Pavilion.

Pehhale, B, & Brown, H (2001) Editorial, *Journal of Adult Protection*, 3, 2, 2–7.

Robb, B (1967) *Sans Everything: a Case to Answer*. London: Nelson.

Rowlings, C (1995) Elder abuse in context. In Clough, R (Ed) *Elder Abuse and the Law*. London: Action on Elder Abuse.

Sobsey, D (1994) *Violence and Abuse in the Lives of People with Learning Disabilities*. London: Brookes.

Social Services Inspectorate/Social Work Services Group. (1991) *Care Management and Assessment: Manager's Guide*. London: HMSO.

Spreat, S, Lipinski, D, Hill, J, & Haplin, M (1986) Safety indices associated with the use of contingent restraint procedures. *Applied Research in Mental Retardation*, 7, 475–481.

Townsend, P (1962) *The Last Refuge*. London: Routledge.

Wardhaugh, J & Wilding, P (1993) Towards an explanation of the corruption of care. *Critical Social Policy*, 37, 4–31.

Williams, C (1995) *Invisible Victims: Crime and Abuse against People with Learning Difficulties*. London: Jessica Kingsley.

Wolfensberger, W (1975) *The Origin and Nature of our Institutional Models*. Syracuse: Human Policy Press.

# Chapter 12

## Monitoring and inspection in social care: Lessons from MacIntyre

Alan Jefferson

This chapter will review regulation's contribution to the promotion of high quality residential care. It will identify some of the current system's shortcomings and consider how the National Inspectorates being planned for the different countries of the UK can help ensure that in the future there are less frequent scandals about residential care.

### Background

The current legislation which governs the regulation of residential care homes for adults with intellectual disabilities, the Registered Homes Act 1984, is over 15 years old and the existing regulatory bodies, local authority Inspection Units, were set up in 1991. The present system was reviewed by Tom Burgner (1996) and judged to be in need of reform. New legislation and regulatory arrangements will be introduced from April 2002 in England, Wales and Scotland (arrangements for Northern Ireland are still being considered). It is, therefore, a good time to review the lessons that can be learned from existing experience.

The Department of Health (DoH) has defined the purposes of regulation as being:

*"To help ensure by a process of evaluation and feedback that:*

- *the quality of life of users meets agreed standards and that individual users and staff are protected from abuse, neglect or exploitation*

- *statutory needs are met and good practice is promoted*

- *action is identified to improve performance against established standards*

- *policies are implemented to ensure that staff recruitment, support and training facilitates service development*

- *services are cost effective."*

(Department of Health, 1991, p 19)

These expectations have been periodically restated in Government publications since that time. There is plenty of evidence to show that inspection units have been effective in meeting these requirements. For example, that National List of Cancelled Registrations contains over 450 names of people whose registration has been either refused or cancelled as a result of enforcement activity by registration authorities. Less obviously, as a result of advice and guidance, counselling, exhortation and threats of enforcement action, many providers have been encouraged to meet and surpass the minimum standards required for registration. These same processes have been used to ensure that potential providers who were unsuitable did not enter the care home market.

However, a consistent and worrying feature of the last decade has been periodic scandals about the quality of care provided in particular residential homes and about the quality of life experienced by the residents who lived in them. Among the most recent of these scandals is Brompton, the home in Medway investigated by Donal MacIntyre in his "MacIntyre Undercover" programme, in which the care regime shown appeared both abusive and demeaning. It was clear that the care offered at this home fell short of realising the Government's Learning Disability White Paper vision that:

> "Good quality services that promote independence, choice and inclusion will lead to good outcomes for people with learning disabilities"
>
> (Department of Health, 2001, p 90)

The programme raised issues about the process and impact of external monitoring of residential homes. It also identified important matters to be taken into account by the new regulatory regimes being planned by the Care Standards Commissions in safeguarding the welfare of vulnerable service users.

## Regulation and Inspection

The difference between "regulation" and "inspection" must be understood. The latter is only one part of a wider range of interconnected activities. Regulation is a five-fold process consisting of the following:

- *Setting standards that identify the minimum requirements for an acceptable level of care*

- *Registration in order to ascertain the suitability of the people responsible for providing the care, of the premises in which the care will be provided, and of the policies and procedures which will underpin the provision of care*

- *Inspection to ensure that the home consistently achieves the required standards*

- *Investigation of any complaints that are made about the service that is provided*

- *Taking enforcement action where services consistently fail to meet the required standards and cannot reasonably be allowed to operate unless remedial action is taken promptly.*

Securing the well-being of service users requires the regulatory system to be effective in all five of these activities, but it should not be assumed that regulation alone can ever be sufficient to guarantee consistently high quality care. Inspectors are only in contact with a home for a fraction of the time it operates. Inspections are therefore only "snapshots" of the care offered. Furthermore, the presence of an inspector inevitably influences the manner in which care is provided during the inspection. In the MacIntyre programme, managers spoke about the efforts they made to present to inspectors and other visitors a false picture of what normally happened in the home. It is generally accepted that announced inspections are less effective than unannounced ones in obtaining a true picture of what goes on in a home. However, as was seen in the programme, even a few minutes' warning (or the opportunity to detain the inspector in the manager's office at the start of the inspection) can lead to frantic activity to hide shortcomings.

Many other people have information about what is happening in a home. Managers have responsibility to monitor the care provided. The statutory regulations that govern the operation of a residential home (The Residential Care Homes Regulations, 1984) include a requirement that, where there is a tier of management above the operational manager of the home, there must be monthly visits, by the person in ultimate control or their representative, to review the conduct of the home. The MacIntyre programme suggested that these managerial quality control functions were not being discharged adequately. The programme also suggested that the staff in the home were aware that some of the things that were happening were unacceptable (eg rolling a resident up in a carpet). Effective "whistleblowing" policies that enable staff to report abuse and bad practice without fear of recriminations from colleagues or fear of losing their job are essential – but all too often absent. Residential homes have many visitors – professionals such as community nurses, doctors and social workers and non-professionals such as friends and relatives – who may also have information about matters of concern which should be reported, but again there may be worries that this could lead to adverse consequences for the residents. The residents themselves may be the best people of all to tell inspectors what is happening in a home and later on in this chapter there will be consideration about what can be done to overcome their difficulties in sharing this information. Inspectors can only act if they know that things are not right in a home and if they have sufficient factual information to substantiate the concerns. Making that information available is everyone's responsibility. As the Report of the Independent Longcare Inquiry into abuse in two residential homes in Buckinghamshire concluded:

> "... the protection of vulnerable adults depends on openness by
> proprietors and managers, vigilance by all who have responsibilities
> towards or contact with residents; encouragement for the communication

*of suspicions; and prompt, co-ordinated action when information about possible harm to the welfare of residents is received or discovered."*
(Buckinghamshire County Council, 1998, p 3)

Good inspection should include advice and guidance on how to improve the quality of life and quality of care being offered to residents. It should not simply identify what is wrong and leave providers to work out what to do to put things right. However, inspections do not have the capacity to "inject" quality into a service that is seriously deficient. The MacIntyre programme suggests that there were serious deficiencies at Brompton. For example:

- The home was large. Any home that accommodates 29 residents in one building is likely to find it difficult to provide individualised care.

- There appeared to be few qualified staff and this included staff with supervisory responsibilities.

- Individuals were allowed to work very long shifts even though prolonged exposure to volatile care settings can reduce people's tolerance.

- The induction of new staff was inadequate. The programme showed staff who were not familiar with the contents of the induction pack, staff who lacked understanding of and commitment to the home's policies and procedures, and some staff who seemed contemptuous of the whole induction process. Donal MacIntyre's own induction experience appeared seriously deficient.

- The programme suggested that some of the staff employed in the home were unsuitable for this type of work. We saw them putting their own needs first, deliberately provoking residents and incidents, and some of the comments they made and attitudes they displayed were entirely inappropriate for care workers. The responses of one member of staff gave rise to particular concerns.

- Managers, at all levels, did not appear to be exercising effective control and, in many instances, were themselves setting poor examples.

- There was no evidence of individualised strategies for handling challenging behaviour, or of attempts at de-escalation and preventive strategies. Indeed, it appeared that challenging behaviours were provoked by inflexible attitudes and low tolerance of fairly minor behaviours.

- There was a "panic culture" which quickly led to the use of physical interventions – or "decking" in the terminology of the staff team. A strong image from the programme was of the regular sudden sounding of the panic alarm and of staff running down corridors to the site of an incident. This would be unlikely to calm the service user involved in the incident nor, for that matter, the other residents in the home.

- Not only were physical interventions used too readily, but also the actual techniques employed, including prone holds, were potentially dangerous. It was not evident that all staff were thoroughly familiar with the techniques they were using, and there seemed to be a degree of "improvisation" and inconsistency (indeed, at one stage in the programme it appears that senior management were actively encouraging improvisation). Some staff had a poor understanding of how physical interventions can cause pain. Though the home clearly had a training strategy for physical interventions, no evidence was offered that suggested that only staff who had been trained in the approved techniques were allowed to use them. The programme also raised concerns about the extent and duration of the use of physical interventions in the home. It was hard to imagine what sort of an incident would justify a resident being restrained for several hours or would require 6 staff to be directly involved.

In residential care there is a distinction between poor practice and abuse, though there is no precise boundary between the two. Poor practice can arise from ignorance, lack of training, poor supervision, misunderstanding or just from tiredness. Often it can be tackled by support and training and by better supervision and monitoring. Poor practice has a detrimental impact on the quality of care provided and the quality of life experienced by residents and needs to be eradicated. Abuse has a much more serious impact on the well-being and safety of residents. It involves a violation of individuals' human and civil rights by someone who has power over their life. This may be physical, psychological or financial or discriminatory. It may be intentional or unintentional or the result of neglect. It causes harm to a person either temporarily or over a period of time. Work in care settings can sometimes attract people who intend to use the presence of vulnerable people in a care setting as an opportunity to abuse. However, abuse is rarely the result of a deliberate action by an individual member of staff who sets out to harm people. As noted in Chapter 11, abuse often has its roots in poor practice that has gone unchecked and unguided. Of particular concern are those care settings where the origins of the abuse are among senior managers who are able to convince more junior staff that it is the correct way to deal with the situations they encounter. Tackling abuse generally requires firmer strategies than those employed to deal with poor practice and it is important for inspectors to be able to distinguish between the two. In March 2000 the Department of Health published "No Secrets" which provided comprehensive guidance on the identification and management of incidents involving the abuse of adults (Department of Health, 2000).

## The Role of Regulation in Preventing Abuse

I shall now move on to consider how each of the five elements of regulation can contribute to ending abuse in homes. I shall contrast what happens now with what we might expect to happen once the new regulatory systems have been implemented. I must, however, stress that my comments must not be taken to be a commentary on how the Medway Inspection Unit regulated Brompton. The MacIntyre programme said very little about what the Inspection Unit was doing and I do not have a significant amount of additional information about what the Medway Inspection Unit was or was not doing in respect of this home so it would be presumptuous of me to comment.

## Setting standards

We are told in the programme that "most of" the local authority's standards were met at the time of the last inspection. This begs a number of questions:

- Should all of the standards have been met?

- Which standards were not met – were they important ones or more minor issues?

- What was being done to ensure future compliance with the standards that were not being met?

Currently each registration authority has been given the responsibility of agreeing its own regulatory standards and there has been only limited guidance about what these should contain. In England alone, there are almost 150 Social Services Authorities, and so there are potentially 150 variations on a common theme. In practice, the variety of content and style of presentation is considerable. This is an unsatisfactory situation and large-scale national providers have long been critical of the fact that they are required to respond to different standards when providing homes in, say, Southampton and Sheffield. They rightly point out that there is little justification for such local variations.

Standards have to fulfil a number of criteria. They have to inform a potential provider about what would be expected of them if they were to enter the care market. In this regard they play a crucial role in the financial and other planning for a new facility. At the point a new home is ready for registration standards must provide "pass/fail" criteria that can be used to judge whether or not a home should be given its "licence to operate". At this stage the facility is not operating and it is only possible to judge its intentions not the actual standard of care it provides. During inspections and the investigation of complaints standards provide essential benchmarks against which to judge the quality of the care that is being provided. When a care facility is considered to be so seriously deficient as to warrant action to cancel its registration, standards have to provide the framework for a successful legal action – an action that will almost inevitably be vigorously challenged by lawyers acting on behalf of the service provider.

Standards fall into three broad categories:

**Input Standards** describe measurable things that the home must provide. Examples include: room sizes; staffing levels and numbers of bathrooms and toilets. Input standards have given rise to the stereotype of an inspector going around equipped with a clipboard and a tape measure. It is fashionable to regard input standards as outmoded but this fails to recognise their importance – especially at the point of registration. High physical standards are not, in themselves, a guarantee of high quality care. Indeed, most inspectors would be able to quote examples of homes where the physical standards are very high but the care provided is not particularly good. Conversely they could identify homes that have physical limitations but highly motivated staff who are able to overcome the disadvantages and provide a high standard of care. There must always be a bottom line. For example it would be readily acknowledged that it would be virtually impossible to provide quality care if one member of staff were expected to care for 15 people with substantial intellectual disabilities or if those 15 people had to share a single bathroom or toilet.

**Output standards** describe quantifiable aspects of the care that is provided. Examples include: activity programmes, care plans and choice menus. Again there are echoes of a "clip board approach" and the existence of a measurable output does not necessarily mean that care is provided in a way that ensures the needs and aspirations of individual residents are being met.

**Outcome standards** describe the actual experience of care of residents and are much harder to assess. "Homes Are For Living In" (Department of Health, 1989) was one of the earliest examples of a methodology for evaluating the outcomes of care and it remains influential. It describes the quality of life and quality of care of residents in terms of 6 values – privacy, dignity, choice, independence, rights and fulfilment. It goes on to define each term, identify what "a good home" would do to promote each objective and includes an aide memoire to enable inspectors to evaluate the extent to which the "good home" criteria are met. Outcome standards acknowledge that there is more than one successful model for the provision of quality care and, as such, introduce an element of flexibility into inspections.

Outcome standards seem at present to be "flavour of the month". Whilst there is much to commend them they cannot entirely supersede input and output standards, since without a core of measurable resources, it is not possible to provide successful outcomes. Outcome standards are also of little use in supporting the registration process since, at this stage, there are no outcomes only promises and good intentions. Outcome standards are of the greatest use in an inspection methodology.

Section 23 of the Care Standards Act (2000) introduces the concept of national minimum standards that are applicable to establishments or agencies and says that these standards shall be "taken into account" when decisions about regulation are being made. National minimum standards are designed to establish a baseline below which no registered facility should be allowed to fall. Because they are nationally applicable they will help eliminate the variations that currently exist and it should be easier for providers and service users and their advocates to know about them. National standards have the potential to strongly influence the quality of care provided and to effectively underpin the other regulatory processes. They can only do this if they are clear and unambiguous, if they appropriately balance input, output and outcome statements and if they are presented in a way that enables them to resist rigorous legal challenges to their validity. At the time of writing this chapter, a working group has produced a draft of the national standards for residential homes for adults in England and Wales but it has not yet been issued for consultation. We are, therefore some way away from knowing their final content and format and until we do, and until they have been tested in practice, it is impossible to say whether national standards will provide a more effective means of regulating care than do the present 150 variations.

## Registration

Preventing unsuitable people from entering the care market in the first place is essential. This requires effective registration systems. Registration involves ascertaining that the persons who are proposing to provide care and the premises in which the care is to be provided are "fit" (ie, suitable) and that the way it is intended to carry on the home will provide all the services and facilities that are reasonably required. Under the provisions of the Registered Homes Act 1984, the onus falls on the registration authority to prove, on "the balance of probabilities", that the applicant is not "fit". It is not for the applicant to prove that s/he is "fit". There is no statutory definition of "a fit person" but it is generally considered to have three aspects:

- The person (and a "person" may also be a partnership, a company or a charity) must not be debarred from providing care, for example, because of a serious criminal offence or as a result of registration being refused or cancelled in the past.

- The person must exhibit qualities such as honesty, trustworthiness, integrity, uprightness, honour and truthfulness.

- The person must possess an appropriate level of knowledge, skills and abilities about the provision of a care service.

Determining the suitability of the premises and the way it is intended to provide the service may involve obtaining the views of other bodies (eg, the Fire Service, the Health and Safety Executive and Environmental Health Departments). It also involves assessing whether or not the standards required for registration are properly met – and I have already made reference to some of the difficulties in applying these consistently.

Registration authorities may find it hard to refuse to register an applicant for a number of reasons. The applicant may withhold relevant information (even though it is an offence to do so). The checks made by the authority may not be comprehensive enough. DoH guidance (DoH, 1991) provides some structure for checking criminal backgrounds, but there is no overall national methodology underpinning the registration process. That said, my experience suggests that a high degree of consistency has developed around the country and that the depth of the registration process is not a significant problem. A third issue is that registration authorities may not be provided with all the information that is relevant to making a decision about the application. Individuals and agencies who are asked for information or references may be over-preoccupied with confidentiality or may wish to give "the benefit of the doubt" to the applicant and may provide bland information. Sometimes poor recording in agencies and key people moving on means that relevant information is lost. Sometimes information is not provided because people are worried that legal action against them may follow if they share factual information and concerns.

By far and away the biggest problem is that the registration authority has to assemble the information that is made available to it in a form that can convince panels of elected members and the Registered Homes Tribunal that there is lack of "fitness". These processes, and particularly the Tribunal, can be highly adversarial with the appellants employing top barristers to argue the case of the applicants and to undermine the registration authority's arguments. It is also a very expensive process - a Tribunal appeal can cost a Local Authority many thousands of pounds. In many registration authorities, particularly the smaller ones, applications are turned down relatively infrequently and this can mean that there is little experience of the meticulous process of preparing a case. It is perhaps not surprising, given the costs and the uncertainty that some authorities – perhaps on the advice of their legal staff – are reluctant to risk refusing registration unless there is very strong evidence of lack of suitability. This is a weakness of the current system and one that can have an adverse impact on the level of protection offered to service users.

And what of the future? The intention to produce National Minimum Standards has already been referred to. Likewise, work is in hand to produce registration methodologies that will be used by the Commissions. The Commissions will employ their own legal staff and expertise in the preparation and presentation of cases will be more universally available. However, the biggest change is to be found in the wording of the Care Standards Act 2000. Section 13 of the Act says that registration shall be granted if the registration authority is satisfied that the requirements of registration "are being and will continue to be complied with (so far as is applicable)". In other words, the focus shifts from the registration authority having to prove unfitness to the applicant having to prove that they are fit. It remains to be seen how this will work out in practice – and in this regards the early decisions of the Registered Care Tribunal will be very important – but on the face of it this change of emphasis ought to make it easier to refuse to register unsuitable people.

## Inspection

This is the area where the greatest inconsistencies exist. Some time ago I was part of a small group of 6 people asked by the DoH to prepare guidance on open reporting for nursing homes. It soon became clear that each of us approached the inspection task in very different ways. One of the main determinants of the type of inspection is the size of inspectors' caseloads within each authority, this influencing the amount of time available to undertake each inspection. The MacIntyre programme tells us that Brompton had "quite a good report" following its last inspection. We learn nothing about the conduct of the inspection, nor do we hear whether the report includes requirements or recommendations for improvements.

The current legal requirement is that registered homes must be inspected at least twice a year, and that one of these inspections must be unannounced. Inspections should involve: examining policies, procedures and records; talking to managers and to staff at all levels; thoroughly reviewing the premises; and, most importantly, talking to service users (and if possible to their relatives and/or advocates). It is also desirable to talk with other professionals who are involved with and visit the home, though the time pressures that are inherent in an inspection can make this difficult. A good inspector will seek information from all these sources, will use the evidence of all their senses, and will identify consistencies and inconsistencies in the available information in order to make judgements, against agreed criteria, about the quality of care provided and the quality of life experienced by residents.

Inspecting homes for people with intellectual disabilities presents a number of particular challenges to inspectors. Often service users are away from the home during the daytime at work, college or day care. If inspectors wish to meet with them, some parts of inspections have to take place during evenings or at weekends. This requires commitment from inspectors and flexible working policies from employers. A second issue is that inspectors may find it quite difficult to talk with intellectually disabled service users. Sometimes this is because they are unfamiliar with the client group and are uncomfortable. Furthermore, getting to know these service users well enough for them to feel confident to share their opinions with inspectors can be a time consuming process that is not easily accomplished when inspectors have got large caseloads and so cannot visit each home as often as they would like. Finally, it is often necessary to make special efforts to communicate with intellectually disabled service users, either by simplifying ordinary language or by using special techniques. Not all inspectors possess these specialist skills. Recently the Department of Health sponsored a project to provide resource material to help service users to participate in inspections. This resulted in the publication of *Let's meet, Let's talk* (Blunden et al, 2001) which contains much useful practical advice. Several of these communication difficulties can be overcome by training and it is regrettable that the existing system does not include a specific and compulsory training curriculum.

Some fairly small-scale research in Buckinghamshire and Medway (Social Services Inspectorate, 2000) found very little evidence that people with intellectual disabilities had any real understanding of inspection and the role of inspectors. Where understanding was demonstrated it focused on the "physical" aspects and safety of the homes rather than quality of life and personal safety issues. Cleanliness was often cited as the main attribute being inspected. There was ignorance about how to contact an inspector directly without the involvement of staff in the home. Another issue that arose from the research was that people who had experienced several moves associated inspection with those moves or with home closures and were fearful of talking with anyone associated with inspection.

Part of the planning for the Commissions includes the development of inspection methodologies. Early drafts suggest that these will be thorough, comprehensive and wide-ranging. What is not clear at this stage is whether or not the extra resources that will be needed to implement the proposed new inspection method will be forthcoming. If they are not, then compromises may be necessary. The Government has stated that, in the long run, it wants regulation to be funded by the fees paid by registered facilities and there are limits to the level at which these fees might reasonably be set. There is an argument that regulation is a "public good" which justifies subsidy and many people think that subsidies will always be needed if an adequate regulatory system is to be achieved. The difficulties that inspectors have in getting to know intellectually disabled people would justify more resources being made available for these kinds of inspections. This would enable longer or more frequent visits to be made to the home and give greater opportunities for preparing and de-briefing service users. It would also reduce the current reliance on using the home's staff to facilitate service user involvement. After all, if a home is employing abusive and oppressive practices, the staff would be in a strong position to intimidate service users into saying nothing about them. Increased availability and involvement of advocates would also help. The Commissions will also need to consider ways of providing accessible information that will help service users to understand what inspections are about. Better training for inspectors will also be important.

## Complaints

The MacIntyre programme does not tells us whether there had been any complaints about Brompton. The two key issues about complaints are getting people to raise their concerns and conducting thorough investigations once issues have been referred to the registration authority.

Reference was made earlier in this chapter to people's reluctance to complain for fear of reprisals against themselves or the service users. If they manage to overcome these psychological barriers, it is by no means clear whether people know how and to whom to complain. The Residential Care Home Regulations (1984) require registered persons to provide written information about how and to whom to complain, to fully investigate any complaints made and to inform every resident in writing of the name and address of the registration authority to whom complaints can be made. Furthermore, there is a requirement (DHSS, 1988) that this information should be readily available at all times to residents and persons acting on their behalf. The previously mentioned research in Buckinghamshire and Medway showed that service users had an almost complete lack of understanding about how to complain, even when attempts had been made to translate the complaints procedure into more accessible formats, including symbols. It is clear that the new regulatory authorities will need to pay much greater attention to making it easy to complain and a useful starting point will be to review current best practice.

One of the things that it likely to give people confidence to complain is the knowledge that the complaint will be dealt with effectively. It is surprising how good "the grapevine" is in communicating about inspection units' successes (and failures). Investigating a complaint properly requires a clear strategy. It is necessary to know what information is being looked for, and how and by whom it will be sought. A complaints investigation strategy should allocate clear responsibilities taking account that investigations may involve other agencies (particularly if the Adult Protection Procedures have been invoked). It is best for at least two people to undertake complaints investigations. Investigation is about gathering evidence – evidence that may ultimately be tested in legal settings such as a Tribunal or the Courts. Evidence must be collected properly. Inspectors need to gain specific knowledge and skills about obtaining evidence, about cautioning, and about the legal framework of the Police and Criminal Evidence Act 1984. There are few things more galling than discovering that important evidence about a registered person's lack of fitness is ruled inadmissible because there are technical flaws in the way it has been obtained.

The Care Standards Act contains an important new provision to facilitate the investigation of complaints. Section 32 of the Act includes a power to seize and remove documentary and other evidence. This will deal with those past occasions when records have changed or disappeared before the inspector could acquire a portable photocopier with which to copy them. Planning for the Commissions includes devising the strategies for investigating complaints and it is intended that proper training will be provided for all inspectors. Hopefully these measures will improve the quality of complaints investigations and encourage people to air concerns about homes like this.

## Enforcement Action

It is easy say that it is "obvious" that a home like Brompton should not have been allowed to continue to operate and that the local inspection unit ought to have closed it down. We do not, of course, learn from the programme whether this was being considered at the time that the programme was made. Taking enforcement action is not, however, a straightforward process.

Almost all the comments about the reasons for some inspection units' reluctance to refuse registration can be applied to decisions about the taking of enforcement action. There are, however, other issues that need to be taken into account.

There are two main forms of enforcement action. The Registered Homes Act 1984 and the Residential Care Homes Regulations 1984 identify a number of offences that can lead to prosecution in the Courts. The normal penalty upon conviction would be a fine though, in the case of obstructing an inspector, imprisonment would be possible. Conviction for some of the offences precludes a local authority from contracting with the home and this may impact on the home's continuing viability. The other form of enforcement action is to cancel registration either by the urgent procedure which involves obtaining an order from magistrates that has immediate effect or by the non-urgent procedure that can take months – or even years – to complete. It should be noted that cancellation of registration does not give the local authority powers to close a home and remove its residents. What it does do is to make it an offence, punishable by a large fine, for the provider to continue to operate.

Quite apart from the difficulties of preparing a sustainable case, there are a number of "ethical" considerations that tend to influence decisions about enforcement action.

Successful enforcement action usually means that the home will cease to operate and inspectors have to weigh up whether the consequences of this will have a greater detrimental effect on the wellbeing of residents. It is known that moving home can cause them a great deal of stress and distress. Some of the press comments made in the context of the debate about the objectivity of the editing of the MacIntyre programme criticised the Local Authority for the speed with which the residents were moved after Brompton's registration was cancelled.

Where there are few alternative placements available, there are sometimes strong pressures to "keep trying" with the home. Sometimes these pressures come from other professionals, but more often they come from service users' relatives and other carers. The reasons for this can be varied. Occasionally carers may be worried that taking enforcement action will result in them having to take more responsibility for their relative than they wish to. More often, however, relatives have difficulty in accepting that the situation is unsatisfactory either because of lack of knowledge, denial, or a poor appreciation of what an acceptable quality of care involves. It is not always easy to pursue an unflinching commitment to enforcement action, particularly when it appears that the majority of the local MPs, Councillors, service users' relatives and friends – and all the local media – are out to portray such action as unreasonable and evidence of a draconian regulatory regime! There is an element of "damned if you do, damned if you don't" surrounding the public's response to enforcement action.

Some inspectors seem to regard resorting to enforcement action as a personal failure – a demonstration that their negotiating and persuasive skills have been found wanting. If this is a view that is shared by their managers, there can be an unjustified reluctance to act. This should be something that the larger scale Commissions should be able to tackle.

Another issue that has to be taken into account is the consequences of failure. Initiating enforcement action often signals the end of the service provider's co-operation and relationship with the inspection unit. If the action is ultimately unsuccessful rebuilding that relationship in order to continue to monitor the home effectively can be very difficult. There are also wider implications. Word of successful enforcement actions soon gets around the area and can act as an encouragement to other providers to improve their performance. Unfortunately, the converse is also true. If a unit gets a reputation of being unable to sustain enforcement action, its credibility and thereby its effectiveness becomes dented.

The length of time it can take to complete the non-urgent cancellation procedure is another deterrent. Representations and appeals hearings that lasted for a few hours in the early years of the 1984 Act can now take several days, and occasionally run into weeks, and this in turn leads to scheduling difficulties that can cause delays lasting several months before a hearing can be arranged. Lawyers acting for providers frequently employ delaying tactics such as asking for last minute adjournments (sometimes to give the provider more time to sell the home). Registered Homes Tribunal decisions can be appealed, on a point of law, to the High Court and this further lengthens the process. I have experience of instances where a home was still legally operating two years after the notice of intention to cancel registration was issued and, of course, during all this time people were still living in a situation that the registration authority considered to be unsuitable.

None of this is intended to justify failure to act when action is needed. The Commissions will need to establish monitoring and decision making mechanisms to achieve an appropriate balance between continuing to support a home and taking enforcement action. They will need to ensure that inspectors have the necessary skills in evidence gathering and in evidence giving in Tribunals and Courts. A number of new provisions in the Care Standards Act will assist. One of the most effective ways of regulating the quality of care is to impose conditions on the registration. They are straightforward and unambiguous. If a home's registration says it can accommodate 25 people and it is found to be accommodating 30, then there is a very clear case for conviction for an offence. Under the existing legislation the only conditions that can be imposed on a home relate to numbers, age, sex and category of residents. The Care Standards Act allows the registration authority to make registration "subject to such conditions as the registration authority thinks fit". In the case of Brompton, this new power could, for example, have been used to include requirements about the qualifications and training of care staff and managers and about the use of physical interventions. The Care Standards Act also reviews the Tribunal processes and the intention is that both the representation and appeals stages of cancellations will be streamlined and speeded up.

Training for inspectors has been mentioned at several points in this chapter and a number of additional factors need to be considered on this important topic. Regulating a home like Brompton is a complex task requiring well-trained Inspectors. Most Inspectors have a professional qualification in nursing, social work or an allied profession that provides a background understanding of the issues surrounding the provision of care. Beyond this, there is no specified training and we have seen that successful regulation requires the exercise of skills that are not usually taught in nursing or social work courses. Regulation is one of the few professional activities that lacks an accepted training curriculum or an agreed means of delivering it. Training has been developed on an ad hoc basis with a few universities and private trainers devising courses that plugged gaps. Access to training is patchy and dependent on whether Units are conveniently located to attend courses and on the (often woefully inadequate) amount of money available in the training budget. There has been no consensus about training priorities and little quality control of the training that is provided. Under these conditions, is it any wonder that the approach of Inspectors has lacked consistency?

This situation has now begun to change. A national competency framework for inspectors (TOPSS, 2000) has been produced and the Open University has been commissioned to translate it into a training curriculum. All Inspectors will, in future, be required to undertake training and to demonstrate that they possess the required competencies. Planning for the Commissions has strongly emphasised the importance of training – this includes effective transition training to ensure familiarity with the new framework as well as commitment to promoting the training curriculum for Inspectors. In future the workforce will be better equipped.

## Conclusions

The MacIntyre programme included harrowing scenes that have no place in a caring environment. This is not the norm in care settings, but this does not make them any less acceptable. The programme did not dwell on the role of regulation but implied that regulation had not been effective. This chapter has identified inherent difficulties that restrict the present regulatory system's capacity to take effective action in these circumstances. The programme raises points for learning, but most of these were not new. Planning for the new national regulation system was already well advanced by the time the programme was made, and measures were already being taken to address many of the lessons raised by the programme. Everyone, and especially people who are vulnerable to abuse and exploitation because they are disabled, has a right to a fulfilling and secure life. The new regulatory arrangements will assist them to achieve this. However, no matter how good the regulatory system becomes it cannot act alone. The paramount lesson that emerges from the programme is that the wellbeing of the residents at Brompton was the responsibility of everybody who came into contact with them. This will remain true in the future.

## References

Blunden, R, Corker, J, & Rice, J (2001) *Let's meet, Let's talk*. Department of Health: London.

Burgner, T (1996) *The Regulation and Inspection of Social Services*. London: Department of Health and Welsh Office.

Buckinghamshire County Council (1998) *Independent Longcare Inquiry*. Buckinghamshire: Buckinghamshire County Council.

Department of Health (1991) *Disclosure of Criminal Background- Proprietors and Managers of Residential Care Homes and Nursing Homes* Circular LAC (91) 4. London: DoH.

Department of Health (2000) *No Secrets: Guidance on developing and implementing multi-agency policies and procedures to protect vulnerable adults from abuse*. London: HMSO.

Department of Health (2001) *Valuing People. A New Strategy for Learning Disability for the 21st Century*. Norwich: Stationery Office.

Department of Health and Social Security (1984) *The Residential Care Homes Regulations*. London: DHSS.

Department of Health and Social Security (1988) Circular LAC (88) 15. London: DHSS.

Social Services Inspectorate, Department of Health (1991) *Inspecting For Quality*. London: HMSO.

Social Services Inspectorate, Department of Health (1989) *Homes Are For Living In*. London: The Stationery Office.

Social Services Inspectorate, Department of Health (2000) *Learning Disabilities Service Users' Survey. Report of a project undertaken as part of inspections of Buckinghamshire and Medway Council's Registration and Inspection Units October 1999 and September 2000*. London: DoH.

Training Organisation For The Personal Social Services (England) (2000) *National Occupational Standards For Regulators Of Social And Health Care For Adults And Children*. London: TOPSS.

# SECTION V:

## From Theory to Practice

# Chapter 13

# Restraint reduction

Peter Sturmey & Ann Palen McGlynn

## Introduction

Skills training, active treatment, increasing on task behavior, and teaching functionally equivalent behaviors to reduce challenging behaviors are the hallmark of Applied Behavior Analysis (ABA). These strategies are used to enhance the person's dignity, and to increase socially valid outcomes, such as competence, age-appropriate behavior, appearance and lifestyle, as well as client happiness and well-being. Ethical and practice guidelines in ABA promote the use of these strategies. Thus, reduction and elimination of restrictive procedures has always been a concern of ABA. However, practitioners in ABA are often involved in the use of a variety of restrictive procedures, including restraint. This can occur because clients are transferred to their caseload from other services that routinely use restraint. Behavior analysts also work with clients who present the most challenging behaviors, such as severe aggression and self-injury. Restraint may be used in this situation as an emergency procedure to protect the client and others. Of course, behavior analysts may also be involved with restraint when it is added to an intervention procedure.

The ongoing debate on restrictive procedures was recently refocused by the Hartford Courant report *Deadly Restraint* (Weiss, 1998). The report identified at least 142 restraint-related deaths in the United States over a ten-year period. These deaths had occurred in state hospitals, state schools and group homes, and various other community settings. Restraint-related deaths occurred in both people with intellectual disabilities and people with mental illness. Weiss estimated that three times as many deaths occurred due to under-reporting and incomplete or inaccurate reporting of the cause of death. In response to Congressional interest in the issue, the General Accounting Office of the USA (GAO, 1999) reviewed the use of restraint. They concluded that conflicting and inconsistent regulations and the failure of states to oversee deaths and sentinel events contributed to the continued inappropriate use of restraint. There was a vigorous response in the USA to these findings. Some states instigated a retrospective analysis of records in which every recent death in institutional settings was identified and the time between death and the last restraint was reported. Any potential contribution of restraint to each death was reviewed. Some states rewrote policies, implemented state-wide staff training initiatives and began centralized tracking of restraints. In October 1999 the American Association on Mental Retardation held a two-day conference in Chicago to identify best practices. Legislation was proposed to Congress and to state legislative bodies to eliminate or greatly restrict the use of restraint. Accreditation bodies in both mental health and intellectual disabilities services also revised and strengthened existing regulations. Thus, *Deadly Restraint* provoked a nation-wide response to this issue.

Restraint is not a new issue for services for people with intellectual disabilities. It has surfaced periodically in legal contexts and in research. Client safety and the use of restraints has been the basis for many law suits in the United States. In special education, community and institutional settings, injuries to clients from restraint devices and personal holds have been identified as liability issues. This is particularly true if the service knowingly, or should have known, that a danger to a client existed, but failed to take responsible action to prevent injury or re-injury to that client. Equally, failure to restrain a client that led to the injury of another client or a staff member can also be the cause of legal action against service providers. It also emerges periodically that a very small number of families use restraint methods such as locking the family members in their bedrooms at night or in garages because of uncontrollable behavior, lack of service support, concerns for the safety of their family members and lack of any alternative. These families are sometimes accused of neglect, and may even lose access to their child with intellectual disabilities. Thus, legal action related to restraint is not uncommon in the USA.

There has been some research into the use of restraint as a planned intervention procedure. Harris (1996) reviewed 25 papers on restraint in people with intellectual disabilities. He concluded that the literature showed that:

(a) contingent and non-contingent restraint can be effective in long-term elimination of aggression or self-injurious behavior

(b) brief restraint is more effective than long restraint

(c) restraint fading procedures can be effective

(d) restraint is sometimes used for a variety of minor, non-dangerous behaviors

(e) planned restraint is safer than emergency restraint

(f) a wide variety of learning processes might underlie restraint as a behavioral intervention.

The literature that Harris reviewed is very limited in a number of ways. For example, often only data on the target behavior were reported, and not data on the use of restraint per se. The duration of follow-up was usually limited or absent. None of the literature directly dealt with the issue of injuries, sentinel events or restraint related death. Generally, the literature reviewed by Harris focussed on two narrow questions: whether the use of restraint as a punisher could eliminate or reduce a challenging behavior, and whether behavioral methods could be used to eliminate chronic restraint in one or two clients. While these are clearly socially valid questions, the issues raised by *Deadly Restraint* are much broader. For example, much restraint is not part of a planned intervention, and is referred to as emergency or unplanned restraint. By definition, relatively little is known about the use of unplanned restraint.

Restraint-related death is a relatively infrequent event, perhaps occurring only one time per state per year. Such an event might occur in a wide number of settings. Although at risk groups of clients can be identified (Sturmey, 1999a), we cannot identify individuals who are at risk for restraint-related death with any certainty. Some clients might receive a lot of restraint, but the form of restraint used might be safer than other less frequent forms of restraint. Thus, using mittens as restraint to prevent hand mouthing may be used continuously for years. Mittens may be safer than some forms of restraint, but this still carries risk from choking on materials from the mittens. However, emergency personal restraint that occurs at a much lower frequency might carry with it a much greater risk of death, at least for some populations. The only good data we have on this issue comes from Hill & Spreat's (1987) study of restraint-related injury. They showed that injuries to clients and staff were more likely when restraint was used on an emergency basis rather than on a planned basis. Thus, it seems safer for everyone to incorporate restraint into planned procedures and to train staff and others in the use of restraint ahead of time on a client by client basis, especially for clients who have high rates of restraint. Unfortunately we have no data on the relative safety of different forms of restraint, although opinions abound in the absence of data. Thus, at the present time we do not have a good behavioral or organizational technology that has been validated to respond to the issues raised by *Deadly Restraint*. Eliminating restraint-related death requires reduction of restraint by reducing its use over a large number of settings and over an extensive period of time. Further it is hard to evaluate these efforts, since the key dependent variable – restraint-related death – may occur at such low frequency that is hard to measure any meaningful impact of intervention, and unreliable because of inaccurate documentation regarding the cause of death.

Sturmey (1999a) recently highlighted the possible importance of organizational factors in the use of restraint. This study reported on the relationship between the frequency and severity of challenging behaviors, such as aggression and self-injury, and the use of restraint in a large state school (institutional) population. Interestingly, consumer challenging behaviors such as aggression and self-injury were only correlated with restraint to a very modest degree. This suggests that variables other than client characteristics might be important in determining the use of restraint. The GAO (1999) reached similar conclusions. In order to reduce the inappropriate use of restraint the GAO called for regulation, reporting, staff training and adequate staffing. However, the GAO did not provide either a concise technological description of the interventions that might reduce restraint. Neither did they provide detailed data to demonstrate the effectiveness of such programmes. Unfortunately, very little has been published on the use of restraint in schools, community settings and within families. Casual observation of these settings quickly reveals that these practices are relatively widespread, although we have no data to measure the extent of these practices in community settings.

There have been some attempts to implement large-scale reductions in the use of restraint, including restraint reduction programs in acute medical care settings (Hancock et al, 2001) and services for the elderly (Dewey & Brill, 2000). Donat (1998) reported the effect of an intervention to reduce restraint and seclusion duration in a psychiatric hospital. Participants were selected because they had high rates of restraint and/or seclusion. He reported that improved data collection and analysis, mandatory behavioral consultation, behavioral reviews and other procedures were effective in reducing the average duration of restraint or seclusion. The use of restraint or seclusion during six months before and after the implementation of this procedure was analysed. The average duration of these reactive procedures fell from 18.8 hours per month per resident to 7.2 hours per month per resident. Thus, interventions based on staff training and monitoring show promise as a means of reducing restraint usage. Similar studies can be found in Allen et al (1997), Luiselli et al (2000), Obi (1997), Oliver et al (1998), Rangecroft et al (1997) and Syndram et al (1994). All of these studies report that it is possible to reduce restraint both for individuals and for groups of individuals by a variety of interventions based on ABA, staff training and changes in policies and procedures.

In this chapter we report three studies on restraint reduction in services for persons with intellectual disabilities. The first took place in the early 1990s as part of routine clinical work to reduce restraint. The latter two studies took place in direct response to *Deadly Restraint*. In the first study we report on the effectiveness of staff training and graphical feedback in reducing or eliminating the use of restraint in two women with intellectual disabilities over a one-year period. In the second study we describe a 7-month intervention to reduce restraint usage at a large institutional setting. The final study then provides three-year follow up data on consumers at high risk for restraint in which a variety of methods to reduce and eliminate restrictive reactive procedures were employed.

## Study 1: Restraint reduction: two case studies

### Participants and setting

Two participants were selected for the study because they had been identified as having high rates of restraint. The first participant, Ms Longoria,[1] was a 36 year-old woman with severe intellectual disabilities. She was restrained on a papoose board – a commercially available restraint device, consisting of a flat wooden board, plastic covers with underlying padding, and velcro wraps to restrain the person's wrists, legs upper and lower torso – for aggressive behavior as part of her behavior management plan (BMP). The second participant, Ms.Anderson, was a 23-year-old woman with profound intellectual disabilities. She was restrained with a basket hold for aggression. The study took place in a large Intermediate Care Facility 650-bed state school. Each participant lived on separate residential units within the facility.

### Procedure

A review of the facility restraint records was conducted to identify consumers with high rates of restraint. The intervention was based on the work of Reid and

[1] All client names used in this chapter are fictitious in order to protect the client's anonymity.

Parsons (1995). Staff received a 10-minute verbal brief instruction from the unit psychologist, who had a Masters degree in psychology. They were instructed to reduce restraint and to keep consumers and staff safe. They were also instructed to redirect precursor behaviors. Alternates to restraint, such as redirection of precursor behaviors or problem solving with the consumer, were emphasized. They were also reminded of each consumer's BMP.

Staff received feedback in the form of weekly graphs for 8 weeks posted in the break room and mailed to their supervisors. During the remainder of study, monthly graphs were used. The lead author met with the Masters psychologist for 8 weeks on a weekly basis to review restraints, verbally reinforce progress and to problem solve if there was no progress or regression. This supervision was faded to routine monthly supervision after 8 weeks. The main dependent variable was the rate of restraints per week. Intervention was staggered across time to form a multiple baseline design across subjects.

## Results and Discussion

The results can be seen in Figure 13.1. For Ms Longoria the mean baseline rate of restraint was 2.3 per week (range 0 to 8 per week). Post intervention, the

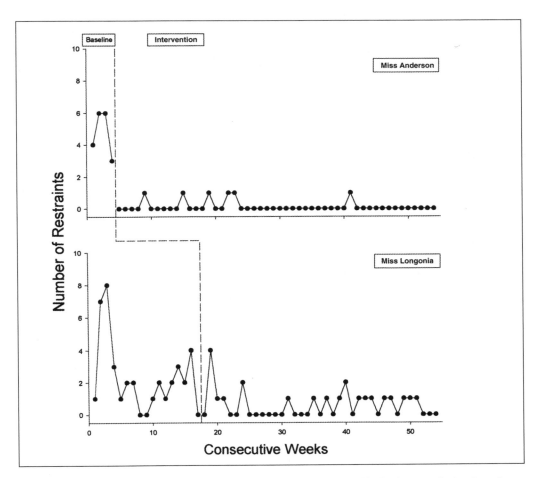

**Figure 13.1:** The frequency of restraint for Ms Longoria and Ms Anderson during baseline and intervention.

mean rate of restraint was 0.59 per week (range 0 to 4). For Ms Anderson the mean baseline rate of restraint was 4.75 per week (range 3 to 6 per week). During the post intervention phase the mean rate of restraint was 0.12 per week (range 0 to 1 per week). During the last 13 weeks of the study restraint was eliminated. A review of the consumers' records and the facility's injury tracking system revealed that there has been no associated increases in injuries to either these two consumers, their peers or staff. No increase in other forms of reactive management practices occurred during this intervention.

## Study 2: Large-scale implementation of restraint reduction

In this study we implemented a facility-wide approach to reducing restraint. We used goal setting, staff training and feedback to reduce restraint for over 300 people with intellectual disabilities over a 7-month period.

### Participants and setting

The study took place in an Intermediate Care Facility –Mental Retardation (ICF-MR) accredited facility for 381 persons in 1999. Fifty (13%) of the group had mild intellectual disabilities, 29 (8%) moderate intellectual disabilities, 50 (13%) severe intellectual disabilities, and 252 (66%) profound intellectual disabilities. There were 249 men (65%) and 134 women (35%). Thirty-eight people (10%) were aged between 0 to 21 years, 124 people (32%) 22 to 35 years, 200 people (53%) 36 to 55 years, and 21 people (5%) 56 years or above. Eighty-eight people (23%) were non-ambulatory. Twenty-five (7%) received additional funding because of medical conditions and 78 people (20%) received additional funding for behavioral needs.

### Procedure

The Texas Department of Mental Health and Mental Retardation's (TXMHMR) Central Office had monitored the use of restraint at each state school in for 2 years. Every quarter, each facility returned restraint data. These data has been analyzed to determine trends within facilities over time and to compare one facility with another. These data were reviewed with each facility superintendent and executive team by Central Office staff once every quarter. On site visits took place to review these and other management data every three or six months.

The facility at which this study took place presented a plan to reduce the amount of restraints was presented to the external review board of the facility. The objectives of the plan were:

(1) By February, 1999, restraint will be reduced by 25% of the total as of August 31, 1998

(2) By May 31, 1999, restraint will be reduced by 50% of the total as of August 31, 1998.

A variety of interventions were implemented. Homes with high rates of restraint were identified and targeted. Each interdisciplinary team worked to reduce the restraint frequency for that home and the need for restraint reduction was presented to staff via individualised training. Finally, the psychology department presented classes on restraint reduction over a one-month period. The classes stressed empathy, current facility practices, alternatives to restraint, and role-playing of redirection techniques. These classes were taught in a central area and were focused on direct contact staff, although all staff were invited to attend.

## Data analysis

Restraints were classified using the categories used to report restraint data to the Texas Department of Mental Health and Mental Retardation's Central office. There were six categories of restraint. Personal restraint was defined as the application of any personal restraint that was included in a BMP. Examples included restraining a hand or limb, basket holds, and two person horizontal restraints. Mechanical restraint was defined as the application of any mechanical device to restrain someone. Examples included papoose boards, jackets, mittens and ties. Personal and mechanical restraints were further classified as emergency if they were not part of a BMP or as programmatic if they were part of a BMP. Medications were also classified as emergency, if there were no guidelines for their use in a BMP or as programmatic, if there were guidelines for their use in the consumer's BMP. Programmed medication included only routinely prescribed psychotropic medication; there were no PRN ('as needed') orders used in these services.

Data were analysed by the number of persons restrained per month and the number of incidents of applications per month. The method of scoring data can be illustrated as follows. Suppose that one consumer was restrained four times in a month. One restraint was with a basket hold in their BMP, one time with a papoose board not in the participant's BMP, and two times with an emergency psychotropic medication. This would be coded as one person with one incident of programmatic personal restraint; one person with one incident of emergency mechanical restraint; and one person with two incidents of emergency chemical restraint.

## Results

*Personal programmatic restraint.* There were 35 people restrained during baseline. At 7-months there were 27 people receiving programmatic personal restraint. This was a 23% reduction over baseline. At baseline there were 99 incidents of programmatic personal restraint. At 7-months there were 41 incidents. This was a reduction of 59%.

*Personal emergency restraint.* There were 11 people receiving personal emergency restraint during baseline. At 7-months there were 18 people who received personal emergency restraint. This was an increase of 63% over baseline. During baseline there were 26 incidents of restraint. At 7-months there were 56 incidents of personal emergency restraint. This was an increase of 115% over baseline.

*Programmatic mechanical restraint.* There were 62 persons who received programmatic mechanical restraint during baseline. At 7-months this had

**Table 13.1:** The frequency of restraints and percentage change in restraint use by type of restraint in Study 2

| | Aug -98 | Sep -98 | Oct -98 | Nov -98 | Dec -98 | Jan -99 | Feb -99 | Mar -99 |
|---|---|---|---|---|---|---|---|---|
| Programmatic personal | | | | | | | | |
| Persons | 35 | 31 (−12%) | 28 (−20%) | 30 (−16%) | 34 (−3%) | 26 (−26%) | 30 (−16%) | 27 (−23%) |
| Incidents | 99 | 81 (−18%) | 59 (−40%) | 81 (−18%) | 108 (+9%) | 62 (−37%) | 60 (−40%) | 41 (−59%) |
| Personal emergency | | | | | | | | |
| Persons | 11 | 9 (−22%) | 11 (0) | 17 (+54%) | 13 (+18%) | 12 (+9%) | 13 (+18%) | 18 (+63%) |
| Incidents | 26 | 12 (−46%) | 18 (−31%) | 28 (+7%) | 31 (+19%) | 22 (−16%) | 20 (−24%) | 56 (+115%) |
| Mechanical Programmatic | | | | | | | | |
| Persons | 62 | 48 (−23%) | 48 (−23%) | 48 (−23%) | 49 (−21%) | 48 (−23%) | 41 (−34%) | 27 (−57%) |
| Incidents | 416 | 387 (−7%) | 484 (+16%) | 350 (−16%) | 364 (−14%) | 271 (−35%) | 228 (−46%) | 160 (−62%) |
| Mechanical emergency | | | | | | | | |
| Persons | 9 | 5 (−44%) | 6 (−33%) | 9 (0) | 5 (−75%) | 1 (−72%) | 7 (−22%) | 5 (−45%) |
| Incidents | 20 | 21 (−30%) | 14 (−40%) | 12 (−75%) | 5 (−75%) | 1 (−95%) | 2 (−90%) | 8 (−60%) |
| Pharmacology emergency | | | | | | | | |
| Persons | 3 | 2 (−33%) | 3 (0) | 6 (+100%) | 2 (−33%) | 5 (+67%) | 1 (−67%) | 7 (+133%) |
| Incidents | 131 | 131 | 134 | 137 | 131 | 131 | 134 | 141 |

reduced to 27 persons. This was a decrease of 57%. During baseline there were 416 incidents of mechanical programmatic restraint. At 7-months there were 160 incidents. This was a 62% reduction over baseline.

*Emergency mechanical restraint.* During baseline there were 9 persons receiving emergency mechanical restraint. At 7-months there were 5 people receiving emergency mechanical restraint. This was a 45% reduction over baseline.

*Pharmacological restraint.* During the course of this study there was no increase in the number of consumers receiving regular prescribed psychotropic medications: it remained stable at 135 persons. There was an increase in the number of consumers receiving emergency psychotropic medications in month 7, however, this was due to the admission of seven new consumers from community settings, all of whom were subscribed medications.

## Discussion

The impact of this programme was most clearly seen in the reduction in the use of mechanical restraint. Large reductions in the number of persons and number of incidents of both programmatic and emergency mechanical restraint were seen. There was no evidence that reductions in programmatic mechanical restraint were accompanied by increase in emergency mechanical restraint.

The impact on the use of personal restraint was less compelling. Whereas the number of people and incidents of programmatic personal restraint reduced there was a concomitant increase in emergency personal restraint. However, a review of these data indicate that the facility received many new admissions during this period, most of whom have had extremely difficult periods of adjustment. In order to get baseline information a BMP is not typically written for at least 30 days after admission. Thus, restraints of newly admitted individuals are considered emergencies. This is particularly true of the increase in month 7. At this time two newly admitted consumers accounted for 56 emergency personal restraints. Some of these emergency personal restraints were also due to an individual with seizures who was extremely aggressive at the end of his seizures. Despite these qualifications, the data on personal restraint remain less impressive than those on mechanical restraints. Nevertheless, this study shows that use of staff training, setting goals, and feedback can be an effective method of restraint reduction.

## Study 3: Reducing restraint using an Organizational Behavior Management approach

### Participants and setting

This study took place in a 310-bed ICF-MR congregate care facility between 1995 and 1999. High-risk participants were identified using the facility's data returns on restraint to the state agency's central office. These restraint data were analyzed to describe the distribution of restraint. An analysis of the frequency distribution of rest indicated that relatively few consumers accounted for the majority of restraint. Only 60 of 310 consumers had restraint in one quarter of the year. Furthermore, 18 of 310 consumers accounted for over 90% of all incidents of restraint (Sturmey & Houdeshell, 1997). These 18 consumers were entered into a programme of restraint reduction. During the first year four other consumers, who were admitted into the facility during the first year, were also entered into the programme. These two consumers were admitted to the facility from community services where they had been restrained 24 hours a day for several years without a BMP.

Twelve men and 10 women participated. The median age was 41 years (range 28 to 69 years). Two persons were diagnosed as people with moderate intellectual disabilities, two persons were diagnosed as people with severe intellectual disabilities, and 18 were diagnosed with profound intellectual disabilities. No one was diagnosed with borderline or mild intellectual disabilities. Fourteen participants were non-ambulatory. The reasons for restraint was SIB for 15 participants and hand mouthing with associated skin breakdown for 7 participants. Interestingly, aggression to others was *not* identified as a reason for restraint in this group of consumers. Most of the restraint used with these clients was mechanical, but some personal restraint was also used. Seven consumers were restrained using short-term restraint, that is several discrete incidents of restraint per month. Fifteen consumers were in long-term restraint, that is they were restrained at least several hours per day or nearly continuously, at some point during the month (cf. Sturmey, 1999a).

## Procedure

The following procedures were implemented over a six-month period. Several OBM procedures were used to reduce restraint. First, all restraint, no matter how brief, was recorded on a standard restraint checklist. In order to facilitate accurate data recording an easy to use data sheet was devised to allow the frequency and duration of restraint to be accurately recorded for those consumers in near continuous restraint. Verbal and graphical feedback was given to direct care staff and managers in the form of frequent in-service training and posting graphs in the staff break room. BMPs for hand mouthing were revised to use restraint contingent on skin breakdown rather than the target behavior of hand mouthing itself. Enhanced supervision and monitoring from the Chief Psychologist and Behavior Therapy Committee was also used initially to review on a monthly basis. If programmes were effective in reducing restraint, the frequency of supervision was faded out to quarterly and then six monthly. If restraint did not reduce review was increased to weekly if necessary until restraint reduction began to occur. Interventions included modifying programmes on the basis of revised functional assessments, ensuring staff implementation through additional monitoring, enhancing the positive components of interventions, and positive feedback for staff when restraint was reduced. After six months the programme was faded to routine monthly supervision and training of the psychologist.

## Date collection and analysis

Restraint data were transcribed from restraint checklists. All residential, vocational and other programmatic staff who restrained a client routinely completed these restraint checklists. If the restraint took place for less than 90 minutes, then the restraint was coded as a short duration restraint. Almost all personal restraints were substantially under 60 minutes. Longer restraint tended to involve mechanical, rather than personal restraints. If the restraint took place for 90 minutes or longer, as in the example of mittens for hand mouthing, then they were recorded either in hours per month or as the proportion of time in restraint. Date were collected at three points: (a) during the quarter prior to the implementation of the programme; (b) during the last quarter of the year, that is, six months after the programme had been implemented; and, (c) during the last quarter of the third year, two years after the programme had been completed.

Change scores were calculated between the first and last quarters of the first year and between the first quarter of the first year and the last quarter of the third year of the study. Changes in restraint use were then calculated as the median and range of change. Data are also presented on the number of consumers who were restraint-free, and who had a 90%, 75% and 50% or better restraint reduction at the end of the first year and at the end of the third year.

## Results

The results are summarized in Table 13.2. At the end of the first year the median reduction in restraint was 72% (range + 62% to − 100%). Two out of 22 consumers were restraint free. Six out of 22 consumers had 90% or better restraint reduction. Eight out of 22 consumers had 75% or better restraint reduction. Sixteen out of 22 consumers had 50% or better restraint reduction. Two consumers had large increases in the use of restraint of 50% and 62%.

At the last quarter of the third year data were available for 21 of the original 22 consumers. At this time the median restrain reduction was 95% (range +213% to −100%). Three consumers were restraint-free. Eleven consumers had restraint reductions of 90% or better. Twelve consumers had restraint reductions of 75%

**Table 13.2:** One- and three-year follow-up data on changes in the use of restraint in Study 3

| Consumer outcome | Follow-up | |
|---|---|---|
| | One-year | Three years |
| Median | −72% | −95% |
| Range | +62% to −100% | +213% to −100% |
| Number with > 50% reduction | 16 | 16 |
| Number with > 75% reduction | 8 | 12 |
| Number with > 90% reduction | 6 | 11 |
| Number restraint-free | 2 | 3 |

or better. Sixteen consumers had restraint reductions of 50% or more. Two consumers had considerable increases in restraint use of + 62% and + 213% over the first quarter of the study.

This study showed that an OBM approach to restraint reduction was quite effective in reducing restraint use within this group of 22 consumers with the highest restraint usage. At three-year follow-up 3 consumers were restraint free for at least the last quarter of that year, 16 of 21 consumers had at least a 50% reduction in restraint use, although 2 consumers had significant increase in restraint use. The two clients with increased use of restraint could be characterized by several very challenging problems and by their being exposed to a number of organisational issues. Individual challenges included rapid, high rate of SIB, essentially life-long SIB, very limited alternate behaviors and reinforcers to incorporate into BMPs and a life long- history of failure to respond to any behavioral, pharmacological or other intervention. Service problems included high rates of staff turn over, very limited staff intervention skills, lack of administrative interest in client outcome, lack of additional staff, external state auditors who did not recognize that there was a problem, and an absence of federal auditors.

## Discussion

The three empirical studies described here show that restraint can be greatly reduced. This is true for both individuals and large groups of service users. Further, with continued effort and oversight these large reductions in restraint can be maintained for periods of up to 3 years. These are clearly meaningful outcomes for service users, staff and family members.

The methods described here and elsewhere in the literature all include some common elements. These common elements can form the basis of good practice.

1.  Ensure that each service provider, including those that apparently do not use restraint, have current and clear written policies on the use of restraint. When service providers do not have policies or they have draft policies this is a bad sign that the issue is not being actively pursued. Ensure that policies are routinely given to all new staff, at annual refresher training and that staff and supervisors are competent in their knowledge and implementation of the policy.

2.  Measure all forms of restraint in an honest and accurate database. Include physical restraints, such as mittens and restraint jackets, personal restraints, such as holding hands down and basket holds, emergency and as required use of psychotropic medications and any other practice that *might* constitute restraint. Distinguish between planned, programmatic use of restraint from emergency restraint. Ensure that service providers do not avoid the issue by mislabeling restraint as physical therapy for posture or special seating arrangements, or by re-labeling a time-out room as a "quiet space", "calming area" or some related euphemism.

3. Similarly document all other related forms of restrictive procedures, such as seclusion. This is useful to ensure that reducing one form of restraint does not lead to increasing other restrictive procedures.

4. Use this database to identify high restraint service users and programme areas. Ensure that these clients and programme areas receive additional and sometimes intense administrative and professional oversight and support. Remember that client behavior is only weakly related to use of restraint. Differences between programme areas and clients are much more likely to indicate differences in local practices, rather than differences between client behavior.

5. The use of restraint can be effectively reduced for high risk clients by combinations of: identifying the service users concerned, publicly posted graphical feedback, staff training in alternatives to restraint, ensuring the behavior plans are high quality, ensuring that these procedures are implemented, ensuring that the client has access to a wide range of pleasurable activities and has a high density of reinforcement in their life. It is reasonable to expect that the half to two thirds of clients with high rates of restraint can have their restraint reduced by 50% to 100% within six months of rigorously implementing these procedures. However, there is a minority of clients with profound intellectual disabilities, multiple disabilities and chronic self-injury, including hand mouthing, for whom restraint reduction is extremely challenging.

6. Service providers for clients with high rates of restraint need special support. These service providers need access to high quality ABA services that can conduct functional assessments and functional analyses of target behaviors that are the basis for restraint. Staff who work with these clients should be able to implement basic behavioral procedures such as shaping and differential reinforcement.

7. Oversight of restraint reduction should be an ongoing part of services. It cannot be dealt with as a special project for a few months.

8. External pressure from accreditation and funding agencies is an essential component to motivate service providers to achieve these client outcomes.

## Limitations to current knowledge

Our knowledge of the evaluation of restraint reduction is relatively limited. Recall that the impetus for the studies reported here was to reduce restraint-related death: none of these studies measured that outcome. Instead these studies, like others in the literature measured only one dependent variable – reduction in all forms of restraint. The reduction of restraint might be viewed as a worthwhile outcome by itself. Indeed administrative and advocacy pressure appeared to focus on this outcome. However, the evaluation of restraint reduction programmes should focus on a wide range of dependent variables. Table 13.3 lists some of them. While there should be a comprehensive set of measures to assess the impact of the intervention on restraint and related restrictive measures, an important question to address is whether interventions to reduce restraint may inadvertently reduce appropriate restraint. Emergency restraint should be used to protect a user or others from imminent danger.

**Table 13.3:** Possible dependent variables for a comprehensive evaluation of restraint reduction programmes

---

**Restraint measures**

1. Number of applications of restraints
2. Duration of restraints
3. Emergency and PRN psychotropic medications
4. Changing from most to least restrictive restraint procedures
5. Appropriate vs. inappropriate applications of restraint

**Other restrictive procedures**

1. Time out, seclusion, calming down in bedrooms etc.

**Target behaviour measures**

1. Rate of aggression, self-injury and target behaviours related to restraint
2. Rate of other target behaviours
3. Rate of replacement behaviours
4. Rate other positive behavioural changes, such as mood etc

**Safety measures**

1. Injuries to self, peer and staff
2. Cost of injuries, including staff lost days and workman's compensation
3. Sentinel events, such as near-death experiences
4. Restraint related death

**Programme integrity measures**

1. Were behavioural intervention procedure carried out accurately?
2. Was the oversight and review procedure carried out accurately?
3. Did treatment teams monitor intervention appropriately?
4. Were policies and procedures implemented?

**Cost measures**

1. Did the cost benefits of the programme exceed the cost of implementation?

---

Programmatic restraint should be implemented accurately if a person's treatment programme indicates its use. Thus, measuring appropriate and inappropriate use of restraint would be a useful refinement of measures to evaluate restraint reduction programmes. Unfortunately at this time no measurement systems have been developed to reliably measure appropriate and inappropriate application and failure to apply restraints. Most publications on restraint reduction have focussed on restraint as the dependent variable, but have not measured challenging behaviors. Thus, it is possible that restraint reduction programmes might inadvertently increase aggression, self-injury or other challenging behaviors. In a similar way restraint reduction programmes might also inadvertently increase injuries to clients and others. In the studies above, we informally monitored injuries through an additional injury database. There were occasions when reducing restraints, especially restraints for chronic self-injury and hand mouthing, may have led to increased injuries to clients. One interesting possibility to address the measurement of restraint-related death might be to measure sentinel events, such as respiratory distress, in response to restraints. However, in the present research we did not collect or systematically analyze data on client target behaviors and injuries for the large samples involved in the second and third studies. It would be possible for future research on small numbers of cases to measure restraints, challenging behaviors and injuries. Implementing such as data collection system for a large, service-wide sample would be a formidable task.

## Context and intervention

A final point worthy of comment is the issue of the context in which OBM interventions were implemented. Sturmey (1999b) has pointed out that behavioral interventions take place in a complex ecology of events. While this is hardly a new observation, Sturmey (1999b) went on to apply Bronfenbrenner's Ecological Model of Human Development to illustrate the cultural, legal and regulatory influences on OBM. In these three studies, several influences at a distance from the point of implementation can be discerned. First, at the time of these studies the government agency that supervised these facilities had been monitoring restraint for over two years. Over time, the progress within each facility in reducing restraint was apparent at public meetings. Additionally, the differences among institutions in the rate and type of restraint use were also apparent. Some institutions used four- five- and six-point mechanical restraint, restraint nets, and restraint chairs. Two facilities used seclusion rooms, but nine did not. Other facilities had comparatively high rates of programmatic mechanical restraint. These observations were not merely apparent to each facility's administration, but were also discussed at the agency's Central Office and even the State Board regulating TXMHMR.

A second external event that triggered continuing sensitivity and impetus to reduce restraint was the Deadly Restraint (Weiss, 1998) article and the media and legislative attention that followed. Such events, though distant in time and space from the implementation of individual BMPs, still influence the allocation of resources such as staff numbers and training, management attention to the implementation of BMPs, and restraint reduction.

## References

Allen, D, McDonald, L, Dunn, C, & Doyle, T (1997) Changing care staff approaches to the prevention and management of aggressive behaviour in a residential treatment unit for people with mental retardation and challenging behaviour. *Research in Developmental Disabilities*, 18, 101–112.

Dewey, K & Brill, C (2000) Decrease in restraint use in a study of a geropsychiatric unit. *Journal of Psychosocial Nursing*, 38, 14–18.

Donat, DC (1998) Impact of a mandatory behavioral consultation on seclusion / restraint in a psychiatric hospital. *Journal of Behavior Therapy and Experimental Psychiatry*, 29, 13–19.

General Accounting Office (1999) *Improper restraint or seclusion use places people at risk.* Washington, DC: General Accounting Office.

Harris, J (1996) Physical restraint procedures for managing the challenging behaviors presented by mentally retarded adults and children. *Research in Developmental Disabilities, 17,* 99–134.

Hancock, CK, Buster, PA, Oliver, MS, Fox, SW, Morrison, E & Burger, SL (2001). Restraint reduction in acute care: An interdisciplinary approach. *Journal of Nursing Administration,* 31, 74–77.

Hill, J & Spreat, S (1987). Staff injury rates associated with the implementation of contingent restraint. *Mental Retardation,* 25, 141–145.

Luiselli, JK, Kane, A, Tremi, T & Young, N (2000). Behavioral intervention to reduce physical restraint of adolescents with developmental disabilities. *Behavioral Interventions,* 15, 317–330.

Obi, C (1997). Restraint fading and alternate management strategies to treat a man with Lesch – Nyhan Syndrome. *Behavioral Interventions,* 12, 195–202.

Oliver, C, Hall, S, Hales, J, Murphy, G and Watts, D (1998). The treatment of severe self-injurious behavior by the systematic fading of restraints: Effect on self-injury, self-restraint, adaptive behavior and behavioral correlates of affect. *Research in Developmental Disabilities,* 19, 143–166.

Rangecroft, ME, Tyrer, SP, & Berney, TP (1997). The use of seclusion and emergency medication in a hospital for people with learning disability. *British Journal of Psychiatry,* 70, 273–277.

Reid, DH & Parsons, MB (1995). *Motivating human services staff. Supervisory strategies for maximizing work effort and work enjoyment.* Morganton, North Carolina: Habilitative Management Consultants.

Sturmey, P (1999a). Correlates of restraint use in an institutional population. *Research in Developmental Disabilities,* 20, 339–46.

Sturmey, P (1999b). History and contribution of organizational behavior management to services for persons with developmental disabilities. *Journal of Organizational Behavior Management,* 18, 2/3, 7–32.

Syndram, C, Stack, EW, & Benjamin, WP (1994). *Restraint and seclusion practices in New York psychiatric facilities.* New York: New York Commission on Quality of Care for the Mentally Disabled.

Weiss, EM (1998). Deadly Restraint. *Hartford Courant,* October 11–15, 1998.

# Chapter 14

# Plenty of gain, but no pain: a systems-wide initiative

David Allen, Tony Doyle & Neil Kaye

## Introduction

A substantial number of specialist services for people with intellectual disabilities and challenging behaviour were developed across the UK in the early part of the last decade (Allen & Felce, 2000; Emerson et al, 1996). In part, these were a response to a series of unofficial (Blunden & Allen, 1987) and official (Mansell, 1993) policy statements that appeared between the late 1980s and early 1990s. The precipitating event for both the policy statements and the services that followed however was hospital closure. As institutions for people with intellectual disability finally began to shut their doors, and new models of community service appeared in their place (Allen, 1989; Mansell & Ericsson, 1996), the 'problem' of providing care for those individuals with severe challenging behaviours increasingly occupied the attention of both service commissioners and providers.

Debates at the time tended to focus more upon the structure of specialist services, and specifically upon the relative merits of specialist teams versus specialist units (Newman & Emerson, 1991 ; Vischer, 1982), rather than upon their function. In parallel with these UK initiatives, a separate movement emerged from the USA concerning the use of non-aversive behavioural approaches. Although not universally embraced (Emerson et al, 1996), this movement helped provide the technology via which the new wave of specialist UK services could deliver their interventions.

Cardiff's Intensive Support Service[1] was one of the first of these 'new wave' services to be set up and hence it is one of the longest established in the country. In addition to a specialist peripatetic team supporting both children and adults in community settings, the service includes an acute admission unit and two long-stay domestic scale residential bungalows; both the unit and the bungalows cater for adults only. The establishment of the service was a key element in the re-provision of services that helped facilitate the closure of the City's Ely Hospital, the institution at the centre of the first of a series of high profile

---

[1] Now part of the services offered by Bro Morgannwg NHS Trust.

scandals that rocked the National Health Service from the late 1960s onwards (Martin, 1984).

The Intensive Support Service has been subject to a number of published studies (Hoefkens & Allen, 1990; Allen & Lowe, 1995; Lowe, Felce, & Blackman, 1996; Allen, 1998) that have provided evidence of its effectiveness with respect to a variety of service user outcome measures. These include reductions in frequency and severity of challenging behaviour, reductions in mental health problems, increases in activity, and reduced dependency on institutional provision.

When the service was first established in 1989, it embraced the positive behavioural philosophy promoted by Gary LaVigna and colleagues at the Institute for Applied Behaviour Analysis (IABA) in Los Angeles. LaVigna's model focused on behaviour change strategies, but also included a reactive behaviour management element for responding to out of control behaviours. While there was already a substantial research literature in place to support the behavioural change strategies advocated by LaVigna & Donnellan (1986), little information was available on behaviour management. At the time, a number of staff working for the service had undertaken Control & Restraint (C&R) training, and this was initially suggested as a possible model for the service. As described elsewhere in this volume, the techniques involved in C&R had originally been devised for use within the UK prison service, and were largely dependent on inflicting pain on the person showing challenging behaviour for their effectiveness. These methods were clearly at variance with the overall non-aversive therapeutic strategy adopted by the service, and several additional concerns surrounded their use:

- There were obvious qualitative and quantitative differences in aggressive behaviour between the population of people for whom the techniques were originally designed and people with intellectual disabilities and challenging behaviour.

- If the challenging behaviours of the latter could be managed via non-painful methods, then the use of these techniques would, by definition, be unlawful.

- The techniques had considerable potential for misuse and abuse.

- The most restrictive techniques required three people for their implementation, a level of resource that was rarely available.

- The approach was in conflict with the values base of the service.

## Developing an Alternate Approach

These concerns led to C&R training being rejected by the service. Although today there are a number of ready alternatives available (BILD, 2000), in 1989 alternative approaches were conspicuous by their absence. Service personnel therefore set about developing a new method of reactive training. The theoretical components were designed to be compatible with and supportive of the IABA model, while the physical intervention procedures were constructed on the basis of an analysis of incident forms collated within the service's admission unit. The rationale behind this decision was that the unit would, by definition, serve a changing population of people with intellectual disabilities and severe challenging behaviour. As such, incident forms completed at the Unit should provide a reasonably accurate sample of the types of physical challenges faced by carers supporting service users with the most severe challenging behaviours. A number of additional forms of physical aggression, not evident from the audit, but which it was thought staff might have to face, were also added to the list. Using this menu of challenges, staff from the service worked in conjunction with a judo expert (who was also experienced in teaching judo skills to people with intellectual disabilities) in order to construct a menu of responses.

The specification for the new training was that it should:

- Embrace a proactive, preventative approach to managing severe challenging behaviours.

- Clearly differentiate between proactive and reactive elements.

- Only utilise physical interventions that avoided the deliberate infliction of pain.

- Utilise a gradient of interventions that could be matched to changes in service user behaviour.

- Reflect the level of challenges posed by the user group.

- Be socially valid, in that they could, if required, be applied in community settings.

- Be capable of being utilised by all key carers, irrespective of size or strength, and with the typical resource levels available within the service.

The initial programme consisted of five major components:

- Understanding aggression – an introduction to the nature and course of aggressive incidents based on the Time-Intensity model developed initially by Smith and cited in Rowett & Breakwell (1992).

- Primary prevention – modifying or removing environmental or individual triggers known to be associated with the production of aggressive behaviour.

- Secondary prevention – responding to early signs of aggression via verbal and non-verbal distraction and defusion strategies.

- Reactive strategies – physical interventions procedures.

- Post-incident support – emotional debriefing for both carers and service users.

Instructional methods included didactic teaching, group exercises, and the repeated practice of physical interventions. With the latter, a task analysis approach was employed via which participants were taught individual steps for each move which were then chained together. In contrast with some approaches to teaching physical intervention that emphasise the use of role play (eg, DiFabio & Ackerhalt, 1978), this training component was conducted under calm, controlled conditions as it was felt that this would enhance skill development and retention. After some initial pilot work, the training was introduced into the admission unit in 1990. The remainder of this chapter will report on studies carried out into the impact of the training since that time.

## Study 1: Impact on Behaviour Rates, Use of Reactive Procedures, and Injuries

Allen et al (1997) reported the first outcome data for the new approach. Their study described the impact of the training over a six-year period and utilised data collated from mandatory clinical records. The data presented suggested that the introduction of the training on the admission unit was associated with improvements on all the key dependent measures studied. Between the start and finish of the data collection, there was some evidence of an overall decline in frequency of behavioural incidents, a 62% decline in the use of physical restraint, 86% decline in the use of as required medication, 75% reduction in staff injuries, and 72% reduction in service user injuries. Data for restraint use and injuries are shown in figure 14.1.

These results could not be explained by changes in the service user group during the course of the study as, contrary to expectations, the unit's population remained largely static during the research period as a consequence of delayed discharges. Furthermore, data collected using a series of behavioural and psychiatric rating scales showed that the users were representative of the wider population of people with intellectual disabilities and challenging behaviour, thus suggesting that the results had a reasonable degree of clinical validity.

Although the results were encouraging, the study had no form of experimental control and it failed to separate out the specific effects of the new reactive training from those of the overall introduction of the non-aversive approach on the unit per se. Furthermore, the study only looked at indirect training outcomes, and failed to assess more immediate and direct impacts on the recipients of the training. The latter concern was addressed in study 2.

## Study 2 Impact on Carer Confidence and Knowledge

In accordance with national policy, the plan for the closure of Ely Hospital involved the majority of users with challenging behaviour being resettled to social care settings. Although the programme was initially designed for use within the admission unit, the bulk of the service's work was therefore conducted in social care settings and with non-NHS staff.

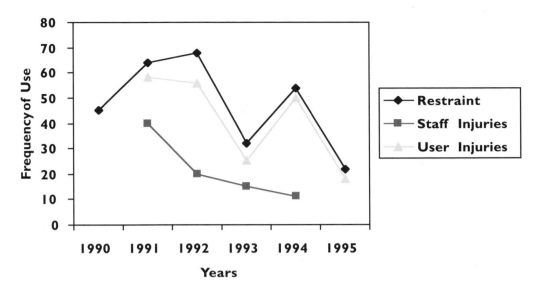

**Figure 14.1:** Restraint use, injuries to staff & injuries to service users during severe behavioural incidents

The initial success of the programme led to increasing requests for staff training by residential service providers. A training for trainers course was therefore developed in order to meet this need, and by 2000, over 50 trainers had been created within these non-NHS services.

This expanded training base allowed for a second study concerned with the impact of the training on staff (Allen & Tynan, 2000). The study was in two parts. First, a group of social care staff that had not received the training (n=58) were compared to a group that had (n=51) in relation to two measures. The first was the Confidence in Coping Instrument (Thackeray, 1987), a questionnaire designed to test participant's confidence in responding to aggressive service user behaviour. The second, the Reactive Strategy Questionnaire, was constructed specifically for the study and designed to assess knowledge of good practice principles in behaviour management. In the second part of the study, the

**Table 14.1:** Score differences between trained and untrained staff

|  | Confidence in Coping Questionnaire | | Reactive Strategy Questionnaire | | |
|---|---|---|---|---|---|
|  | Mean | Median | Mean | Median | Z |
| Untrained (n=58) | 49.7 | 49 | 13.9 | 14 | −7.2* |
| Trained (n=51) | 83.1 | 83 | 15.9 | 14 | −4.3* |

*All measures significant at P < .0005*

**Table 14.2:** Pre & Post-training scores for untrained group (n=58)

| Measure | Training Status | Mean | Median |
|---|---|---|---|
| Confidence in coping Questionnaire | Pre | 49.7 | 49.0 |
| | Post | 74.5 | 76.5 |
| Reactive Strategy Questionnaire | Pre | 13.9 | 14 |
| | Post | 15 | 16 |

*All measures significant at P < .0005*

confidence and knowledge of the untrained group was reassessed after they had also been exposed to the training. Their results were then compared to their pre-training scores. The study therefore provided two separate tests of the impact of the training programme. The results are shown in tables 14.1 and 14.2. ·

Significant differences were evident between both the trained and untrained group and between the pre and post results for the previously untrained group on both measures. These results therefore suggested that the programme was effective both in terms of helping carers feel more confident in working with challenging individuals and in improving their general knowledge concerning behavioural management. The former is likely to be a critical concern when working with individuals who pose severe challenges.

## Study 3: Placement Breakdown

This study provided an indirect measure of the impact of the training programme. Despite the evidence that the Intensive Support Service was achieving clinically effective outcomes for its users and, in particular, had contributed to a reduced dependency on institutional care, it remained the case that periodically, care situations for users with intellectual disabilities and challenging behaviour were subject to placement breakdown.

Allen (1999) investigated factors associated with breakdown by comparing the personal and service characteristics of a group of users with severe challenging behaviour who had been successfully maintained in community settings with those of a group that had experienced breakdown with a subsequent long-stay episode in an institutional setting. It was hypothesised that the breakdown group would display higher levels of behavioural and psychiatric disturbance and that they would come from services that were less well structured and resourced.

Contrary to what had been predicted, the behavioural and psychiatric profiles of the two groups were remarkably similar. The only statistically significant differences evident were that the maintained group had higher rates of stereotypic behaviour while the breakdown group showed more frequent and severe anti-social behaviours. There were major differences in levels of adaptive behaviour however, with breakdown group being significantly more able.

Important differences in service provision were also identified. In general, the services that broke down were rated as less well resourced and organised than those that did not. Of particular relevance was the fact that almost 82% of carers in the maintained group had received training in the behaviour management programme, whereas only 36% of those in the breakdown group had. This suggests, perhaps not surprisingly, that training staff to manage behavioural crises is one factor that may help to insulate against placement breakdown.

## Studies 4–6: Auditing the use of physical interventions

Over time, a number of important changes were made to the training programme. The most significant of these involved the removal of any procedures involving taking users to the floor and then restraining them in the prone (face down) position. These modifications were driven by increasing general concerns over the safety of these procedures (Weiss, 1998; Patterson, 1998; Pollanen et al, 1998) rather than by specific experiences within the service. Other procedures (eg escapes from strangles on the floor) were removed because anecdotal evidence suggested that the behaviours for which they were designed occurred at very low frequencies. In addition, they were both complex and risky to teach. The cost-benefit of including them in the training was therefore low.

In 2000, some 10 years after the launch of the programme, the first of a number of audit exercises to assess the use of the physical interventions taught was conducted (Kaye & Allen, 2002). This was carried out over a nine month period in the admission unit where the procedures were originally devised.

The audit was conducted by attaching a monitoring form that recorded the frequency of use of each specific intervention to the case notes of each user attending the Unit. This was completed following every incident requiring the use of physical interventions by the staff member or members involved. Data were collated for all users each month and their reliability checked by cross-referencing the monitoring forms with other recording systems (ABC forms, nursing process etc) that were in place.

At the time of the audit, a total of 42 different physical interventions were available in the programme. These were normally delivered on a bespoke basis; that is, staff were only taught the techniques required for users whom they supported. On the admission unit however, where the user population would be more changeable,[2] it was felt necessary to teach the staff the whole range of procedures in order to help them meet the varying challenges that they would face. This meant that both the initial and refresher training for staff was lengthy and complex. Staff had a potentially bewildering array of interventions to remember, and their chances of successfully recalling them under field conditions were therefore compromised. It was hoped that the audit would help

---

[2] 18 admissions occurred during the audit period.

differentiate between essential and non-essential techniques, thereby enabling the training to be condensed to a more practical level.

While it was anticipated that some techniques would be used infrequently, the results of the audit were extremely surprising. Only 15 techniques (36% of techniques taught) were utilised during the audit period, thereby leaving 27 techniques (64% of those taught) unused. Of the techniques that were used, 90% involved the use of procedures for evading or escaping from assaults, 4% concerned procedures for moving service users from one location to another, and 6% concerned minimal restraint.

While these results appeared to provide a clear basis for making radical reductions to the contents of the physical intervention component of the training, a more cautious approach was required given that the results obtained may have been a specific function of the time that the audit was conducted. It was possible, for example, that the users of the Unit at the time that the audit was carried out presented atypically low levels of aggression, and that the levels observed at the time that the training was originally designed were in fact more representative of the usual forms of aggression seen by staff.

In order to explore this possibility, users resident on the Unit throughout the audit period were assessed using the Aberrant Behaviour Checklist (Aman et al, 1985) and their scores on this measure compared with those of users attending the Unit at the time of the original study (Allen et al, 1997). Only the scores on the Stereotypy subscale were significantly different, with higher rates being seen in the original sample. This difference would obviously be very unlikely to explain any differences in the use of physical interventions, as stereotypic behaviour would not warrant the implementation of the physical procedures taught in the programme. Further analysis of the specific scale item concerned with aggression indicated slight variations in the number of users presenting with aggressive behaviour that was rated as either a moderate or severe problem. In the original study sample this figure was 71% and in 2000 it was 61%. Viewed overall, there was no compelling evidence to suggest that the low rate of use of certain procedures was a function of major changes in the population served. Indeed, the perception of staff was that the audit had been conducted at a time when the Unit was supporting a particularly difficult group of users.

Kaye & Allen (2002) speculated on the reasons why this discrepancy between the moves taught and used occurred. Two possibilities were put forward:

- Minor episodes of aggression often tend to be under-reported. Incident reports therefore tend to capture more severe episodes. Basing a training curriculum on incident forms, as essentially happened in this case, is therefore likely to skew the training towards high-intensity but low-frequency behaviours which may not be reflective of day-to-day patterns of aggression.

- The original training analysis added in risk behaviours that it was thought may be encountered by staff. As such, this analysis was inaccurate in that it over-estimated the variety of aggressive behaviours presented by this population of service users.

In a further attempt to validate the results, the audit was repeated over a further 12 month period between mid 2000 to mid 2001 (study 5). The profile of physical intervention use during these two periods is shown in figure 14.2. The horizontal axis represents the total range of techniques available, and ranges from least intrusive procedures (evasive and self-defensive) on the left of the axis to most intrusive procedures (moving procedures and minimal restraint) on the right. The figures for the original 9 month audit were pro-rated in order for them to be comparable with the new 12 month data.

Although some variations in the use of physical interventions were evident at the two audit points, the overall profile was remarkably similar. Consistent with the above data, the profile shows a relatively high frequency of use of evasive and some self-defensive procedures (left side), together with a lower frequency use of some procedures for moving and restraining users (right side). Furthermore, there were a whole series of self-protective procedures (shown in the middle of the graph) that were never or hardly ever used, and these were essentially the same at both points.

In a further attempt to validate these findings, data were collected from another three agencies trained in the procedures detailing their use of techniques over a 12 month period (study 6). Each of these agencies provided domestic scale community accommodation for people with intellectual disabilities (including people with severe challenging behaviour). A total of over 12,000 physical interventions were recorded across these services during the audit period. The profile of usage is shown in figure 14.3. As in figure 14.2, the horizontal axis represents the total menu of techniques available, and ranges from least intrusive procedures (evasive and self-defensive) on the left of the axis to most intrusive

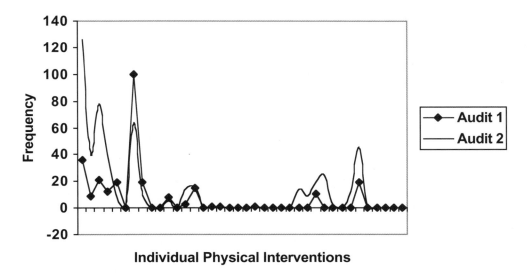

**Figure 14.2:** Use of Physical Intervention on the Admissions Unit at the two audit points (n=807 interventions)

procedures (moving procedures and minimal restraint) on the right. Each separate line on the graph represents a single agency.

Although there was again some variation evident between the agencies in terms of their frequency of use of individual procedures, the overall profile was once again very comparable with that seen on the ISS admission unit. Most notably, there was a whole raft of self-protective procedures in the middle of the graph that remained unused.

Taken in conjunction, these audit exercises have provided the basis for making a significant reduction in the content of the training programme to 18 core procedures. This has a number of benefits:

- The techniques now taught are based on a much more comprehensive and, therefore, more valid empirical analysis of the behavioural management needs of service users

- The amount of training time required to achieve mastery of the identified physical interventions has been greatly reduced, thus making it easier to meet initial training and refresher targets

- Within training sessions, the amount of time available to practice individual techniques has increased.

- On trainer courses, the scope for more in-depth analysis of trainee competence has increased.

The audit exercises have allowed the training to be modified in such a way that it is more likely to meet the requirements for optimal training in physical interventions suggested by Bell & Stark (1998). Based on a analysis of training

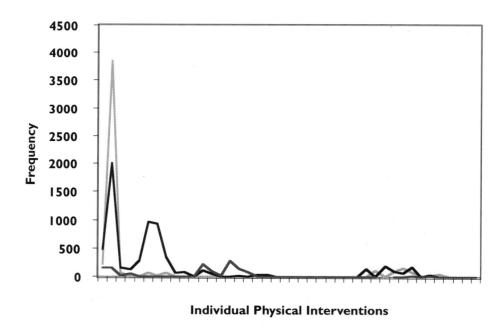

**Figure 14.3:** Use of Physical Interventions across 3 services (n=12,640 interventions)

effectiveness in relation to instruction in cardio-pulmonary resuscitation, these authors suggested that physical intervention training would be enhanced by training only one technique at a time, by allowing maximum training time and teaching to saturation, by building in regular update training, and by systematically assessing the competence of trainees. It is clear that, the more techniques that are taught on a training course, the more difficult it will be to achieve these requirements.

## Discussion

The need for evidence-based approaches is as great, if not greater, in relation to behaviour management strategies as it is for behaviour change strategies. Despite this need, there is a comparative dearth of research evidence available on the former as compared to the latter.

None of the studies described above are particularly robust in experimental terms, and there is considerable scope for improving both the breadth and scientific rigour of work in this area (Allen, 2001). Nevertheless, the research presented here represents an attempt to develop an empirically based approach to behaviour management that was tailored to the needs of the specific requirements of the population served. The studies described have also attempted to measure both direct and indirect training outcomes. Direct outcomes refer to the impact of training on immediate recipients (ie impact on trainee skill, confidence, knowledge etc), while indirect outcomes concern the impact of training in the workplace (ie impact on rates of challenging behaviour, rates of reactive procedures, injuries to carers and service users etc). The results suggest that the training programme achieved beneficial outcomes in a number of these areas.

The work completed to date reflects the ISS commitment to delivering high quality care in relation to behaviour change and behaviour management, and the studies reported form part of an ongoing research portfolio. Other research carried out to date includes a study on the use of reactive procedures with children (Adams & Allen, 2001), and another which identified links between good behaviour management practice and the ability to reduce levels of anti-psychotic medication (Ahmed et al, 2000). Research currently in progress includes a comparative study of the views of carers and service users regarding the use of physical interventions, and a controlled evaluation of the use of the programme within a unit for young people with mental health problems.

Objectives for future research include an investigation of whether the observed increases in confidence immediately post-training endure once staff return to the work place, and an examination of the extent to which competence at physical skills decays over time. The latter has particularly important implications for refresher training. Research on training into cardiopulmonary resuscitation (see Bell & Stark, 1998) indicates that physical skills may decline significantly within six months of training, and it would seem highly probable that the same effect will be observed in relation to physical intervention training.

In conclusion, it is important to stress that the results described here apply to one particular training approach which delivers a particular form of training using particular teaching strategies. The number of different training models in behaviour management is now legion, and no general assumptions about the effectiveness of training can be made from the data reported here. If we are to fulfil our commitment to providing the highest quality, evidence-based behaviour change and behaviour management interventions for people with intellectual disabilities and challenging behaviour, it is essential that both providers and commissioners of training take steps to evaluate its impact. It is also essential that grant giving bodies regard this area of research as one worthy of financial support; there is no evidence that this is the case to date. If this situation prevails, then opinion and the 'hard sell' will continue to predominate, and service users and staff will continue to be exposed to inappropriate and, in some instances, potentially dangerous practices.

## Acknowledgement

Our thanks are due to Colin Dunn, Linda Newton, Wendy James, and John Hadley for their invaluable contributions to developing, running and revising the training programme since 1989. John Dwyer also provided significant assistance in collating the audit data.

## References

Adams, D & Allen, D (2001) Assessing the need for reactive behaviour management strategies in children with intellectual disability and severe challenging behaviour. *Journal of Intellectual Disability Research*, 45, 4, 335–343.

Ahmed, Z, Fraser, W, Kerr, MP, Kiernan, C, Emerson, E, Robertson, J, Felce, D, Allen, D, Baxter, H & Thomas, J (2000) Reducing antipsychotic medication in people with a learning disability. *British Journal of Psychiatry*, 176, 42–46.

Allen, D (1989) The effects of deinstitutionalisation on people with mental handicaps. *Mental Handicap Research*, 2, 18–37.

Allen, D (1998) Changes in admissions to a hospital for people with intellectual disabilities following the development of alternative community services. *Journal of Applied Research in Intellectual Disabilities*, 11, 156–165.

Allen, D (1999) Success and failure in community placements for people with learning disabilities and challenging behaviour: An analysis of key variables. *Journal of Mental Health*, 8, 307–320.

Allen, D (2001) *Training Carers in Physical Interventions. Research towards evidence-based practice.* Kidderminster: British Institute of Learning Disabilities.

Allen, D & Felce, D (1999) Service responses to challenging behaviour. In N Bouras (Ed) *Psychiatric and Behavioural Disorders in Developmental Disabilities and Mental Retardation* pp. 279–94. Cambridge: Cambridge University Press.

Allen, D & Lowe. K (1995) Providing intensive community support to people with learning disabilities and challenging behaviour: A preliminary analysis of outcomes and costs. *Journal of Intellectual Disability Research*, 39, 67–82.

Allen, D & Tynan, H (2000) Responding to aggressive behaviour: Impact of training on staff members' knowledge and confidence. *Mental Retardation*, 38, 2, 97–104.

Allen, D, McDonald, L, Dunn, C, & Doyle, T (1997) Changing care staff approaches to the prevention and management of aggressive behaviour in a residential treatment unit for persons with intellectual disability and challenging behaviour. *Research in Developmental Disabilities*, 18, 101–112.

Aman, MG, Singh, NN, Stewart, AW, & Field, CJ (1985) The Aberrant Behaviour Checklist: a behaviour rating scale for the assessment of treatment effects. *American Journal of Mental Deficiency*, 89, 485–491.

Bell, L & Stark, C (1998) *Measuring competence in physical restraint skills in residential child care.* Edinburgh: Scottish Office Central Research Unit.

British Institute of Learning Disabilities (2000) *Providers of Training on the Application of Physical Interventions.* Kidderminster: BILD.

Blunden, R & Allen, D (1987) *Facing the Challenge: An Ordinary Life for People with Learning Difficulties and Challenging Behaviours.* London: King's Fund.

DiFabio, S & Ackerhalt, EJ (1978) Teaching the use of restraint through role play. *Perspectives in Psychiatric Care*, 16, 218–222.

Emerson, E, Forrest, J, Cambridge, P & Mansell, J (1996) Community support teams for people with learning disabilities and challenging behaviours: results of a national survey. *Journal of Mental Health*, 5, 395–406.

Hoefkens, A & Allen, D (1990) Evaluation of a special behaviour unit for people with mental handicaps and challenging behaviour. *Journal of Mental Deficiency Research*, 34, 213–228.

Kaye, N & Allen, D (2002) Over the top? Reducing staff training in physical interventions. *British Journal of Learning Disabilities*, 30, 3, 129–132.

LaVigna, GW, & Donnellan, AM (1986) *Alternatives to Punishment. Solving Behaviour Problems with Non-aversive Strategies.* New York: Irvington.

Lowe, K, Felce, D, & Blackman, D (1996) Challenging behavior: The effectiveness of specialist support teams. *Journal of Intellectual Disability Research*, 39, 117–127.

Martin, JP (1984) *Hospitals in trouble.* Oxford: Blackwell.

Mansell, J, (1993) *Services for People with Learning Disabilities and Challenging Behaviour or Mental Health Needs: Report of a Project Group.* London: HMSO.

Mansell, J, & Ericcson, K (Eds) (1996) Deinstitutionalization *and Community Living. Intellectual disability services in Britain, Scandinavia and the USA.* London: Chapman & Hall.

Newman, I & Emerson, E (1991) Specialised treatment units for people with challenging behaviours. *Mental Handicap,* 19, 113–19.

Patterson, B (1998) Restraint and sudden death from asphyxia. *Nursing Times*, 94, 44, 62–64.

Pollanen, MS, Chiassen, DA, Cairns, JT, & Young, JG (1998) Unexpected death related to restraint for excited delirium: a retrospective study of deaths in police custody and in the community. *Canadian Medical Association Journal*, 158, 1603–1607.

Rowett, C, & Breakwell, G (1992) *Managing violence at work. A course leader's guide.* Windsor:NFER Nelson.

Thackeray, M (1987) Clinician confidence in coping with patient aggression: assessment and enhancement. *Professional Psychology: Research and Practice*, 18, 1, 57–60.

Vischer, JC (1982) Problem analysis in planning a community-based behaviour management programme. *Journal of Practical Approaches to Developmental Handicap*, 6, 22–28.

Weiss, EM (1998) Deadly restraints. *Hartford Courant*, October 11–15, 1998.

# Postscript

These are remarkable times for people with learning disabilities. Never before has there been a greater and more intelligent debate about their welfare across the public service spectrum. Although much remains to be done, the quality of life for those with learning disability is improving all the time.

In Britain a new wave of awareness has been generated at a primary level by many of the contributors to this book and their colleagues. Together with some of the major charities, they have revolutionised the approach of carers, legislators, and providers. Even more critically, they have helped change the way the world views people with disabilities.

This book is a signature to a decade of change and revolution. It is a salute to a community which has moved mountains and faced up to difficult and traumatic issues and found imaginative and exciting solutions.

Signing off on this book for me represents the end of a traumatic and difficult road – a road well travelled on by David Allen,, who became a mentor of sorts over the last four years. My journey here started on December 21st 1998 when I started my first day as a care worker in the Brompton Care Home in Kent. My investigation was to centre on one of the key issues confronted in this book – how do we deal with the issue of restraint in a caring environment, pursuant to health and safety regulation, welfare concerns, and quality of life considerations, whilst at the same time delivering empowerment and social inclusion?

It was an investigation into abuse in a home where the above considerations were not evidently a priority. Our investigation received an audience of seven million viewers, a remarkable figure for such a difficult subject in this fickle age. The programme revealed a culture of neglect at the home and broadcast evidence of physical abuse. The help line established afterwards received a larger response than any other individual programme in BBC history. The Kent Police investigated and found five cases of assault on five different residents in just 15 days of filming.

Bizarrely, some months later they attacked the programme, saying that it wasted Police time. First to the defence of the programme was David Allen. Fast in his slip stream were Martin Gallagher (MENCAP), Richard Mills (NAS), and John

Harris (BILD), who had all seen the undercover rushes. When our programme was under assault an academic and public service experts stood behind the evidence and, at some critical risk, defended the BBC and my investigation.

The BBC commissioned a special report from David Allen which went some way to convincing the Senior Law officers in Kent that their own force had got their investigation in to the Brompton Care Home wrong.

Late in 2002, the Kent Police apologised in an unprecedented fashion. I am sure that they, along with other Police forces, will take more time and give more consideration in the investigation of care cases involving vulnerable adults in future. Without the support of above colleagues and friends, I would not have had the personal reserves of strength to carry on the good fight. It was a fight that nearly broke me in two, but a line has now been drawn under those events and I can look to the future with some fortitude – a fortitude absorbed from the contributors to this book and their colleagues in the care community.

Their strength of character and dedication to the cause, their determination to move society towards recognising as a priority the care of the learning disabled, and their insight to do so with considered debate and intellectual rigour demonstrates how appropriate it is that the authors of this volume help lead the debate and set the welfare agenda of the last great civil rights movement in this country.

I with others will take the authors' dedication to continue to fight the good fight to heart and rely on it for inspiration to continue to work in the field.

Donal MacIntyre
BBC Reporter

# Index

Aberrant Behaviour Checklist 226
abuse, 156
    anti-professionalism 172–73
    best practice and 165
    conceptual underpinnings 165–66
    conditions for 169–73
    culture of 169
    euphemisms 166
    evidence interpretation 167–69
    failure to act on 182
    fallacies about 167, 168
    financial 164
    historical evidence 166
    impact of 190
    individual characteristics of 181
    individual client level 174
    individual service co-ordination 179
    inexperience and 172
    inquiries 168
    institutionalised practice 171–72
    internal management 166
    intimidation 171
    isolation and 170, 180
    management failures 170–71
    medication and 164
    multiple 168
    neglect and 164
    passive 165
    physical 164, 166
    policy level 177
    response to 178
    revelations of 115
    scandals 166, 187
    serial 168
    service level 175
    service quality and 164–65, 181, 190
    service quality, scrutiny of 178–79
    sexual 156, 164
    staff level 175
    staff supervision, ineffective 170–71
    systems level 176–77
    testing boundaries 168–69
adolescents 12–19

adult protection practice 168, 173–77, 178, 181, 182
Adult Protection Procedures 196
adults 19–25, 116–18 *see also* adult protection practice; Adult Protection Procedures;
Afro-Caribbean people 120, 126
aggression 7, 71, 72
    physical 5
    predicting 74–75
    prevention 41
    risk factors 74, 75–76
Allen, D 47, 81, 222, 224, 233, 234
Allen et al 51, 206
American Association on Mental Retardation 204
Applied Behaviour Analysis (ABA) 6, 203
Association for Persons with Severe Handicaps 3
autism 22, 108, 159
Ayecliffe secure unit 118

Baker & Bissmire 160
basket holds 118, 122, 209
behaviour, ignoring 96–97, 105
behaviour change 3–11, 109
behaviour management 7–9, 15–27, 159–61, 206
behaviour management plans (BMP) 206, 207, 209, 212, 217
behavioural technology 89
Bell & Stark 228
Best Value 180
Biggs et al 166
BILD (British Institute of Learning Disabilities) 9, 39
    *Code of Practice for Trainers* 32, 43, 124, 135–36, 137, 138–42 (Table 9.1; 9.4), 148
    law and 40
    *Physical Intervention: A Policy Framework* 32, 40, 43, 48, 51–65 (Table 4.4; Table 4.5)
    evaluation 51–65
    policy principles 40–42 (Table 3.2)
    trainers' directory 65, 136–37
    training and 121
    tunnel vision criticism 60–61
"blame cultures" 128